# Virtual Weaponry

Aaron Tucker

# Virtual Weaponry

The Militarized Internet in Hollywood War Films

Aaron Tucker
Department of English
Ryerson University
Toronto, ON, Canada

ISBN 978-3-319-60197-7          ISBN 978-3-319-60198-4    (eBook)
DOI 10.1007/978-3-319-60198-4

Library of Congress Control Number: 2017944177

Cover design by Ran Shauli

Printed on acid-free paper

This Palgrave Macmillan imprint is published by Springer Nature
The registered company is Springer International Publishing AG
The registered company address is: Gewerbestrasse 11, 6330 Cham, Switzerland

*For Julia, all of everything*

# ACKNOWLEDGEMENTS

I need to begin by thanking my parents, Cam and Sherrie Tucker, for all their incredible and constant support. Thanks as well to Dr. Christine Daigle for her invaluable recommendations and advice at the outset of this book and to Shaun Vigil and Glenn Ramirez at Palgrave Macmillan for guiding this book home. I also would not have been able to complete this text without the generous financial and spiritual support of the Ryerson University English Department and my CUPE union sisters and brothers.

Chapter 2, "The Hard Technological Body in the Exoskeletal Soldier," was first published in *Cinema: Journal of Philosophy and the Moving Image* (Issue 7) as "The Hard Technological Bodies of *Elysium* and *Edge of Tomorrow*." Earlier versions of these chapters were also presented at the 2015 and 2016 Society for Cinema and Media Studies conferences, as well as the Pop Culture Association conference in 2014 and 2015, and the 2017 Film Studies Association of Canada.

# CONTENTS

# LIST OF IMAGES

# CHAPTER 1

# Introduction: Virtual Weaponry

After watching a TV news report about men terrorizing a village, industrialist-playboy Tony Stark flies from his home in the United States to that village in Afghanistan in his robotic Iron Man suit. After he is shot out of the sky by a missile, he pulls himself up out of a crater, dodges another giant shell, fires a tiny explosive into the tank and walks away as it explodes spectacularly. As he is being shot at by another terrorist soldier, he flies up into the air and pauses. The movie switches to a shot from Stark's perspective, looking out through the suit's eye slits; the audience watches as the computer system within the suit scans the landscape, outlining each individual with a digital red silhouette indicating potential targets while popping up annotative information beside objects ("Jericho missiles"), after which Stark fires his hand-mounted weapons at his enemies. The movie then cuts to a group of men rounding up civilians, and just as one is about to shoot a father in front of his screaming son, Stark lands and punches one man so hard it launches him dozens of feet backwards. As he comes upon another hoard using civilians as shields, he powers his weapons down and stands with his arms at his sides. While completely still, the movie again cuts to the interior point of view of Stark within the suit, and this time the computer system separates the people into the binary of "Hostile" (identified by a red bull's-eye) and "Civilian" (identified by white text); guns then rise from each of his shoulders and he expertly snipes just the terrorists out of the group, leaving the civilians unharmed (Image 1.1).

© The Author(s) 2017
A. Tucker, *Virtual Weaponry*,
DOI 10.1007/978-3-319-60198-4_1

1

**Image 1.1**   Tony Stark and his Iron Man suit separate ally from enemy

This scene from *Iron Man* (Dir. Jon Favreau 2008) involves a number of actions and cinematic effects that are common throughout the very popular series of films that feature the character of Tony Stark as Iron Man. What is that audience to make of the fact that Stark just flies to another country to carry out vigilante justice with his own military-style technologies? What is the audience who watches such a scene being encouraged to think about their relationship to their digitally networked technology in such scenes? In what ways do Stark's violent acts on the battlefield affect those relationships? With all these questions in mind, broadly, as bell hooks writes in her introduction to *Reel to Reel*, "Whether we like it or not, cinema assumes a pedagogical role in the lives of many people. It may not be the intent of a filmmaker to teach audiences, but that does not mean that lessons are not learned" (2). Beyond this, hooks adds, "Movies not only provide a narrative for specific discourses of race, sex, and class, they provide a shared experience, a common starting point from which diverse audiences can dialogue about these charged issues" (3). To this end, Kellner states that "contemporary cinema can be read as a contest of representations and a contested terrain that reproduces existing social struggles and transcodes the political discourses of the era" (2); as such, he continues,

> films are an especially illuminating social indicator of the realities of a historical era, as a tremendous amount of capital is invested in researching, producing and marketing the product. Movie creators tap into the events, fears, fantasies, and hopes of an era and give cinematic expression to social experiences and realities. (10)

Their mass scale makes them especially important texts as their "lessons" reach an enormous, global audience in a manner that few other forms of entertainment are capable of. From this perspective, considering that each movie is a capsule of an era's attitudes and reflects a number of cultural forces and voices, this text then begins to answer what arguments are being constructed and reproduced within movies like *Iron Man* and the other war films discussed throughout this book, with a more specific focus on the "fears, fantasies, and hopes" that emerge from the portrayals of digitally networked technologies within those movies.

Broadly, "war has served as the aesthetic as well as the technological laboratory of modern films" (Der Derian *Virtuous War* 165). Barry Langford points out that "the invention of cinema coincided with a decade of imperialist military conflicts" and that "warfare has been one of the movies' principal subjects since their infancy" (105). He contends that D.W. Griffith's *The Birth of A Nation* (1915), one of Hollywood's first blockbusters and examples of the war film genre, "relocated the audience's relationship to screen warfare away from the simple consumption of war-as-spectacle towards narrative participation and empathetic participation in the terrifying experience of modern war" (106); this film provides the visual and affective template for films in the genre to follow and replicate. With war as a main focal point of much of cinema's development, and therefore at the heart of much of the medium's cultural "lessons," it is useful to begin with a definition of the war film genre. Jeanine Basinger, in her indispensable *The World War II Combat Film*, argues that "because a genre story is a kind of shell to be filled, many subtle variations on plot are presented from film to film without damaging the basic units of its presentation" (16). Speaking more specifically to the war film, as Neale summarizes in *Genre and Hollywood*, early genre scholars insisted that combat scenes be a "requisite ingredient" (125). However, upon sustained examination, that definition is too narrow. A far more useful, and simple, definition is that "war films are films about the waging of war" (Neale 125). This obviously broad definition is illustrative in that such a genre (the basic "shell") covers a wide range of movies through subgenre and cross genre mixing[1] and fits well with David LaRocca's understanding of the contemporary war film:

[War] films regularly involve the portrayal of political decision making, so the workings of war can always in some measure trace back to the ideas, ideologies, and decisions of individuals and their interests, loyalties, obligations, or factions … commanders and soldiers, but also to politicians and policymakers, diplomats and lobbyists, the intelligence and clandestine services, and even journalists and image-makers. (16)

Further, Neale utilizes R.E. Shain's work in the 1970s in pointing out that "a war film [deals] with the roles of civilians, espionage agents, and soldiers in any aspect of war (i.e., preparation, cause, prevention, daily life, and consequences or aftermath) … war films therefore do not have to be situated in combat zones" (as quoted in Neale 125). From this, Basinger argues that "the war film does not exist in a coherent generic form. Different wars inspire different genres. 'War' is a setting, and it is also an issue. … 'War' can be a metaphor, or it can be a background to other stories" (9). LaRocca makes the point that, "If war is now part of our daily lives, then arguably any film that emerges out of a contemporary context might qualify—or recommend itself in some fashion—as a war film" (26). It is because of this ubiquity that LaRocca contends that there must be an urgency in the immediate analysis of the genre: "Given the radical degree to which war films have propagated, splintered, hybridized, found variants and versions, it is highly pertinent to invite scholars to think anew about the philosophical significance of the genre and its myriad representatives" (14) and, as such, he has collected up what he calls "The Multifarious Forms of War Films: A Taxonomy of Subgenres" (489) in an initial attempt to parse through the many multiple splinters of the genre. All together, the war film needs to be identified as a shifting and sprawling genre, with further recognition given to how war is an incredibly widespread and ubiquitous cultural force.

Thinking further about war movies as "social indicators" and the reciprocal potential "dialogues" they may encourage, Langford argues:

The evolution of war films is marked perhaps more directly than any other [genre] by developments in the world beyond the frame … changing perceptions of particular wars and of war itself, arising from cumulative shared cultural experiences of different conflicts and their embedded politics, elicit unusually direct effects in the shifting tenor, iconography and generic verisimilitudes of war films. (107)

This reciprocity between the world "beyond the frame" and real conflicts becomes even more complicated when considering that, as Rosi Braidotti states, "The post-Cold War world has not only seen a dramatic increase in warfare, but also a profound transformation of the practice of war"

(122); equally as troubling, as the headline for *The New York Times* article "U.S. War Footprint Grows in Middle East, With No Endgame in Sight" makes clear, the American military is not only expanding but has no intention of "ending" any of the conflicts it is embroiled in (Hubbard and Gordon 2017). It is important then to closely examine the deeply pervasive war film in order to unpack the "specific discourses" present and the rhetorical "lessons" that the films themselves teach via the audience's "shared experience," especially in the midst of this "dramatic increase," expanded "war footprint," and the "profound transformation" of war via the inclusion of Internet-enabled technologies. Movies about the real or imagined conflicts become extremely useful documents to analyze because they do an excellent job encapsulating an audience's attitudes and emotions, a potential time capsule of their zeitgeist that captures the "tenor" and "iconography" around the particular conflicts that surround the production and viewing of a movie.

Importantly, as hooks writes, "Movies do not merely offer us the opportunity to reimagine the culture we most intimately know on the screen, they make culture" (12). Filmmakers do not simply "tap into the events, fears, fantasies, and hopes of an era"; films are not just records or reflections, but are active creators and/or reinforcers of cultural values, wishes and concerns. War affects movies but movies also affect war. More specifically, cinema and warfare have a long and reciprocal history, wherein the technology and iconography of Hollywood filmmaking has been harnessed, or at the very least monitored, by the American military in order to shape civilian culture. As an example of Hollywood's effectiveness Der Derian points to the example of the military base STRICOM (Simulation, Training, and Instrumentation Command) as one example of where the American military comes to "Hollywood to find the tools and skills for simulating and, if necessary, fighting the wars of the future" (*Virtuous War* 163). The American military does not just borrow from Hollywood, however; they also give to, and create with, the American moviemaking industry. Lawrence H. Suid's *Guts and Glory*, a thorough recounting of the overlaps between the American military and Hollywood,[2] contends that

> the symbiotic relationship between filmmakers and the military began almost as soon as the new medium became a part of American life. The armed forces quickly realized that movies in which they appeared would aid their recruiting campaigns as well as their efforts to inform the public and Congress of their activities and procedures. (12)

Martin Barker's compact summary in *A Toxic Genre* reminds us that the Office of War Information was formed in the 1940s in order to undertake "the development for using film (identified as the medium most likely to reach soldiers and the general population) to propagate its messages" (9) and therefore "any understanding of the 'genre' of Hollywood war movies has to begin by seeing the conditions of their production as an institutionalised compromise" (11). This "development" continues to this day, as the American military has set up a series of liaisons and offices tasked with coordinating with Hollywood.[3] Using these lines of communication, many war films are given time to shoot in military spaces and/or given military personnel as "technical advisors"; as one example among many, the movie *Stealth*, discussed in Chapter 5 of this text, was given time to shoot on the aircraft carriers USS *Abraham Lincoln* and USS *Carl Vinson* by the US Navy (Cook 2004; Fahey 2004). However, this involvement is obviously self-serving and potentially dangerous: citing David Robb's 2002 text *Operation Hollywood*, Barker points out how "the Pentagon successfully steered film scripts in some very precise directions ... [and] regularly overruled historically accurate elements of films in favour of what might enhance the military image" and in turn have "become virtual advertisements for 'America' and its military" (11). Again, this has long been the case: Suid states that the hundreds of Hollywood films released during and just after World War II "created the image of combat as exciting, as a place to prove masculinity, as a place to challenge death in a socially acceptable manner" and, by doing so, the "screen victories reinforced the image of the American military as all-conquering, all powerful, always right. In a real sense, then, Hollywood war films have helped justify war and the use of violence to achieve national goals" (12). Žižek updates this thought into the contemporary by arguing that "a series of meetings between White House advisors and senior Hollywood executives" was organized to synchronize "the war effort and [establish] how Hollywood could help in the 'war on terrorism' by getting the right ideological message across not only to the Americans, but also to the Hollywood public around the globe" (*Welcome to the Desert of the Real* 19). This coordination, he writes, is "the ultimate empirical proof that Hollywood does in fact function as an 'ideological state apparatus'" (19).

Considering what exactly an "ideological state apparatus" might be, it is useful to draw some lines between this text's use of "military," "the War Machine," the "State War Machine" and the "Total War Machine." This book's theoretical understanding of the War Machine and the military is taken primarily from Deleuze and Guattari's *A Thousand*

*Plateaus* (*ATP*) and Manuel De Landa's *War in the Age of Intelligence Machines* (*WAIM*) and, in more practical applications, is near synonymous with President Dwight D. Eisenhower's understanding of the Military Industrial Complex. To begin, Deleuze and Guattari explain that the "War Machine" is "a tool of the nomad. ... Rather than the military (which is a State appropriation of the war machine), the war machine is a collection of nomad-warriors engaged in resistance to control, war being only a consequence—not the intended object" (*ATP* 420); David Heckman clarifies: "Unlike the military, the war machine is not influenced by the economic and political concerns of the State. The war machine is a 'grass roots' affair which bubbles up from common concerns for freedom to move, and as a result it is part and parcel of nomadic life" (para. 23). Mbembé in "Necropolitics" adds,

> War machines are made up of segments of armed men that split up or merge with one another depending on the tasks to be carried out and the circumstances. Polymorphous and diffuse organizations, war machines are characterized by their capacity for metamorphosis. ... A war machine combines a plurality of functions. (32)

This is an important distinction to draw: the War Machine itself is an entity that is not necessarily designed for war, but is rather a collection of warriors that exist outside of geographical and State concerns. Because pre-Industrial nomad forces were significantly smaller and more fractured than larger States that were based in territory, as well as in expansive and permanent infrastructures, the nomad aimed "to destroy the State-form and city-form with which it collides" (*ATP* 418). Yet, as a rule, the State is more powerful and "developed" than the nomad force and subsumes and appropriates the War Machine; the War Machine then "changes in nature and function, since it is afterward directed against the nomad and all State destroyers, or else expresses relations between States, to the extent that a State undertakes exclusively to destroy another State or impose its aims upon it" (418). While the nomad-warriors are largely based in the organizational principle of lineage, Deleuze and Guattari maintain that within the archaic State and State War Machines "lineages remain very important, and numbers take on their own importance. But what moves to the forefront is a 'territorial' organization, in the sense that all the segments, whether of lineage, land, or number, are taken up by *an astronomical space or a geometrical extension* that overcodes them" (authors' italics 388). Such an appropriation is a commandeering of territory and mercenary action, and this new version of the

War Machine is what is meant by a "military" or a State War Machine: the military, by contrast, is an organization formed by the State specifically "to wage wars and immobilize adversaries (which are determined by the State)" (Heckman para. 21). The modern form of the Total War Machine beings when "the State apparatus appropriates the war machine, *subordinates* it to its 'political' *aims*, and gives it war as its direct *object*" (*ATP* authors' italics 420). More, the factors that make State War into Total War are closely connected to capitalism: "It has to do with the investment of constant capital in equipment, industry, and the war economy, and the investment of variable capital in the population in its physical and mental aspects (both as war-maker and as victim of war)" (421). Total War is the result of what Manuel De Landa describes as "the slow militarisation of civilian society, a process in which schools, hospitals and prisons slowly came to adopt a form first pioneered in military camps and barracks, and factories came to share a common destiny with arsenals and armories" ("Economics, Computers and the War Machine" para. 1); the Total War Machine then is not just the hardware, soldiers, tactics, and command employed in direct conflicts, but is also a completely interdependent melding of the mechanics of civilian life, "a plurality of functions," to the needs of the military. This is precisely what Eisenhower warned against in his famous 1961 presidential parting speech in which he spoke at length about the establishment and dangers of the Military Industrial Complex, wherein the

> conjunction of an immense military establishment and a large arms industry is new in the American experience. The total influence – economic, political, even spiritual – is felt in every city, every Statehouse, every office of the Federal government. In the councils of government, we must guard against the acquisition of unwarranted influence, whether sought or unsought, by the military-industrial complex. (para. 14)

This Military Industrial Complex, and the notion of Total War and the Total War Machine, has only expanded since 1961, and when considering the aforementioned symbiosis between Hollywood and the American military, the "compromise" that Barker mentions between viewers, producers, politicians and the military is indicative of the type of dense interweaving that results from the activation of a Total War Machine. At a very basic level, LaRocca points to the seemingly inherent overlap in the acts of making war and making a movie in that the two cultural forces "encode a shared lexicon of 'loading,' 'cocking,' 'aiming,' and 'shooting,' among other familiar and evocative terms" (9).

Der Derian calls the expansion from the overlap of the two forces the "military-industrial-media-entertainment network" (786) which recognizes all forms of military entertainment, video games, TV, movies, etc., as being a function of Žižek's "ideological state apparatus" (19); this is best exemplified "when the simulations used to train fighter pilots show up in the special effects of the film *Independence Day* [and] four-person Marine fire-teams train with the videogame 'Doom'" (Der Derian 786). Expanding from this, De Landa, in *Deleuze: History and Science*, explains that an army "should be viewed as an *assemblage of assemblages*, that is, an entity produced by the recursive application of the part-to-whole relation" (author's italics 68). Here, and in my previous work, I've used the term "assemblage" to refer to the hybridization created by a person's organic body and their Bodies without Organs, with Bodies without Organs acting as "an abstracted projection of a person's identity that underlies the physical organism/body" (Tucker 19) that Deleuze and Guattari highlight as "adjacent to [the organism] and ... continuously in the process of constructing itself (*ATP* 164).[4] When the bodies and Bodies without Organs join with other virtual and physical technologies, they form a larger assemblage; when that assemblage bonds with another assemblage, say in an army, they form an "assemblage of assemblages"; when that army joins with the movie-producing and movie-watching-audience assemblages, the "military-industrial-media-entertainment network," which also includes functions of military and civilian assemblages, then we begin to see larger assemblages merging with larger assemblages and the expansive Total War Machine at work, a military force that cuts across forms and informs culture on a massive scale.

This leads to a global production and reproduction of war, with the war film serving as a key influencer in shaping the attitudes of war making and State making (patriotism) in its audiences. The constant ubiquity of Total War should be united with the definition of the war film genre given earlier in this introduction and acknowledges the deep and extensive tendrils war has as a cultural power. As well, given the military's history of active involvement in war films, movies then are a component of that Total War Machine, spreading and reinforcing the rhetoric of the State War Machine.[5] Cinema, as a double-edged reciprocal reflector of conflicts and constructor of culture, is especially effective because it is so similar, in its use of the camera and visual image, to the modern State War Machine: as Paul Virilio argues in *War and Cinema*, contemporary warfare is "a war of pictures and sounds [that is] replacing the war of objects (projectiles and missiles)" (5); he writes that the State War

Machine becomes a "watching machine" fueled by drones, "reconnaissance aircraft and remote seeing satellites" so that "the eye's function is the function of the weapon" (4). LaRocca adds: "The camera is not just a mechanical, chemical, or digital means of representing war; it is also, necessarily, a component of war machinery. And the camera has become, progressively with each new war, as necessary—or at least as prevalent— as the guns that shape the unfolding course of events" (9). With this involvement of the camera in "real-life" warfare, war movies, as similarly visual documents, often based in the spectacle of combat, can potentially become a weaponized form of cultural rhetoric, a successful civilian-watcher element of a Total War Machine.

To this text's focus, Eisenhower speaks to the specific "technological revolution" he sees in which "research has become central; it also becomes more formalized, complex, and costly" (para. 16), situating part of this revolution in the costly and State-funded labs where "for every old blackboard there are now hundreds of new electronic computers" (para. 15). The chapters in this text stem at least originally from the tangled military-civilian history of the "electronic computer" and the Internet. Both Christos J.P. Moschovitis and Johnny Ryan have written thorough texts that outline the basic trajectory of the Internet[6] and its integration into civilian life, so we do not need to rehash that here.[7] However, as they and popular texts like Andrew Blum's *Tubes* and Katie Hafner and Matthew Lyon's *Where Wizards Stay Up Late* demonstrate, while the Internet was perhaps not immediately used for military purposes, the funding for creating and maintaining it and its infrastructure came through military channels; in addition, a large percentage of the small population of pre-1990 users would have had roots in the military.[8] The central premise of Manuel De Landa's 1991 *WAIM*, a book returned to multiple times throughout this text, is that the American State War Machine had been using computers and the Internet as a central part of its organizing and tactical principles, and here it is worth noting that by the time the technology exploded in the mid-1990s into a common-use, civilian one,[9] the American military had been using it for nearly three decades. In fact, within the first Gulf War, it was the Internet, at least in part, that granted the American State War Machine its spectacular dominance; in support of this thought, Mbembé states that "the growing gap between high-tech and low-tech means of war has never been as evident as in the Gulf War ... [where] a military-technological revolution ... has multiplied the capacity for destruction in unprecedented ways" (29). The State War Machine expanded then to include "smart bombs and bombs coated with depleted uranium (DU), high-tech stand-off weapons, electronic sensors, laser-guided missiles, cluster and asphyxiation bombs, stealth capabilities, unmanned aerial vehicles, and cyberintelligence [that] quickly crippled the enemy's capabilities" (29). While this book will give some basic histories of Internet-enabled weapons like the ones Mbembé lists, alongside analysis of how the Internet itself has been repurposed toward the Total War Machine, its focus will be on the digitally networked American State War Machine and the contemporary notion of Network-Centric Warfare (NCW), which Mary Sterpka King outlines in depth in "Preparing the Instantaneous Battlefield". She asserts that NCW is "designed to mobilize information into a competitive fighting advantage through the networking of operations and forces" and "signifies the integration of human systems and technical capacity into a networked, joint-command structure" (305). Such an approach to warfare demands that all elements of that "networked, joint-command structure" must "observe, orient, decide, act, loop" (318), and depends upon a pervasive networking of all elements of the Total War Machine, using the "public" Internet or an Internet created by a military, in order to link human soldiers to their technologies (and provide information about weather, enemy conditions, and mission updates, for example), and bond those soldier assemblages to other parts of the chain of command. Such a structure also allows for networked simulations of battles (wargames) to be run and considered, granting greater tactical knowledge to the Total War Machine (321). From this, this complete interweaving between civilian and military that is present in the Total War Machine is because, as Tsirigotis continues,

> Warfare, as society, is mainly based on the impeccable use of networks through which information flows undisturbed to every operational level: to the higher command echelon and to fighting squadrons, as well. This constitutes the kernel of Information warfare and which has already been implemented in real life battlefield heralding fundamental changes to war paradigm. (389)

All the connection, production, distribution, and consumption of digital information within the Total War Machine relies on some form of the Internet, and, with this understanding, the porous relationship between the civilian and military Internet mirrors the war film's similar ability to slide easily over the barriers of the two.

The war film and the Internet also overlap in their pervasive and persuasive nature, as both are core examples of the Total War Machine enabled by the Military Industrial Entertainment network. Analyzing the use of the Internet in war films then provides, at first, an initial site to analyze and/or critique the American military's use of the technology as well as to begin to understand the Internet's impact on the genre of the war film. Both Jean Baudrillard in *The Gulf War Did Not Take Place* (1991) and Paul Virilio in *Strategy of Deception* (2000) argue that the American State War Machine was already based firmly in the principles of war-as-simulacra by the first Gulf War, principles that pushed both the fighting and the depictions of "real-life" war into the realm of unreal model and constantly mediated simulation. In an effort to fight a war without having to fight a war, Virilio sees a shift toward a "clean" war, "beyond the principle of the *just war*," aimed at "ensuring victory without bloodshed, at least of reducing the symbolic/media impact of the blood" (author's italics 53). This leads to what he calls the "tele-war," one that uses many of the principles of a Network-Centric Warfare, based on "information warfare" that is dependent on satellites gathering data from around the globe in real time, with computers performing "rapid analysis" on that data (18). This "information" would have largely been produced, consumed and distributed by the Internet, creating a culture of "over-information" (48), one in which the American military was constantly bombarded with information, while civilians, safely away from conflict, were also immersed in a constant stream of information (as well as disinformation, Virilio points out) about the distant combat. All this culminated in a dystopic version of McLuhan's global village built on the constant "interactive feedback between the global and local" (48). Little has changed in 2017: this unwavering feedback, running alongside "the guidance of missiles using 'electronic warfare,'" parallels and utilizes the globalizing nature of the Internet, and its focus on the binary logic of its software and hardware underpinnings; problematically, as well, this "electronic warfare" is based on a reduction of the world, via the militarized gaze of tactics, strategy and the literal aiming scope of the weapon, into digital units. Extending Deleuze and Guattari's explanations of how new technologies affect the State War Machine, the State War Machines of the 1990s and beyond, aided by the Internet and virtual weaponry, "overcoded" the segments of its battlefields (populations, resources, landscapes) with numerical, rather than the older "territorial," organization. There has been an increasing exaggeration of this overcoding post-9/11, with the "war on terrorism" and the rise of non-territorial States of terrorist groups like al-Qaeda, ISIS and Boko Haram, where groups do not fight or define their sovereignty by national borders, as an older State War Machine might, but rather by a decentralized and non-geographical notion of ideology. To this end Mbembé argues:

> An important feature of the age of global mobility is that military operations and the exercise of the right to kill are no longer the sole monopoly of states, and the "regular army" is no longer the unique modality of carrying out these functions. Instead, a patchwork of overlapping and incomplete rights to rule emerges, inextricably superimposed and tangled, in which different de facto juridical instances are geographically interwoven and plural allegiances ... abound. (31)

It should come as no surprise then that the integration of a popular Internet into a civilian life has made it so that these terrorist groups' War Machines often use the civilian networks of the Internet to distribute, communicate, recruit and globally reinforce their "patchwork" and "geographically interwoven and plural allegiances."[10] Chapter 6 of this text explores in more detail the fact that State War Machines, and to a lesser extent terrorist groups, utilize the civilian Internet, and its inherent public networked nature, as a weapon to attack other States' civilian and military infrastructures in acts of cyberwarfare; as Klaus-Gerd Giesen reminds, older notions of warfare, sovereignty and territory are scrambled "due to the decentralized nature of the Internet, [where] any malware can actually cross many borders within a fraction of a second before finding its target" (66). Der Derian worries deeply about the Internet's proliferation in the Total War Machine, as he sees it as one, and perhaps the primary, example of "new technologies of imitation and simulation as well as surveillance and speed [that have] collapsed the geographical distance, chronological duration, the gap itself between the reality and virtuality of war" (774). With this, "new media, generally identified as digitized, interactive, networked forms of communication, now exercise a global effect if not ubiquitous presence through real time access ... war reaches not only into every living room but splashes onto every screen, TV, computer and cinema" (775). The Internet, as a part of the Total

War Machine, ensures not only that both civilians and the military weaponize the Internet, but that the battlefield and spaces of war are everywhere, at all times.

While the Internet has generated virtual worlds that have transformed the Total War Machine, so too have cinema and the war film transmogrified the understanding and justifications for war. In Paul Patton's introduction to *The Gulf War Did Not Take Place*, Baudrillard is said to have flagged this new warfare as "the birth of a new kind of military apparatus which incorporates the production and circulation of images as well as the power to direct the action of bodies and machines" (5). This centers upon the actions of stripping out images of bloody (actual) warfare because it doesn't fit into "the script of … [a] high-tech clean war" (13) constructed in order to maintain the support of those civilians at home. This then completely destroys the actual violent events of war, as "the involution and encrustation of the event in and by information" (48) eradicates it by suffocating the actual real victims and actions within war; within this destruction, civilians "remain fascinated by the evidence of the montage of … war with which we are inoculated everywhere: through the eyes, the senses and in discourse" (68). This focus on the eradicating and distancing power of the image in the State War Machine parallels the cinematic images created within war films, "montages of war," and the similar construction of warfare within Hollywood movies. Using as an example the overlapping montage of drone warfare imagery in both the State War Machine and the war film, military intelligence officer Lieutenant Colonel Douglas A. Pryer, in "The Rise of the Machines," writes that he was scared that "because of the small, gray viewing screens that came with these drones as well as their limited loiter time … we were physically removed from the action, maybe such an event would not affect us much. Would it look and feel, I wondered, like sitting at home, a can of Coke in hand, watching a war movie?" (14). On the other side of this, soldiers engaged in "real" war and combat were left with "an impression of the surreal, the hyperreal, or the unreal" wherein "even soldiers who experienced combat firsthand will sometimes later relate incredulously that at the time, even on the battlefield, life seemed 'like a Hollywood blockbuster'" (LaRocca 4). As "real" war footage/experience and the war film become increasingly identical, movies become a form of virtual simulation aimed primarily at civilians, with the filmic treatment of "real" footage that adds verisimilitude to the movies further blurring the real and the fictional to the point where the "real" becomes "a war movie."

Speaking further to the modern digitization of war, Virilio describes the use of satellites to gather information, computer simulation and the increased reliance on long-range air strikes as coming closer and closer to "acts of war without war" (*Pure War* 32). This text argues strongly that movies are potential "acts of war without war," are modes for (mostly) civilians to access and experience war, and to achieve some form of sensory and narrative similarity to that of actual warfare, without actually having to physically engage. Baudrillard goes further, arguing that "we have a pressing need for simulation, even that of war … what we require is the aphrodisiac spice of the multiplication of fakes and the hallucination of violence, for we have a hallucinogenic pleasure in all things" (75); Suid clarifies that "war films do more than serve as a means for vicariously experiencing the proximity of death, the romance, and the adventure of war. They offer an escape from reality, the same appeal that war itself offers those who are involved in combat" (6). With the aforementioned American military's active participation in Hollywood, including lending locales, technical know-how, and materiel to movies, war films themselves can give the illusion of reality, of involving "realistic" hardware and software in "realistic" environments. As such, there is a blurring between the fictional and non-fictional of the world that has, as mentioned previously, been used to promote a civilian involvement and justification for (ongoing and ever-present) war. The "pleasure" of the simulation, the "aphrodisiac spice" of escapist and "vicarious experience" are always created within a space of virtual unreality but also with the knowledge that the "choices" within Hollywood films are always also "distorted and clouded by a medium that, after all, places before its audiences a commodity emphasizing entertainment" (Scott 5). As LaRocca reminds us, "War films lie at the junction of two multibillion-dollar industrial complexes: the military and the movies. Thus, while governments around the world wage war overtly or covertly, Hollywood and other moviemakers continue to explore and celebrate the dynamic features and implications of war" (4). Not only does this cinematic commoditized document, a key output of the Military Industrial Entertainment network, reduce the real suffering of people and landscapes via a distancing and fictionalizing mediated representation, warping the ethics and attitudes around contemporary warfare, but these documents also form deeply influential scripts that affect how an everyday movie-watching audience relates to their Internet-enabled technologies.

The representation of technologies within war films has always been part of the spectacle of combat and an essential part of entertaining the movie-watching audience, and it deserves attention if only for that fact. However, more complexly, Mead, addressing the long history of militaries promoting the literal literacy of reading and writing as a means to empower their own armies, speaks to the emerging "literacies" that are required within the State War Machine as "new technologies and duties have emerged" in which the term "literacy" has shifted to "encompass whatever skills are needed to handle [those technologies and duties]" (60). Mead argues that "video games represent one of the more culturally prominent examples of a new sort of literacy" (60), and this text extends his thinking to contend that war movies grant the same "literacy" as video games to their audience; when returning to the focus of this text, war films that showcase the Internet and Internet-enabled technologies are creating "literacies" and making arguments about how a civilian user should relate to her/his technologies in his/her everyday life. In *Interfacing with the Internet in Popular Cinema*, I call this contemporary audience the machinic audience. Drawing from Deleuze and Guattari's sense of the word "machinic" as reflecting how identity is formed through the interaction of various invisible and visible infrastructural and conceptual machines, I define the machinic audience as the contemporary movie-watching audience, itself an example of an assemblage, that is "savvy to their soft and hard networks of networks … an audience comfortably draped in the virtuality of Web 2.0 … and [that] understands/appreciates/invites the digitization of themselves and the world around them."[11] Within my previous work, I argue that this hybridization within a modern movie watcher was largely a product of their physical body and their virtual Bodies without Organs (or avatars), and that film representations of such assemblages construct arguments, both positive and negative, around Internet usage. The most positive version of this assemblage is built with what Deleuze and Guattari would call full Bodies without Organs, entities that the authors characterize as "intense," "unified" and having the potential to be "full of gaiety, ecstasy and dance" (*ATP* 150), which ultimately create a creature that is "open and allows other Bodies without Organs and information/sensation to flow through it" (Tucker 20). By this, Deleuze and Guattari contend that identity is a rhizomatic collection of Bodies without Organs that interweave with the physical body to produce a person's self.

Such an understanding of identity is synonymous with Hayles' "posthuman," a modern construct that is a symbiotic combination of biological and technological, "an amalgam, a collection of heterogeneous components, a material-informational entity whose boundaries undergo continuous construction and reconstruction" (*HWBPh* 3). In many ways, Hayles' posthuman owes a great debt to Donna Haraway's "cyborg" that she established in "A Cyborg Manifesto" (first presented in 1983; collected in her text *Simians, Cyborgs, and Women: The Reinvention of Nature* 1991).[12] Haraway allows for the cyborg to incorporate the virtual or "fictional" elements of technology, stating that "a cyborg is a cybernetic organism, a hybrid of machine and organism, a creature of social reality as well as a creature of fiction" (291). This hybrid, like the posthuman, is a network of different technological and biological components, Bodies with and without Organs, which are in contact with other humans who are also networks of technological and biological components. Considering all this, what is most important when utilizing the concept of the posthuman/cyborg is recognition that such an entity is reliant upon an interdependence between physical bodies and technological elements: there can be neither a physical-only version nor a technology-only version, and the unbalancing of one side of the material-informational/technological partnership generates unhealthy forms of identity.

This book then unpacks the linking together of the machinic audience and the Total War Machine at the site of the war film genre, in particular with the understanding that each is an individual "machinic phylum" and they join together to form a larger machinic phylum. For Deleuze and Guattari, a machinic phylum is dependent on "singularities," which De Landa describes as when technological-biological assemblages bond with other such assemblages in a self-organizing fashion until there is a large system in which all become part of a "common phylogenetic lineage" that culminates in a machine (in Deleuze and Guattari's sense of the term, that "blurs the distinction between organic and non-organic life" (*WAIM* 7). This assemblage of assemblages is the machinic phylum, which Deleuze and Guattari clarify further: "The machinic phylum is materiality, natural or artificial, and both simultaneously; it is matter in movement, in flux, in variation, matter as a conveyor of singularities and traits of expression" (*ATP* 409). In its more positive forms, De Landa sees the machinic phylum as a unifying process: "The idea of a 'machinic phylum' would then be that, beyond biological lineages, we are also related to non-living creatures (winds and flames, lava and rocks) through common 'body-plans' involving similar self-organizing and combinatorial processes" ("The Machinic Phylum" para. 10), adding that the concept of a "machinic phylum" "refers to both the process of self-organization in general and to the particular assemblages in which the power of these processes are integrated" (*WAIM* 20). For De Landa one of the primary examples of the machinic phylum is the simultaneous "materiality, natural or artificial" of the State War Machine: as he outlines, the State War Machine as a machinic phylum incorporates "weapons, both offensive and defensive"; "tactics, the art of assembling men and weapons into formation"; "strategy, the art of assembling single battles into a coherent war"; and "logistics, the art of military procurement and supply" (23). The State War Machine is an assemblage of all these machines, both virtual and physical, into a machinic phylum of assemblages interacting and organizing. The computer, at both the hardware and software levels, plays an essential role in tying all the levels of the State War Machine together, giving the State War Machine materiel; actual weapons (or computerized weapon components); an ability to communicate quickly and efficiently (core to Network-Centric Warfare); an ability to store, generate, retrieve and display data (AR displays); the modes, spaces and technology to produce, design, improve and distribute weapons (and soldiers); and a virtual space to simulate battles in order to decide on the best tactics, strategy or logistics (to name just a few items of a seemingly endless list). Chapter 3 of this text more completely unpacks these ideas, but here, it is enough to pose the question of what happens when the machinic audience, itself a machinic phylum of its own civilian versions of Internet-enabled technologies and biological components, links together with the State War Machine? What then happens when those two machinic phyla join with the machinic phylum of Hollywood cinema (an assemblage of assemblages that includes movie production, promotion, distribution, etc.)?

Answering these questions and understanding the dense networking of assemblages that takes place within the machinic phylum of the Total War Machine means returning to the arguments from the beginning of this introduction. When Kellner argues that "Hollywood films provide important cinematic visions concerning the psychological, sociopolitical and ideological make-up of US society at any given point in history" (18), he is speaking to both the reflection of war within a specific era of a society, and he is also arguing that these visions encompass representations of technologies, like the Internet, and Hollywood's impacts on attitudes toward those technologies. As such, the entirety of my previous book makes the argument that films are effective cultural documents that make arguments for how the machinic audience might celebrate or fear their technological elements. This text's specific focus on the intersections between war films and Internet-enabled technologies is built on Haraway's argument that "modern war is a cyborg orgy, coded by C3I, command-control-communication-intelligence" (292), adding that "the main trouble with cyborgs, of course, is that they are the illegitimate offspring of militarism and patriarchal capitalism" (293). With this "modern war" and "militarism" in mind, Haraway outlines the two paths for the cyborg:

> From one perspective, a cyborg world is about the final imposition of a grid of control on the planet, about the final abstraction embodied in a Star Wars apocalypse waged in the name of defence. … From another perspective, a cyborg world might be about lived social and bodily realities in which people are not afraid of their joint kinship with animals and machines, not afraid of permanently partial identities and contradictory standpoints. (295)

So the machinic audience is already steeped in a historical military parentage, then representations of those cyborgs in cinematic warfare will potentially be powerful tools in shaping which of Haraway's two paths the movies' audiences would choose to take. The more cynical path of "a Star Wars apocalypse waged in the name of defence" stems from the fact that the cinematic representations of (Internet-enabled) technologies serve Žižek's "ideological state apparatus": speaking to the naval war film, Rayner paraphrases Patrick M. Regan when arguing that "the pervasiveness of war films, war toys, and popular images of conflict … [is] a prerequisite for the heightening of patriotism, the identification of enemies and the propagation of ideological norms" (203). Rayner calls this a "fetishistic treatment of military hardware" in which "reintroduction of such features transforms the civil war and the presence of the reluctant American hero into a scenario in which American forces can intervene clearly and decisively, and reconfirm their superiority in the process" (203). As discussed in the upcoming chapters of this book, the asymmetrical gap between the American State War Machine and their enemies is often portrayed cinematically as a way to reaffirm American superiority and heighten the "ideological norm" of militarized technological development—in particular, the weaponizing of civilian digital spaces that use the Internet. With this weaponizing, the machinic audience is complicit in actual and cinematic warfare. Revisiting the war film's abilities to parallel conflicts "beyond the frame" and Langford's earlier insistence that war films move toward "narrative participation and empathetic participation," the repetition of the word "participation" is key: watchers of the genre are active (victims? perpetrators?) in the warfare on screen, and are therefore as much involved in the creation of the culture around the document as those involved in the movie itself. Because of the war film's audience's special (complicit) "participation," it is especially imperative that the machinic audience take a critical position in this text's analysis of the war film and the types of arguments, "lessons," being activated.

When considering the cyborgs of cinematic warfare, and their effects on the machinic audience, this text focuses most often on the soldier, a figure who is often the audience surrogate and the portal for encouraging participation in the movie, and therefore the most valuable rhetorical figure. Describing the first three main cycles of the war film genre, Isenberg argues that war films centered around WWI tended to focus on "contemporary liberal values" with a more humanist individual girded by "the emphasis on honor, duty and valor" (as paraphrased in Neale 128), while a WWII-era war film is marked by "its regular stress on cooperative goals, its frequent critiques of extreme individualism," which are then contrasted with Vietnam war films by marking them and their characters with a characteristic lack of control of over the "environments, their activities, their enemies and their fates" (Neale 133). While Basinger agrees that the WWII combat film was most often built around the collective components of a State War Machine, Barry Langford explains that in Vietnam war films, in order to deal with this lack of control, the protagonists often become "loners" whose actions are based on "implicit individualism" based more around "self-preservation" in the face of "the combined strain of military failure and increasingly strident domestic political opposition" (120). Langford, publishing in 2005, points out that this characteristic of war films have not changed much, with WWII films being anomalous for a number of previously theorized reasons,[13] and this text contends that this construction of the soldier remains largely true into 2017. However, Deleuze and Guattari expand on the soldier's struggle within the State War Machine: "Trapped between the two poles of political sovereignty, the man of war seems outmoded, condemned, without a future, reduced to his own fury, which he turns against himself" (355). The "two poles of sovereignty" are, then, the individual soldier and her/his personal ethical system, set against the State's infrastructure and larger machines of war-making at the other end of the spectrum. This tension is exactly what Susan Jeffords sees in her construction of the cinematic "hard body" in Reagan-era films, wherein the hero of the text is the sole rational individual that is tasked with carrying out near-impossible tasks, and despite the ineffective infrastructures of the State War Machine in the name of American and masculine superiority. The hard body was not, obviously, the only cinematic representation of masculinity emerging from the 1980s, but it was and continues to be resoundingly significant. According to Jeffords, such a markedly white, masculine and American body, exemplified by the *Rambo* films, was a distinctly militarized projection of a unified national identity; the hard body, despite the sometimes cartoonish markers of "muscular physiques, violent actions, and individual determination" (*Hard Bodies* 21), are representatives of "average citizens" who are "thrust forward into heroism … in defiance of their governments and institutional bureaucracies" (19) and then wish to recenter power back to the "heroic, aggressive and determined" (25) citizens who populate the country. Such a body was, if nothing else, "a strong one, capable of confronting enemies rather than submitting to them, of battling evil empires rather than allowing them to flourish, of using its hardened body—its renewed techno-military network—to impose its will on others" (25). The extreme popularity of hard-body films, such as the first three *Rambo* films (Dir. Ted Kotcheff 1982; Dir. George P. Cosmatos 1985; Dir. Peter MacDonald 1988), *Die Hard* (Dir. John McTiernan 1988) and *Batman* (Dir. Tim Burton 1989),[14] makes it an important concept that constructed and maintained notions of the male body, in particular within action-adventure, war, and combat films, throughout the majority of the movies analyzed in this text.

However, as explored in this chapter, the biologically based hard body becomes a relic with the introduction of increasingly intelligent hardware and software and Internet-enabled networked weaponry and warfare and, as such, the pure version of the hard body became at best a nostalgic touchpoint and at worst a cartoonish satire of itself. Yet this hard body figure did not disappear, but has evolved as a reflection of how the "real-life" soldier has also evolved. Returning to Basinger's assertion that "different wars inspire different genres," with the hard body as its hereditary bedrock, the representation of a milita-rized Internet in Hollywood war films has shifted to include the cyborg while also acknowledging that there is an expectation (need?) for the machinic audience to see their heroic soldiers mixed with their tech-nological devices in a spectacular fashion. This new technological hard body, explored more fully in Chapter 2, is one that uses the "muscles" of networked hardware and software in combat; such combat is not always physical and acknowledges the globalized nature of the Internet, and the paranoia and surveillance, that comes with a constant and ever-present cyber-battlefield.

Chapter 2, "The Hard Technological Body in the Exoskeletal Soldier," uses Susan Jeffords' work on Reagan-era action movies to establish the "hard body" as the overmuscled biological spectacle that functioned as a unifying force for both "a type of national character" and "the nation itself" (25). The "mastery" that the hard body repre-sents is echoed in the equally spectacular hard technological bodies of the exoskeleton-enhanced protagonists of *Elysium* (Dir. Neill Blomkamp 2013) and *Edge of Tomorrow* (Dir. Doug Liman 2014). The hard tech-nological body arises in reaction to the increased globalization of the world and terrorist attacks that have made international borders and con-flicts far murkier. Simultaneously, such a body also reflects the extreme interpenetration that computerized technology has had both in global-national militaries as well as in the average posthuman Western mov-iegoer's life. Different than the all-encasing machine "suits" of *Pacific Rim* (Dir. Guillermo Del Toro 2013) and the *Iron Man* films (Dir. Jon Favreau 2008, 2010; Dir. Shane Black 2013), the exoskeleton, specifi-cally as combat weapon, is one that deliberately melds the human and the machine so that both biological and technological are visible simul-taneously. The chapter briefly traces the representations of cinematic exoskeletons through *Aliens* (Dir. James Cameron 1986), *The Matrix Revolutions* (Dir. Lana and Andy Wachowski 2003), and *Avatar* (Dir. James Cameron 2009). A focus on the recent use of exoskeleton com-bat in *Elysium* and *Edge of Tomorrow* shows that biological muscle com-bined with and augmented by a technological apparatus generates a spectacle reminiscent of the '80s hard body. In this, the hard technologi-cal body has morphed its focus of mastery from international and physi-cal conflicts to virtual and borderless ones. Such a transition encourages the contemporary machinic movie audience not to view themselves as a healthy symbiotic posthuman; instead, the hard technological body, in an attempt to heroically reassert human exceptionalism and a human-centric transhumanism, treats his/her computerized technology, specifically the Internet, as a tool to be conquered and a weapon to conquer with.

Chapter 3, "The Soldier Interfaces on the Digitally Augmented Battlefield," begins with the fears, documented by Manuel De Landa and N. Katherine Hayles, of cutting humans "out of the loop" in military operations, which have almost completely dissipated within films and have been replaced by a new model of soldier that is exemplified by the near-literal man-in-the-middle suits of the *Iron Man* films and the cyber-connected dual Jaeger pilots in *Pacific Rim*. Different than the hard technological body, the suits present an entirely different interface and symbiosis with its human user(s) in that the human is shrouded entirely within the technology itself. Beginning with D.N. Rodowick's theorizing on digital filmmaking and "perceptual realism," the suits present the user with an objective and "framed" vision of the world that is then further filtered through the lens of military organization and combat. When the machinic audience looks "through the eyes of these suits" there is a doubling of Judith Butler's understanding of the war photograph's frame, so that anything within that view is distanced and completely dehumanized from the cinema audience. These immediately mediated perceptions of the characters' worlds, presented as supra-human tools completely under user control, encourages a dangerous remilitarization of the Internet, in an outdated model that promotes an overly simplistic nationalism and too-basic posthuman evolution. The chapter ends by exploring what happens, as harbingered by contemporary real-world advances in Internet technologies, when Internet and technological interfaces dissolve into the biological body, using *Transcendence* (Dir. Wally Pfister 2014) as a core example. *Transcendence* proposes a military entity that is completely unable to separate its biological from its mechanical components, instead generating a completely symbiotic assemblage. Much like how the formerly clear enemies of earlier war films have become increasingly complicated in recent examples of the genre, what constitutes a soldier and a military use of everyday technology has similarly blurred, generating a virtually connected Total War battlefield that is equal parts civilian and soldier and is at all times constant and everyplace.

If, as Chapter 3 argues, civilian and military technological use are converging to the point of being indistinct, then Chapter 4, "War Films, Combat Simulators and the Absent Virtual Soldier," will take up combat that is represented as completely virtual through cinematic representations (or lack thereof) of combat simulators. The American military has long been invested in single-soldier and networked simulation technology, early examples of which include SIMNET and "The Battle of 73 Easting" (to say nothing of flight and tank simulators), as a means to train its soldiers and expose them to the speed and visceral nature of warfare. Yet these simulators are almost completely absent from movies within the war film genre. Interesting, then, that the cinematic representations of the technology, when they do show up, come under the guise of civilian military-styled video games and virtual reality in movies like *Brainstorm* (Dir. Douglass Trumbull 1983), *The Lawnmower Man* (Dir. Brett Leonard 1992) and *Gamer* (Dir. Neveldine and Taylor 2009). The chapter explores these films' critiques about the use of popular combat simulators' functions within a culture of Total War, as well as raises concerns around the virtualizing of the modern American State War Machine as both dehumanizing and overcorporatized applications of military brainwashing. The movies present conflicts that further enhance the theme of enemy-ally disintegration by turning civilians against other civilians in the role of soldier in militarized combat, generating an Internet-enabled space, via the games themselves and the cinematic representations of these virtual spaces, wherein the dense networking capabilities of the Internet becomes a normalized facilitator of military violence. The end of the chapter explores the reasons why, despite its normalized placement within a contemporary War Machine, combat and warfare simulators do not show up in war films. While first touching on the obvious differences in the mediums of film and video games, the chapter then looks at the intertextual nature of movies like *Jarhead* (Dir. Sam Mendes 2005), and how soldiers watch other war films, to argue that cinema itself functions as a form of "virtual reality" training that potentially indoctrinates soldiers in much the same way a combat simulator does.

Chapter 5, "Ender's Wargames: Drones, Data and the Simulation of War as Weapon and Tactic," expands from Chapter 4 into how the rising acceptance of game theory in combination with increasingly complex and sophisticated computer simulators has drastically changed the modern State War Machines. While such a shift was popularly reflected in *WarGames* (Dir. John Badham 1983) and the publication of Orson Scott Card's novel *Ender's Game* (1985), simulated war, with the possible exception of the war movie, was kept largely from the public eye. Yet, as Jean Baudrillard and Paul Virilio have theorized, beginning with the Gulf

War, recent warfare has pushed the depiction of real-life war into the realm of unreal model and constantly mediated simulation, transforming the landscape and its combatants into distanced sets of data points. Using the science fiction example of *Stealth* (Dir. Rob Cohen 2005) and the more "realistic" *Eye in the Sky* (Dir. Gavin Hood 2016) and *Good Kill* (Dir. Andrew Niccol 2014), the chapter argues that all three films echo much of the critique of the movie version of *Ender's Game* (Dir. Gavin Hood 2013) of a "data-driven" simulated war via their representations of distanced drone strikes. Unlike the previous three chapters, this chapter explores what it means to have filmic representations of military use that are completely abstracted from soldier-to-soldier combat; instead the conflicts are rendered as drone strikes and/or computer-modeled battles wherein the "soldiers" are in fact continents away from their weapon's actions and consequences. Acknowledging Manuel De Landa's work alongside the shifting genre of the war movie and the simulated roots of cinema itself, such a dangerous shift is reflected most clearly in *Ender's Game*, wherein the simulation itself becomes the war, which then reveals the traumas caused, on both civilians and soldiers alike, by a distanced military overdependent on technologies, specifically the Internet.

The final chapter, "The Civilian Soldiers of Cyberwarfare," extends in the other direction from Chapter 5, and questions what happens when the densely generated networks that the military has used to completely abstract war into distanced data points begin to be repurposed by civilian users and turned back upon the State War Machine as a means to combat and expose that military machinery. My previous work in *Interfacing with the Internet in Popular Cinema* establishes the cinematic hacker as a civilian too easily reappropriated back into Total War. However, recent films such as *Blackhat* (Dir. Michael Mann 2015), *Snowden* (Dir. Oliver Stone 2016) and *The Fifth Estate* (Dir. Bill Condon 2013) present civilian protagonists that effectively hijack secret and dense digital military networks and expose that normally top secret information to the public in heroic fashion. With this shift, the contemporary war film begins to blend with the political thriller and the biopic, wherein there is little "traditional combat" and the focus of the film is on conspiracy and the exposure of, and degrading of trust in, Gilles Deleuze's notion of Societies of Control. These films, then, address one of the key alternatives of an Internet-enabled War Machine, shifted toward an increasingly globalized enemy (terrorists, other hackers, etc.), wherein information and data, and the protection/privatization thereof, are just as important to military infrastructure and effectiveness as soldier-to-soldier combat. Superficially, the civilian protagonists within the discussed films are necessary and are the aware and active machinic users of the Internet, but at the core, each of the films still uphold the biological human as the most important part of any biological-technological assemblage.

Across all the aforementioned chapters, problematically, the key heroic figures are deeply rooted in a traditional sense of humanism. Pramod K. Nayar critiques that humanism, as centered around the exceptionalism of "the universal human," "is constructed through a process of exclusion" that leaves humans as the only species capable of "autonomous rationality" and "the agency of the individual" (11). As such, humanism, Nayar argues, becomes an ideological system that (morally) classifies other races, genders and species and in doing so becomes a "system of *differentiation* in which some forms of the body were treated as 'human' and others as 'not human'" (author's italics 12). Thinking about the archetypical war film with a universal human soldier at the center as the positive protagonist, the humanism of the movies allow the audience to easily dehumanize the enemies of that protagonist as Other, and therefore justify the actions and/or violence against that "lesser" group. Mbembé locates this ethics more specifically in the process of colonization, an ideological state whose core tenets resonate and structure much of the Western world today:

> In the same context, colonies are similar to the frontiers. They are inhabited by "savages." The colonies are not organized in a state form and have not created a human world. Their armies do not form a distinct entity, and their wars are not wars between regular armies. They do not imply the mobilization of sovereign subjects (citizens) who respect each other as enemies. They do not establish a distinction between combatants and noncombatants, or again between an "enemy" and a "criminal." It is thus impossible to conclude peace with them. (24)

The enemies of that State War Machine are non-humans, are savages populating a frontier to conquered, and, as such, all occupiers of that space are enemies, with no "distinction between combatants and noncombatants." Returning to Jeffords, this human-centric approach is most clearly seen in the '80s hard body, where there is a whole ethical system built into this: the humanistic soldier, as appropriated by a State War

Machine under the guise of "civilization," is an individual and full of the aforementioned "honor, duty and valor"; he/she is righteous and justified in his/her actions in war. Placing this ethical system within a contemporary environment of globalized and Internet-networked warfare, Der Derian makes clear that

> unlike other forms of warfare, virtuous war has an unsurpassed power to commute death, to keep it out of sight, out of mind. In simulated preparations and virtual executions of war, there is a high risk that one learns how to kill but not to take responsibility for it, one experiences "death" but not the tragic consequences of it. In virtuous war we now face not just the confusion but the pixilation of war and game on the same screen. (773)

The "frontiers" and "savages" are then further distanced by virtuous warfare and made less human by this "pixilation," and the responsibility for the killing within those spaces dissipates further when filtered through a (cinematic and/or computer) screen, which Braidotti argues clearly in stating that "new forms of warfare entail simultaneously the breath-taking efficiency of 'intelligent', un-manned technological weaponry on the one hand, and the rawness of dismembered and humiliated human bodies on the other" (122). The soldier then is "a form of information technology" (Mead 4); however, this contemporary military unit is an extension of a post-WWII cybernetics that stressed placing a "man-in-the-middle" of any biological-technological military personnel, with the "'human-machine system,' not just the machine itself," being of the utmost importance. Still, it is the liberal and individual human at the core that is the most valuable and trustworthy. Returning to the figure of the cyborg and this text's focus on the Internet and Internet-enhanced machines, what is important to understand then is that the liberal human/biological components of the soldier are by far the most important elements of the soldier assemblage, the only parts capable of honor, duty and individual free will. As reflected in the movies discussed in this book, within this construction, the machine species of the film (guns, tanks, computers, etc.) are most often relegated to simple weapons under full control of that "free" (biological) human. However, an intriguing trend that courses through many of the movies examined in the book is that this soldier assemblage very rarely begins as a military figure. Instead, the soldier-protagonists of the films are often civilians that are then repurposed into the machinic phyla of State and Total War Machines, usually because of their technical expertise. While the following chapters will go further into depth with individual movies and examples, this trend is also a reflection of how the Total War Machine effortlessly melds itself to civilian life, with the Internet itself being a prime example, so that civilians are themselves, directly or indirectly, participating in the war effort. However, in relation to the notion of humanism, this move to integrate the civilian into the Total War Machine is perhaps a reflection of the aforementioned distrust, post-Vietnam, in both the military and governmental apparatuses; it is only the liberal and individual civilian, who is outside of both of these infrastructural entities, that is able to solve the problems that these two corrupted and ineffectual forces cannot.

So with this humanistic system undergirding the war film genre, Langford further defines war films about post-Vietnam conflicts, such as *Enemy of the State* (Dir. Tony Scott 1998) and *Swordfish* (Dir. Dominic Sena 2001), as having evolved to something akin to "techno-thrillers" that are "closer to the espionage thriller's shadowy world of surveillance and covert action than the combat film's terrain of pitched battles and firefights" (126). Obviously, cinematic soldier-to-soldier combat does still exist, but the soldier within the American modern military is going to be augmented with a series of networked communication and weapon-enhancing technologies.[15] Yet despite this shift in the genre (and in actual warfare), the central figure of the soldier-assemblage and the ethical systems within the movies have only superficially (at best) evolved to consider complex versions of the posthuman/cyborg. As mentioned previously, the '80s hard body is a near-cartoon, but the hard technological bodies that intertwine through the movies analyzed in this book use their own Internet-enabled technologies, like steroids, that transform the "average" citizen into the same spectacular soldier as the biologically-based hard body. While this cinematic construction superficially highlights the type of cyborg or posthuman a modern machinic audience would identify with and perhaps admire, the concentration on the individual liberal human within that cyborg assemblage resists a posthumanism based in Guattari's "new virtual social ecology, which includes social, political, ethical and aesthetic dimensions, and the traversal links between them" (quoted from Bradotti 93). Instead, most of the movies analyzed in this text fall back upon an anthropomorphic humanism, a

> structurally unattainable form of self-identity which conceals or attempts to repress its own difference. Its main 'agent'—the free universal and at the same time singular and unique individual—thus exposed or undone, the

'liberal humanism' itself becomes incredible as a grand narrative, as ideology, as myth, or as historical or political discourse. (Nayar 11)

In *Iron Man 3, Pacific Rim, Elysium* or *Edge of Tomorrow*, movies closer to the action-adventure or combat film genres, the liberal biological individual is the literal center of the soldier assemblage; the superficial posthuman soldier is controlled fully and completely by its human/biological components, with the victories of those films' protagonists being directly attributed to humanist qualities of sacrifice and honor. Movies that are closer to what Langford flags as techno-thriller, like *Blackhat*, showcase hackers and/or whistleblowers as the most incorruptible figures, the only ones upholding the values of "duty" and "honor." However, they are only able to do this because they are humans who have mastered the machine species around them, and they are able to control and manipulate computers and computer networks in order to uphold their humanistic ethics. The conflicts within films that engage with the virtuous Network-Centric Warfare, like *Stealth, Good Kill* and *Eye in the Sky*, are primarily driven by the biological human as a liberal and individual human, with that figure being the only one capable of fighting off the perceived contemporary vulnerability generated by being increasingly mediated by computers. While the movies do include the types of Internet-enabled technologies a machinic audience might recognize and/ or appreciate (wearable technology, software such as games and browsers, smartphones, etc.), there are still relatively clear lines in each between the human/biological and technological/machine components, with the greatest value clearly being placed on the "human" in the middle of it all.

Nayar would flag these hard technological body movies as a type of "pop posthumanism" that he further defines as "transhuman" (7).[16] Texts with a transhuman ethics argue that "technological and biological modifications ... improve the 'human.' This implies that there is a distinctive entity identifiable as the 'human,' ... [refusing] to see the human as a construct enmeshed with other forms of life and [which] treats technology as a means of 'adding' to already existing human qualities" (6); through this, however, the transhuman "retains the key attributes of the human—sensation, emotion, rationality—but believes these characteristics might be enhanced through technological intervention" (8). At the core, then, "transhumanism relies on human rationality as a key marker of 'personhood' and individual identity" (7), and, in Nayar's critique, is simply an extension of humanism that still retains too much of its traditional "Enlightenment ideals" in its hierarchical pursuit of the exceptionalism of the human species via the mastery of other non-humans, animal, and, in this case, machine species. Though the techno-logical is present and the protagonists of the movies mentioned in the previous paragraph are a version of the cyborg or posthuman, they are a too-simple, non-porous version, still placing "human rationality," and the moral, justified and heroic decisions that arise from the choices of that rationality, as the unique ethical rulers of self-identity. More simply, however, "war, after all, is as much a means of achieving sovereignty as a way of exercising the right to kill" (Mbembé 12); as established earlier in this introduction, this self-identity is an extension of Mbembé's necropo-litics, in which the State War Machine is a force determined to dehu-manize its enemies and strip them of their sovereignty in order to kill and conquer them and their landscapes. Not only are these movies often upholding and celebrating militaristic means and violence as a mode of global problem solving and nation building (again, in opposition to the enemy Other), but the healthy balance between biological and techno-logical is rarely present and instead, in most of the films, the machinic audience is encouraged to take a (biologically) human-centric view in which machine cooperative co-species are reduced to weapons necessarily under complete control in order to conquer and control.

This text critiques these movies and complicates these initial conclu-sions with detailed analysis, and, in doing so, upholds critical posthu-manism as the alternative model for human-technological interaction. Nayar, as well as Stefan Herbrechter and Rosi Braidotti, have written excellent texts outlining what is meant by critical posthumanism: in reaction to the distinctly European "classic ideal of 'Man'" (Braidotti 13), focused on the "unshakable certainty [in the] boundless capacity of humans to pursue their individual and collective perfectibility" with high faith in "the unique, self-regulating, and intrinsically moral powers of human reason," such critical posthumanism rejects this "hegemonic cultural model" (14) and instead rests "on an enlarged sense of inter-connection between self and others, including the non-human or 'earth' others. This practice of relating to others requires and is enhanced by the rejection of self-centered individualism" (48). Within this system

> humans and their humanity are historical and cultural constructs rather than transcendental concepts free from ideology and they therefore must be placed within larger contexts like ecosystems ... where the human is no longer seen as the sole hero of a history of emancipation, but as a (rather improbable but important) stage within the evolution of complex life forms. (Herbrechter 9)

But, as this introduction has argued, this "evolution" is irradiated by the cultural force of war. More specifically, Martin van Creveld argues that contemporary warfare generates "a 'flattened' image of reality that may prove fatal when the real thing [war] comes about" (*Wargames* 203). More, Baudrillard saw the mediated warfare undertaken with the weapons of longer-range bombers and, just as importantly, 24-hour news cycles and mediated representations of the conflict, as creating a fake war, with "fake and presumptive warriors, generals," to the point, Baudrillard argues, that the war is so abstracted from the real events, such a stunning and complete simulacra itself, that it does not exist, is simply a projection, an empty simulation and that "the day there is a real war, you will not even be able to tell the difference" (59). When this "flattened" image is composed of "real" and "fake" battlefield footage, and then repackaged as a commercial entertainment product, the simulacra that materializes, the subject of war, as reified through the war film and the Internet technologies within, demand critical posthumanism as a means for analysis. Nayar describes critical posthumanism as

> an *ethical project* that asks us to ponder, and act, upon the acknowledgement that life forms have messy intertwined histories. ... It asks us to acknowledge that human hierarchization of life forms has resulted in catastrophic effects for/upon animals, forests, plant life and some groups of humans in the form of genocide. (author's italics 31)

As an "ethical project" that recognizes the ongoing "process of technologization, based on the idea of a radical interdependence or mutual interpenetration" between human, animal and machine species (20), critical posthumanism understands that engaging texts (and the worlds in which they are created) while they are still in the process of being generated and ingested is an urgent and crucial undertaking. For this text, a critical posthumanism is a robust ethical system that allows the machinic audience to best analyze the effects of both the technology interpenetrating the machinic audience and the ways that the films are encouraging their audiences, through the saturation provided by the Total War Machine, to think of and utilize those technologies. However, given the interdependent relationship between the film genre and the "real" world, analyzing the texts with these ethics will allow that same audience to see the ways in which those same technologies are employed for violence in actual conflicts and to be further critical of the mediated modes in which warfare is presented to them (in other mediums like video games, TV or books, but also through the non-fiction modes, such as print or TV news). LaRocca asserts that

> a war film, then, in short, is an artificial ordering and construction, and a highly partial and specific vision of war that may be made available to, and in some sense appraised by, viewers. By contrast, the scope of actual war is inconceivable—even and especially for those who live it, witness it, or survive it—and so war films create satisfactions for the felt need of comprehension (28).

If war movies are a way of fighting a war without fighting a war, but are by their nature unable to even remotely capture the inconceivable "scope of actual war," then they are a problematic extension/manifestation of the "contemporary death-technologies" that Braidotti outlines as the main weapons of modern warfare, and the machinic audience's contribution to them must be reflexive and resistant (9). While this introduction has discussed how the war film rhetorically recontextualizes past conflicts and reflects current military engagements, it is important to remember too that war films might also "anticipate what future wars may encompass" (18). It is with this forward-looking gaze that LaRocca articulates that "since the nature of war-making and the nature of image-making are always evolving, such a question suggests that our understanding of war—as firsthand experience and as representation—requires continual, vigilant, and exacting analysis" (5). Settling for the illusionary "satisfaction" that comes with the shallow "comprehension" that the war film provides is not enough. This is especially true as, according to a comprehensive survey on the relationships between civilians and the military by the Triangle Institute, "military elite officers, far more than elite civilians, are prone to view civilian society as troubled and in need of reform. Elite military officers, far more than elite civilians, are prone to think that civilian society can be repaired if only military values were more widely accepted" (40). As the American State War Machine, via its active involvement in Hollywood productions of the war film, attempts to impose its "military values," a self-aware audience rooted in "continual, vigilant, and exacting analysis" and attuned to their own participation in the war film would be especially critical of the networked nature of Total War, and the place of war movies within this structure, and best be able to oppose its mechanics and refuse its rhetoric. It is unreasonable to think that the war film, a genre as old as the medium, will disappear anytime soon, but there is hope that a machinic audience engaged in a critical posthumanism can encourage and create cinematic reflections of warfare that are more sympathetic to the ecosystems of species and identities that make up the globe and, by doing so, complicate or eradicate the celebration of militarized violence.

## NOTES

1. Rick Altman's work on film genres, in particular the chapter "Why are generes sometimes mixed" within *Film/Genre* (London, Britain: British Film Institute, 1999), was especially useful to my thinking here, especially when considered with Rayner's work in *The Naval War Film* (28–29).
2. Because Lawrence H. Suid's *Guts and Glory* focuses on, for the most part, pre-Internet war films, I use it sparingly; however, his history of the interconnection between the military and Hollywood cinema is excellent and thorough, in particular his first chapter "Beginnings" (12–23).
3. As examples, Mirrlees lists "The Army's Hollywood liaison is called the Office of Army Chief of Public Affairs; the Navy's is called the Navy Office of Information West; the Air Force's is the Office of Public Affairs-Entertainment Liaison Office; the Marine Corps' is the Public Affairs Motion Picture and Television Liaison; the Coast Guard's is called the Motion Picture and TV Office" (7).
4. For further definitions of what I mean when I use the terms "assemblage" and Bodies without Organs, see the introduction to *Interfacing with the Internet in Popular Cinema*. In short, my construction of the the Body without Organs (BwO) comes first from Deleuze and Guattari's *Anti-Oedipus* (trans. R. Hurley, M. Seem and H. Lane. New York: Penguin Books, 1977, 9–16), but the somewhat negative characterization of the BwO in the text leads me to more actively use their version of the BwO in *A Thousand Plateaus*, in particular their construction of the term in the introduction and the chapter "Nov. 28, 1947: How Do You Make Yourself a Body Without Organs?" (149–168).
5. James Der Derian's article "Virtuous War/Virtual Theory" (*International Affairs* 76.4 (2000): 771–788. Website 3 September. 2016) and his full text *Virtuous War* (New York: Basic Books, 2009) are excellent further discussions of the military entertainment complex. Further definitions and discussion can be found in "Theatres of War" by Tim Lenoir and Henry Lowood (http://www.stanford.edu/class/sts145/Library/Lenoir-Lowood_TheatersOfWar.pdf) and "The Military-Entertainment Complex: A New Facet of Information Warfare" by Stephen Stockwell and Adam Muir (http://one.fibreculturejournal.org/fcj-004-the-military-entertainment-complex-a-new-facet-of-information-warfare).

6. Moschovitis, Christos J.P. et al. *History of the Internet: a chronology, 1843 to the present.* Santa Barbara, CA: ABC-CLIO, 1999; Ryan, Johnny. *A History of the Internet and the digital future.* London: Reaktion Books, 2010.

7. A brief history of the Internet and its progression to and introduction of the Popular GUI interface can be found in my introduction in *Interfacing with the Internet in Popular Cinema* (6–22). The key technology in the Internet's popularization that most scholars point to is Mosaic, the first Graphical User Interface (GUI) for the Internet, released in 1993. Once this GUI interface was publically released, the population of the Internet went from 10s of thousands to 10s of millions by the turn of the millennium.

8. As many histories of the Internet make clear, while the Internet was not invented solely for military purposes, it was funded throughout the 1960s by the militarily-rooted Advanced Research Projects Agency (ARPA), which, in 1972, added "Defense" to its title to becomes DARPA. In 2017, DARPA is housed under the United States Department of Defense.

9. See note 7.

10. Der Derian, in *Virtuous War* (2009), makes the point that in reaction to this globalized warfare wherein "states dematerialize and deconstruct, as national identities becomes more fluid, as simulations and scenarios reach for a credible threat, the public image of the enemy is (only) reducible to a wanted poster...all that is left as the last manis criminalized demon" (101). This is especially true of the enemy in *Blackhat*, allegedly a globalized terrorist group that is in fact a lone hacker who the protagonist of the film must eventually defeat, one-on-one, in order to avenge the death of his friend and claim his freedom.

11. Drawing from Deleuze and Guattari's sense of the word "machinic," I further define the machinic audience in the introduction and within Chapter 3 of my *Interfacing with the Internet in Popular Cinema*.

12. The term "cyborg" originates in Clynes and Kline's 1960 paper "Cyborg and Space" and is used to explain an entity that, via an exterior mechanism, incorporates its "own homeostatic systems [with]...an organization system in which such robot -like problems are taken care of automatically and unconsciously" (27). While I much prefer Haraway's definition of the term, Clynes and Kline's usage, while sterile, provides the bedrock for considering the hard technological bodies that run through Chapter 2 of this text.

13. Langford argues that the nature of World War II was different from every other war in how it was popularly constructed as a "moral" war of good versus evil. The communal comradery that the war films of this era are built around is the desperate need to pull together and expunge that evil.

14. *First Blood* made $125 million+ worldwide; *Rambo: First Blood Part II* made $300 million+ worldwide; *Rambo III* $189 million+ worldwide; *Batman* made $411 million+ worldwide; *Die Hard* made $140 million+ worldwide. All numbers via www.boxofficemojo.com. Accessed May 4th, 2016.

15. One example, The Future Combat System, as outlined by Roderick, "Putting the Post-Human in the Loop: Future Combat Systems and Post-Disciplinary Training." (*Journal for Cultural Research* (October 2008), 12 (4), 301–316), outlines how such a soldier, surrounded by Internet-enabled networked weapons and communication devices, would engage in combat. Such a real world assemblage is a good template for how contemporary examples of cinematic war combat are portrayed. Further work on this can be found with the discussion of the Land Warrior System (LWS) in Chapter 3.

16. Nayar is more critical of Hayles than I am, pointing to her work as "techno deterministic" and centering around a "human-machine interface" which still maintains the human/biological as the primary bastion and creator of identity (6). Based on her later critique of the Macey Conference and the foundational tenets and proponents of cybernetics in *How We Became Posthuman*, as well as her later discussions in *my mother was a computer* (Chicago: University of Chicago Press, 2005), "Traumas of Code" (*Critical Inquiry* (Autumn 2006), 33 (1), 136–157), and "Waking Up to the Surveillance Society" (*Surveillance and Society* (2009), 6 (3), 313–316), I see her theorizing as falling much more in line with the critical posthumanism Nayar is arguing for.

# CHAPTER 2

# The Hard Technological Body in the Exoskeletal Soldier

## INTRODUCTION: THE CYBORG'S EXOSKELETON

Through the 1960s, the American field of cybernetics began to solidify into a number of "real-world" applications and systems: The 1969 *Survey of Cybernetics* (ed. J. Rose) interweaves philosophical discussions with engineering formulas, ranging through a variety of examples, from flight simulator systems (280) to automatic computers and numerical calculating methods (233) to discussions of ergonomics (271) to the improvement of the management and business practices of industrial production in plants (313). This balance between philosophical and practical is embodied by the text's definition of the "cybernetic revolution": "It is introducing machines which augment our human capacity for rational data processing on a scale analogous to that which on steam, electrical and internal combustion engines augmented our physical powers in the Industrial Revolution" (Demczynski 23). Looking specifically at this chapter's focus of the exoskeleton, the practical application of augmenting "human capacity" is rooted deeply in Clynes and Kline's 1960 paper "Cyborg and Space." Its construction of the cyborg, via an exterior mechanism, generates an entity that incorporates its "own homeostatic systems [with] … an organization system in which such robot-like problems are taken care of automatically and unconsciously" (27). Clynes and Kline's question of whether "it will be possible to achieve [the altering of bodily functions to suit different environments] … *without alteration of heredity*" (authors' italics 26) is central to this

© The Author(s) 2017
A. Tucker, *Virtual Weaponry*,
DOI 10.1007/978-3-319-60198-4_2

application and is illustrated by the writers' point-by-point problem solving of how humans can survive in space while augmented with, not replaced by or fully enclosed within, their technology. They point to the Rockland Rat, which has, "under its skin, the Rose osmotic pump designed to permit continuous injections of chemicals at a slow, controlled rate" (27); in the picture the authors provide, the rat can be seen physically spliced with the pump and, while the divisions between technological and biological are simple, it does provide the groundwork to imagine an external device, one that doesn't rely on biological "heredity" or even the limits of "human capacity," welded to an organism as a symbiotic prosthesis that extends/enhances that organism beyond its natural abilities.

The focus on not altering the "heredity" of the biological aspect inside the exoskeleton and the ways in which the technological aspects are only there to extend that biological entity, not cooperatively interpenetrate, is indicative of the anthropomorphic humanism that the introduction to this text outlines as problematically pervasive in transhumanist projects. The thinking around developments like the Rockland Rat was the product of early cybernetic work and thought that emerged from the Macy Conferences (1946–1953) and Norbert Wiener's texts, namely *The Human Use of Human Beings* (*HU*; 1950; revised in 1954) and *Cybernetics, or Control and Communication in the Animal and Machine* (*Cybernetics*; first edition 1948; Second edition 1961). Both the Macy Conference and Wiener's ground-laying work are expertly summarized in Steve Heims' *The Cybernetics Group* (1991) but are more actively reconstructed in N. Katherine Hayles' *How We Became Posthuman* (*HWBPh* 1999), in which she dedicates a great deal of time to focusing on Claude Shannon and Warren Weaver's mathematical model of communication[1] and Norbert Wiener's theoretical constructions of human-robot entities. Hayles points specifically to *HU* as addressing the movements "from the physiology of living organisms to the electrical engineering of a cybernetic machine" (98) and blurring the "borders" between organic and mechanical: by way of a "prosthesis," such as the "hearing glove," cybernetics could potentially balance the "embodied experience, noisy with error" with "the clean abstractions of mathematical pattern" (98–99); this then spans everything from a man walking with a cane, to hearing aids, to a "voice synthesizer for someone with impaired speech [to] ... a helmet with a voice-activated firing control for a pilot" (84). In reading Hayles' paraphrasing alongside *HU* and *Cybernetics* (as well as the aforementioned Wiener-dedicated *Survey of Cybernetics*), it is apparent how seamlessly the authors, Wiener specifically, problematically mix military applications and metaphors with civilian examples. For example, in the space of a page in *HU*, Wiener juxtaposes the use of an elevator with a gun-pointer in combat (36); in another instance, his examples of "modern machines" cover "the controlled missile, the proximity fuse, the automatic door opener, the control apparatus for a chemical factory" (33). This casual blending of military and civilian was perhaps a product of the time in which he was writing (immediately post-WWII; the beginning of the Korean War and a protracted Cold War) wherein the aura of warfare and the lived experiences of being at war were ubiquitous. From within this specific zeitgeist, he states later in the text, "All this changed in the war" (201), and the "scientific war effort" (201) was most often the driver of civilian use of cybernetic technologies and systems; it therefore makes sense that a good amount of the practical applications of cybernetics were, at least initially, seen as weapons ("more effective killing machines"), such as Wiener's work in "self-correcting radar tuning, automated antiaircraft fire, torpedoes and guided missiles" (Hayles 86). Perhaps superficially, Wiener's later writing attempted to dismiss the issues with such weaponization by emphasizing the need for a humanistic approach that firmly planted a "liberal humanist subject" in the middle of any cybernetic apparatus. Hayles summarizes these projects as converting man from "an open-ended system into a portable instrument set" within which "the human as an information processing machine [is] spliced into a closed circuit [of technology]" (68); within this circuit, the presence of the "liberal humanist subject" creates a literal "man-in-the-middle ... splicing humans into feedback loops with machines" (68), which maintains much of the hierarchical anthropomorphism central to transhuman military applications that are then reflected and recreated in the movies analyzed in this text.

More specifically, this chapter explores a number of those problematic transhuman projects through cinematic representations of the exoskeletal assemblages across a number of decades.[2] While the exosuits discussed herein are not densely networked via Internet or Internet-like technologies, as the other more obvious depictions of warfare and soldiers are throughout this text as whole, they do provide a bedrock ethical system that structures the networked technological-biological assemblages that populate the rest of this text. The exosuits, and their relationship to the liberal human, provide a resonating model for how the machinic audience is encouraged to view and use their civilian networked technologies as weaponized tools that they are complete masters of. This weaponry and mastery begins with the fact that exoskeletons allow the biological body, and most importantly the face, to be viewed simulta-neously alongside the technological body, which then generates a more immediately literal and visible "man-in-the-middle" than the sealed *Iron Man* and *Pacific Rim* suits discussed at length in Chapter 3 of this text; these figures also remain more "human" than, for example, the com-pletely mechanical titular figures of *Terminator 2: Judgment Day* (Dir. James Cameron 1992). Generally, LaRocca argues that "these mobile, metal exoskeletons—full metal jackets of a different sort—often incorpo-rate advanced technologies of sensory perception as well as armaments that make the individual soldier into an arthropod, and an army unto himself or herself" (10). It is this notion of being "an army unto himself or herself" that focuses the ethics of the hard technological body films toward the liberal and individual human, resulting in an overfocus on the biological ("human") components of the hybrid assemblage, unbal-ancing the body–Body without Organs assemblage[3] too far toward the biological ("human"). In doing so, the movies miss the opportunity to enact a critical posthumanism that would provide their machinic audi-ences with more complex and critical engagements with their own (wear-able) technologies, as well as explore the ethical implications of using such devices in actual "real-world" warfare.

In terms of how a cinematic human-exoskeleton assemblage looks, the General Electric (G.E.) Hardiman Exoskeleton is deeply illustra-tive. General Electric attempted to build a "Prototype for Augmentation of Human Strength and Endurance" (1971) (Image 2.1). Rather than focusing on maintaining the chemical balances of the human body, the G.E. Hardiman would be

> worn as an outer mechanical garment, [and] the exoskeletal structure will be powered to dramatically amplify the wearer's strength and endurance by a factor of approximately 25 to one. ... The device will provide him with a set of 'mechanical muscles' that enables him to lift and handle loads in excess of 1000 pounds. The human operator will 'feel' the objects and forces he is working with almost as if he were in direct body and muscle contact. ... [It] mimics the movements of its wearer, presenting a literal union (man and machine). Thus the human's flexibility, intellect, and ver-satility are combined with the machine's strength and endurance. (5)

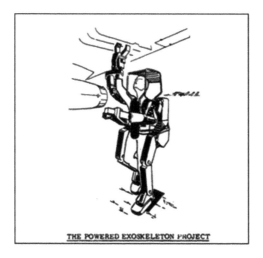

**Image 2.1** A prototype sketch for the G.E. Hardiman exoskeleton

The "master-slave" device was an imagined military technology built from a "joint Army-Navy program in November 1965" (4); the device was going to be used to load bombs into aircrafts or, more generally, to simply move cargo. Though an arm was allegedly completed, a full suit was never constructed. Still, the illustrations included in the reports are very useful in creating the iconography of the powered exoskeletons that appear later in *Aliens, The Matrix Revolutions* and *Avatar*. While interesting and worth exploring briefly later in this chapter, the exoskeletons of those three movies do not play nearly as central a role as they do in the more recent *Elysium* and *Edge of Tomorrow*; the exoskeletons inhabited by Max (Matt Damon), Kruger (Sharlto Copley), Cage (Tom Cruise) and Rita (Emily Blunt) are unique in their deliberately predominant, spectacular and heroic blend of the visible human with augmenting technology. Grounded in imagery of contemporary DARPA prototypes such as the Warrior Web,[4] these later portrayals are an evolution of the encoded rhetoric within the "hard bodies" of 1980s action films that Susan Jeffords outlines in *Hard Bodies: Hollywood Masculinity in the Reagan Era* (*HB*). As outlined in the introduction to this text, Jeffords' hard body was a figure meant to reflect the "average citizen" and her/his resistance to ingrained ineffective military and corporate infrastructures in service of a global American superiority. Eberwein, after praising Jeffords' concept, clarifies further by using Rambo as his example and stating that the title figure "and the film itself can be seen as ideological instruments that use his body … to reassert America's power in the world" (34); Steve Neale ties the "hyperbolic bodies" within the hard-body films as key contributors to the genre of action-adventure ("Action Adventure as Hollywood Genre" 71), while Holmlund, borrowing also from Tasker's work in *Spectacular Bodies* (1993), adds that the hard body is a "fantasy … masquerades of masculinity [that] are eminently popular, and undeniably potent" (225; also quoted in Neale "Action Adventure…" 73). Yet even in 1994, Jeffords flagged the shifts away from the hard body into a "more internalized and emotional kind of heroic icon" (*HB* 22). Whether the heroic bodies in post-Reagan film became softer is beyond the scope of this chapter.[5] It is, however, worth noting that the extreme explosion of Internet usage and infrastructure from the mid-1990s onward parallels this internalization, turning Americans into a more virtual and globalized populace in the 2000s. Alongside this change in national post-Y2K identity, America's "enemies," terrorist groups like al-Qaeda and ISIS, have become equally untethered from nationalistic borders, instead united by virtual spaces built around constructions of ideology rather than geographical space. As a starting point for understanding the cinematic representations of military exoskeletons, the hard body and its ripples of influence through nearly three decades of movies provide the (biological) core necessary to deconstruct the problematic portrayals in the movies of this chapter.

The "fantasy" or "masquerade" of the hard body is centered in both the unachievable physical state of the hard body, its unreal muscles and physique that generate literal power, and the fantasy of action, of being able to change the world and reinforce American ideals. To this end, as Jeffords writes in *The Remasculinization of America*, Rambo's "body mediated by technologization, can become … its own spectacle," and his body *is* the weapon, a "Ram-Bow" fitted with knives and guns (11–15). The exoskeleton-human assemblages in *Elysium* and *Edge of Tomorrow* should be viewed as evolved versions of that hard body. The exoskeleton-enhanced soldiers similarly construct their bodies as spectacular military hardware, carrying the initial technologization of the hard body much further by blending that body with far more sophisticated weaponry and technologies than their '80s counterparts. This is in line with Wiener's early fears of the employment of prosthetics wherein these technological tools "give new and potentially dangerous powers to the already powerful" (*HU* 229): The already physically spectacular soldier is then given more powers via its exoskeleton. It is clear that the technologically augmented hard bodies resurfacing in contemporary cinema encourage the machinic audience to combine the spectacular and fetishistic physical bodies with the new "muscles," equally spectacular, of flexibly wearable technology in much the same hierarchical "master-slave" transhuman relationship that the G.E. Hardiman was constructed with. The augmentation via the exoskeleton gives the same "fantasy" of super-human capabilities, the same exaggerated speed and strength as the '80s hard body, while evolving it to include the types of (wearable) technology that the machinic audience would be familiar and comfortable with. This transhuman portrayal reflects neither the "joint kinships" nor the cooperative modes in which the machinic audience engages with their hardware and software and instead regresses back to the human exceptionalism found in early cybernetics where man has "mastery over the planet" (much as "the hard-body hero masters his surroundings" [Jeffords 28]). As troublingly, then, the "mastery" and "total control" of the hard technological body is an "ideological instrument" that exalts the increasing militarizing and weaponizing of the Internet, over-focusing on the material/physical components of the posthuman/cyborg, while doing little to represent the complex and messily internalized ways a 2017 user of the Internet and computerized hardware, engaged in a critical posthumanism, actually interacts with his/her technology. Instead, the movies promote the notion that computerized technology (both networked and non-networked) is a tool to be utilized as a weapon to heroically go to combat with.

## INITIAL CINEMATIC EXOSKELETONS

The key to understanding the hard body is to recognize that it encourages the movie watcher to co-identify herself/himself as "masterful, as in control of [her/his] environments (immediate or geopolitical), as dominating those around [her/him]" (*HB* 27). For Jeffords, this manifested in the overmuscled bodies that had "mastered" their own biology and shown themselves as being in "control" (a word used often in early cybernetics) of the various weapons they wield, technological (guns, vehicles) and biological (fists) alike. However, the relationship between the hard body and technology, Jeffords points out, is fraught, as belied by the tensions between being an "individual" versus being a (literal and figurative) "fighting machine" (*HB* 40). She typifies the relationship between hard body and technology as falling into two categories: in the first, more positively, technology is "a military resource"; in the second, more negatively, technology is meant to "circumvent human 'freedoms'" (*HB* 54). This means that hard-body users should not over-rely on "technological innovation" to establish mastery of his/her environments, but rather should "rely on individuality ... as the true basis for American superiority" (*HB* 40). Jeffords' theorizing echoes Wiener's sentiment (as summarized by Hayles) that "the ultimate horror is for the rigid machine to absorb the human being, co-opting the flexibility that is the human birthright" (*HWBPh* 105). Behind the hard body must be a "free" and (biological) "human" mind. Simply put, being the "man-in-the-middle" of a radar display or antiaircraft guy is not the "best" use of military technology; the "best weapon" is "not then a tank or nuclear bomb but the 'free' American mind inside a hard body" (*HB* 41); it is only "'free-thinking' human individualism [that] can put technology to good uses" (*HB* 54). It is here that the exoskeleton, revisiting the earlier quote describing the G.E. Hardiman, combines "the human's flexibility, intellect, and versatility ... with the machine's strength and endurance." In addition, exoskeletons are more visually in line with the hard body than enclosed Iron Man–style suits, as the ability to see the physical body, in particular the face, through the exosuit makes obvious the humanist ethics that are constructed through a lauding of the "human mind" and "individuality." Within cinematic representations, the exoskeleton potentially takes the best of both machine and biological and combines them, while still granting the immediately visible human and liberal elements the control of the whole assemblage.

However, one key difference between the hard body and the hard technological body is that "hard-body films display sophisticated military hardware only in the hands of enemies ... and [are] used only to deny human 'freedoms'" (Jeffords 54). Yet there was a relatively small population of "average" 1980s movie watchers who had access to "sophisticated" home technology, like personal computers; for that moviegoing audience, those technologies would likely be foreign, other, and their appearance might seem especially unnatural and threatening. However, as home computers became cheaper in the early 1990s and the Internet moved from private institutes (military, government, university) to public use, computerized technologies came into the private home and, increasingly and, at an exponential rate, became normalized components of an average citizen's life.[6] As Haraway's characterization of modern war as a "cyborg orgy" (295) and texts like Manuel De Landa's 1991 *War in the Age of Intelligent Machines* make clear,[7] artificial intelligence and networked computing had long ago "migrated" over to State War Machines, symbiotically restructuring and melding with individual soldiers, larger strategic planning, weaponry, communication systems, etc. Though this prism, the hard technological body is shaped by the "mastery" of those newly normalized Internet-enabled technologies, which, in turn, shifted the hard bodies' "immediate or geopolitical" concerns to more globalized and virtual ones surrounding the avatars and humans' relationships with an exploding machine population.

The notion of "borders," both national and corporeal, becomes exceedingly important during this transition. Jeffords argues that the hard body resists being "messy" or "confusing" and instead responds by "having hard edges, determinate lines of action, and clear boundaries for their own decision-making" (*HB* 27). As such, the initial film representations of the hard technological body showcase very distinct and clean boundaries between the technological and biological elements: in Ripley's use of the exoskeleton in her fight against the queen alien in *Aliens*, the film goes to great length to make sure her biological body, though united with the machine, is clearly separated; in particular, the repeated shots of her expressive face and her dialogue clearly delineates her machine parts from her human parts and makes it obvious she is in total control of that machine (Image 2.2). However, Ripley's exoskeleton is a repurposed civilian technology, a cargo loader very similar to the G.E. Hardiman[8]; in contrast, the exoskeletons used by the last human inhabitants of Zion in *The Matrix Revolutions* are used only as weapons. Similarly, *The Matrix Revolutions* gives a clear divide between biological and technological as each soldier-assemblage has the human centrally situated and clearly visible within the exoskeleton. For users in the 1990s and early 2000s still coming to grips with the interpenetration of visible and invisible/virtual technologies into their everyday actions, this reassuringly present human body, clearly separated, would be necessary. Most importantly, the imagined cybernetic systems/circuits remain under human control, demonstrating that the augmented human has mastered the machine as a tool.

The exoskeleton's observable human also lines up with Jeffords' insistence that the hard body be capable of vulnerability in order to justify "arms buildups, weapon development, [and] billion-dollar military budgets" (*HB* 50); additionally, this vulnerability reinforces the

**Image 2.2**   Ripley in her exoskeleton about to square off against the alien queen

resilience and strength necessary to construct the hard body. For Ripley and the inhabitants of Zion, being vulnerably and visibly human at all times, instead of an indestructible machine or alien, is the root of their self-identity, the audience's relation to the characters, and the main motivation for continuing to battle against their vastly more formidable enemies. These divisions between machine and human "species" are made exceptionally clear, with the human/biological being valued most. While this does not justify the same militarization the hard body might, seeing that vulnerable human in the exoskeleton reminds the audience that there is a person, not a machine intelligence or hyper-murderous alien, at the controls of the technology.

While susceptible and clearly separated, there is the beginning of spectacular and heroic small steps toward the hard technological body in *Aliens* and *The Matrix Revolutions*. In *Aliens*, the exoskeleton is briefly established earlier in the movie, but its actual use comes near the end of the film when Ripley is chased by the alien queen and is forced, in desperation, to don the exoskeleton. When she does, she is revealed slowly, from the bottom up, dramatically backlit. The machine itself is imposing: the claws are obviously artificial and slow but menacing when they are raised in preparation for an attack. While the monstrous walk forward is awkward and overtly mechanical, far from the "feeling" and mobility of the G.E. Hardiman, Ripley's first blow is extremely powerful, striking the seemingly indestructible queen to the ground. The speed and agility of the queen is offset by the lumbering force of the exoskeleton's amplified muscles, expertly wielded by Ripley, and the repeated shots that exchange between Ripley's concentrating face and the movements of the machine give the audience a sense of their combined power. Less spectacular than later portrayals, Ripley's exoskeleton, repurposed as weapon, is still the heroic assemblage that defeats the queen and saves herself and the traumatized child Newt (Carrie Henn).

Fifteen years later, the exoskeletons of *The Matrix Revolutions* are amplified and militarized versions of Ripley's. The claws of Ripley's exoskeleton are replaced by guns, and as the soldiers prepare for combat in the climactic Zion fight scene, the music swells heroically and the camera stares into the barrels as they point up in anticipation of the oncoming enemies. Captain Mifune's (Nathaniel Lee's) cry of "For Zion" just as the machines enter recalls the same clichéd patriotic shouts soldiers cry out before battle scenes in the traditional war film. The automatic gunfire that follows echoes the firing of Rambo's gun, the men aiming their blazing barrels into the advancing enemy (Image 2.3). The score underlines the battle and the camera swoops over to show three of the

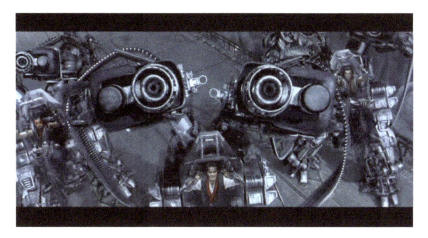

**Image 2.3** Captain Mifune fires from inside his exoskeleton in *The Matrix Revolutions*

exosuit-human assemblages fighting together; the guns never pause as the camera alternates between shots of the men's faces and the gun barrels firing. As the battle continues and more and more human casualties fall to the exponentially increasing army of the machines, Captain Mifune becomes the movie's focal point: his contorted face and primal yelling are underlined by the constant gunfire from his exoskeleton and his heroic sacrifice takes place amidst a literal cloud of enemies. The military battle's cinematic treatment, from the music to the special effects to the tropes that echo the war film genre, is intended to encourage a positive portrayal of this militarized exoskeleton. More so than Ripley's, *The Matrix*'s exoskeletons are obvious combat weapons and even though they are ultimately defeated, their portrayal moves closer to Jeffords' heroic hard body. With the (male) liberal human at its center, the exoskeleton and its hardened "muscles," its added strength and overpowered, constantly present guns, give an initial template that is expanded upon later in *Elysium* and *Edge of Tomorrow*.

It is essential to note that the Ripley-assemblage acts alone while *The Matrix Revolutions* establishes the army of exoskeletons with one shot showing dozens of the exoskeletons shooting up, together, as a unit. In the portrayal of this later army there is an acknowledgment of the communal nature of a 2000s technological/Internet usage, that there is no longer one isolated user of the technology but rather a complete, albeit overtly militarized, network. It is worth noting as well, though it is beyond the scope of this text, that there is more to be written (and that has already been written)[9] about how Ripley being female and playing a maternal role in protecting Newt, and Nathaniel Lees, the actor playing Captain Mifune, being of Samoan heritage, clashes with Jeffords' distinctly white, male hard body. However, with this chapter's focus on the technology of the exosuit, it is important to note that while the portrayal of Captain Mifune and his soldiers are framed positively, the army of exoskeletons in *Avatar* house the main antagonists of the film. The portrayal of the hard technological body in *Avatar* is centralized in Colonel Miles Quaritch (Stephen Lang), and while he bears the same filmic markers of spectacle in the focus on guns and super-human strength as Captain Mifune, he and his army are vilified.

This runs parallel to *Avatar*'s release year of 2009, a period where the post-9/11 American machinic audience had been engaged in a protracted war in Afghanistan and Iraq that the newly elected president had promised to extract them from; the negative portrayal of a corporate military aligns itself with that audience's pessimism and fatigue with war-fare.[10] The difference between the portrayals of Quaritch and Mifune can be further parsed by examining the crisis that each technologically hard body is responding to and the threat that each entails. Returning to Jeffords, she states that the hard body is "justified" only when there is "a 'hard' external opponent" and that the hard body then needs to be called upon in order to "meet that threat" (*HB* 38). Within war propaganda, which is extended here to include war films, Neale adds that it is important to "invest the enemy with an attribute of power ... to mobilize a population against an enemy in time of war" ("Aspects of Ideology..." 39). The mobilizing of, and subsequent sympathy for, the human-exoskeleton assemblages in *Aliens* and *The Matrix Revolutions* is generated by the external threat of an invincible alien and a seemingly inexhaustible machine army; human survival justifies the hard techno-logical body while also changing the unifying rhetoric of the national American hard body to a unification of the globalized human species within the hard technological body.

In *Avatar*, however, Quaritch's corporate and military crisis is purely capitalistic and provides none of the unifying that the hard body requires in order to be rhetorically effective. Further, the "threat" of the "soft" Na'vi, a lithe species without sophisticated armor and equipped with bows and arrows, is not one that "justifies" the use of the tech-nology; this aligns Quaritch's version of the hard technological body as closer to the overpowering alien and machine forces of *Aliens* and *The Matrix Revolutions*. If the hard body's enemy is made hard by their use of sophisticated technology, the human army's exoskeletons in *Avatar* are actually a hard external threat to the protagonist Jake Sully and his adopted Na'vi, an echo of the previously stated fear of Wiener that tech-nological augmentations can give "new and potentially dangerous pow-ers to the already powerful" (*HU* 228).

The heroes of the more recent *Avatar* and *Matrix* trilogy, to some extent, are rooted in an internalization of networked technology that par-allels the machinic audience's expectations that a relatable hero embraces (embodies) the same internal and symbiotic relationship they have with their own various networked devices and software. As argued in Chapter 3 of *Interfacing with the Internet in Popular Cinema*, the char-acters in *The Matrix* films are able to enter into a networked computer-generated world and interact with each other (and other humans), while in *Avatar* the Na'vi literally plug into their world (trees, animals) and each other, networking together. While the end of Chapter 3 of this text explores this extreme Internet-of-Everything networking and the dissolving of any machine interfaces in *Transcendence*, within this chapter it is important to recognize the immense popularity demonstrated by the financial success of the *Matrix* films, and the fact that *Avatar* is among the largest-grossing movies of all time cannot be ignored.[11] To this end, the movies marginalize or vilify their versions of the hard technological body because they are too-simple representations, too "literal," in their union of technology and biology; the ending of *Avatar* makes this even clearer as Jake sheds his physical body, an overt man-machine assemblage made by the use of his wheelchair, and instead chooses to live as his avatar Na'vi body; Quaritch, in contrast, dies in his exoskeleton. The pure weaponization of Quaritch's assemblage simplifies the relationships between technology and biology that the machinic audience has and ignores the myriad of uses that an audience undertakes when interacting with their surrounding hardware and software and struggles.

However, less than five years later, built upon the figure of the hard body, there is a reemergence of the physical and visibly human soldier augmented by an exoskeleton in *Elysium* and *Edge of Tomorrow*. There are a number of shifts that may have contributed to this new positively constructed version of the hard body. Speculatively, the literal and overt recentering of the human subject in a technological frame is a reaction to the changing shape of warfare and the public's awakening to progressively "virtualized" combat; the humanist ethics centered around the "human mind" and "liberal subject" that are so key to Jeffords' hard body are much more difficult to locate in warfare built around remote, unmanned drone attacks and hacking cyber armies. Therefore, cinematic portrayals of assemblages that clearly highlight the biological components within a militarized technological-biological assemblage would be a reassuring (traditional) image, one that centralizes a visible human as master of technological tools.[12] Perhaps, as well, it is because both films show the human-machine assemblage in close combat in a style much closer to the combat film genre, perhaps a more familiar and comfortable (traditional) way to visualize and process warfare in movies.

Within this framework of virtual warfare and the protracted War on Terror, Cynthia Weber's *Imagining America at War* and her writing on war films post-9/11 argues that often portrayals of Americans in war films "get charted back through our WWII past, a seemingly simpler time when bad guys were bad guys (Fascists, Nazis) and *we* were the undisputed good guys" (author's italics 117); she contends that this simplicity resurfaces after 9/11 as the construction of "Osama bin Laden, the Taliban, and Saddam Hussein were all bad to the point of being morally irredeemable and all were out to get America and Americans" (117); America was then the "undisputed good guys" in opposition. This urge toward a binary "simplification" within a post-9/11 environment makes sense when reconsidering the non-national terrorist groups that America was/is fighting and the muddling of the identification of enemy and ally already mentioned that was/is taking place. Mathias Nilges argues that "the terror of a new world" is born from a post-1970s notion that "we must abandon tradition in favor of the new, at which point this mandatory, functional abandonment is less associated with liberation than with loss and instability," which then begins to be "characterized by representations of the struggle with a large-scale transition into a world that is widely perceived as chaotic, complex, confusing, and threatening" (27); the political realities of a post-9/11 atmosphere were a "chaotic, complex, confusing, and threatening" environment, and this would have been further amplified by the aforementioned explosion and normalization of Internet-enabled, always-on devices and the software and apps made possible by such hardware, a shift that was tumultuous and that greatly changed values around the construction of individual and national identity.

Narrowing back down to the reemergence of a new form of the hard body, Nilges further explains that the impulse to return to "simpler times" via future depictions, such as the ones in *Elysium* and *Edge of Tomorrow*, reveals that "cultural representations of future solutions to present problems that regressively seek answers in a return to an idealized past can provide us with valuable insights" (30); these regressions, he claims, most often move towards paternalism, "traditional concepts of masculinity ... that [re-legitimize] traditional gender roles and norms" (30). He states that the return to these "traditional roles" is often undergirded by a "hypermasculinity" (31); it makes sense then that within the chaos of a post-9/11 world, made more "complex, confusing" by the large-scale integration of Internet-enabled devices, there would be a regression back to the "simpler" rhetoric and portrayals embodied by the 80s biologically centered hard body.

However, Nigles, using *Live Free or Die Hard* (Dir. Len Wiseman 2007) as an example, states, "The apparent trauma from the inability to formulate stable traditional life narratives, hence, becomes nowhere near as obvious as in the general crisis of the figure of the white male action hero, who, especially in the aftermath of 9/11, is portrayed as increasingly unable to avert threats to family, community and nation" (28). While the hard body never disappeared entirely in the decades following the height of its popularity, the ineffectiveness of the "traditional" hard body that Nigles identifies can be explained by returning to Wiener, when he prophetically argues that "the man who has nothing but his physical power to sell has nothing to sell which it is worth anyone's money to buy" (*HU* 209). In a Web 2.0 world, the biologically based '80s hard body is a futile relic rooted too deeply in its "physical power," and, therefore, rhetorically ineffective until it could harness and master the technology (or projected technology) a machinic audience engages with. From this, *Elysium* and *Edge of Tomorrow* start with the template of the traditional hard body by generating a simplistic binary construct of warfare (Us Versus Them) that is still largely rooted in hypermasculine spectacle, but then evolves that body to include a control of the types of technologies that would be familiar to a machinic audience, constructing a hard technological body that is potentially more persuasive to a contemporary movie audience.

However, the hard technological body, still embedded in "paternalism," "hypermasculinity," and militarization, reaffirms the same problematic spectacle that the hard body provided. Instead of cooperating with their technology, like Neo and Sully, the heroes of *Elysium* and *Edge of Tomorrow* clearly separate their machine bodies from their biological ones and, like the hard body, simply wield the technology as a weapon, using it strictly in a master-slave hierarchy as a prosthetic and external tool to augment their physical muscles of speed and strength, rather than utilizing their technologies as intimate partners for further critical posthuman evolution.

## The Hard Technological Bodies of *Elysium* and *Edge of Tomorrow*

The evolutionary step of the hard body in *Elysium* and *Edge of Tomorrow* is established by returning to the notion that the hard body represents "average citizens ... in defiance of their governments and institutional bureaucracies" (Jeffords 19). The "average" member of the machinic audience has many reasons to be suspicious of the use of technology surrounding their "governments and institutional bureaucracies," including the National Security Agency's tracking of global citizens' Internet usage, as well as the proposed SOPA and PIPA laws surrounding net neutrality.[13] Like their audiences and Jeffords' hard-body figures, the conflicts within the two movies showcase heroes that are fighting against many infrastructural frustrations. In that fighting, both celebrate the individual's will in the face of a corrupt and ineffective set of infrastructures: in *Elysium* the protagonist Max's triumph is over the corporate makers of the robot police force that oppresses the earth's population, as well as over the ultra-rich citizens of Elysium that are hoarding all the wealth and resources for themselves. Similarly, the protagonist of *Edge of Tomorrow*, Cage, must resist the unwilling and slow-moving military infrastructure, headed by a defiant General Brigham (Brendan Gleeson), that seems hell-bent on knowingly sending troops into a slaughter despite Cage's protestations. As discussed in the introduction to this text, this trope of the lone soldier breaking away from corrupt/ineffective military and corporate infrastructures is very common in post-Vietnam war films; with this in mind, both Cage's and Max's breaking away from their infrastructure and their individual sacrifice/death in defeating the Mimics, an alien race that Earth's military battles throughout the movie, demonstrates the same valuing of individuality and trust in the "free" human mind as the traditional hard body.

While the independence of the hard technological body harkens back to Jeffords' theorizing, the move to recognize a machinic audience's communal (global) identity, beyond strict national identity, marks an evolution from the '80s counterpart. *Elysium*, not so subtly, is a movie about class relations, not otherworld invaders, and it sets clear divides between the ultra-rich inhabitants of the space station Elysium and the overcrowded and extremely poor inhabitants of Earth. This clear enemy, singularly embodied by Delacourt (Jodie Foster), has quarantined themselves from Earth in an impregnable space fortress; further, they use an army of preprogrammed robots that mercilessly keep the inhabitants of Earth in line. Therefore, the battles that Max fights are battles for all of Earth's inhabitants (not just Americans). *Edge of Tomorrow* has a similarly clear enemy in the Mimics. As the Mimics run over Earth in conquest, the United Defense Force (UDF), a Total War Machine made up of Earth's remaining humans, rally the global population together and begin to fight back, headed by a ground force of soldiers equipped with battle combat "jackets" (or exosuits). Again, Cage's fighting is done on behalf of the remaining population of Earth. Cage's exoskeleton is applied with the same desperation against an impossibly superior enemy as Max's donning of a similar device in *Elysium* is; in the mold of the '80s hard body, both films treat the exoskeletons as a necessary weapon in the face of a dominant enemy. These binary enemies create a similar unity to the hard technological bodies in *The Matrix Revolutions*: instead of uniting around a nation as the hard body did, the hard technological body reflects the increasing globalization (and subsequent recognizing/exposure to other cultures as well as the lessening of nationalistic borders) that comes with the contemporary expansion of the Internet.

This reflection of increased globalization found in the hard technological body of the two films is confused by the movies' contradictory and extreme forms of posthumanity: on a small scale, as discussed later in this chapter, when looking just at the protagonists in *Elysium* and *Edge of Tomorrow*, there is an extreme valuing of the physical body that focuses too heavily on the physical components of the posthuman; however, on a larger scale, the films generally treat the physical body as disposable and therefore undermine the necessary material/physical components of the posthuman. As argued above, the hard body needed to evolve beyond its status as a nostalgic relic in order to again be effective, and therefore the inclusion of virtual Bodies without Organs into the human-technology assemblage makes sense; while the two films construct their protagonists using the template and iconography of the hypermasculine spectacle of Jeffords' hard body, the other physical bodies in the films are at times oddly marginalized, creating a bedrock of unbalanced relationships between the technological and biological entities of the film. For example, the human bodies of *Elysium* are potentially immortal: there are "Lazarus beds" on the space station that can cure any illness and mend any physical wound almost instantaneously; the villain Kruger uses one of the beds after having his face blown off and is effortlessly brought back to full health. The human body within this world is without stakes, rendered as machinelike, its material "parts" (organs, limbs, faces) as replaceable as the robot army tasked with patrolling Earth in the film. One of the conflicts is that only residents of Elysium are able to use these beds and the residents of Earth are not allowed their miraculous resurrecting powers. At the end of the movie, Max fights his way through the security of the space station Elysium and enters the core of its computer databases; as he dies, he is able to register every Earth citizen as a resident of Elysium, and the movie finishes with a number of spaceships flying down to Earth filled with enough Lazarus beds to cure all of the humans. Yet, such access actually celebrates the eradication of death and illness: the human body becomes unimportant, or interchangeable, which effectively destroys the unique physical body and its experiences that are such a key component of the posthuman. This postbiological future, initially explored by Hans Moravec (*Mind Children* 1988) and Ray Kurzweil (*The Age of Intelligent Machines* 1990; *The Age of Spiritual Machines* 1999) and denounced by N. Katherine Hayles (*HWBPh*), is also generated in *Edge of Tomorrow*: as Cage and Rita are able to manipulate the Mimics' abilities, resetting their bodies and going back in time with each death, their bodies too become disposable. While the film eventually does away with this conceit for the culmination of the movie, the first hour upholds this ability to die without penalty, to shed the biological body, as Cage uses each non-death as a means to become a better fighting machine. While such portrayals recognize the virtual body/bodies that emerge from an Internet-enabled globalization, perhaps in an effort to reflect the avatars a contemporary machinic audience creates and values, the postbiological bodies and technologies of the films overcompensate and establish the films too far within a moviegoing audience's online existence without reflecting the healthy symbiotic blend between avatar and body that a posthuman assemblage experiences.

If the human bodies and the traditional biological-only hard body are too outdated and weak, and the postbiological body is too unbalanced, then the exoskeleton-warriors and the versions of the technologically hard body in both movies are efforts to situate their heroes between those two poles. Interestingly then, both choose to shrink the exoskeletons considerably from previous depictions: unlike Ripley's giant Hardiman-style prosthesis or the bulky, oversized extensions of *The Matrix Revolutions* and *Avatar*, the exoskeletons of *Elysium* and *Edge of Tomorrow* are far less immediately mechanical and shape themselves more closely to the contours of the human body inside (Image 2.4). Additionally, far more of the human operator can be seen inside them: not only are the faces of the operators more visible but so too are the muscular arms and legs, especially within Max's and Kruger's. This increased human presence obviously offers counterfigures to the "inhuman" enemies of *Elysium*'s robot police force and *Edge of Tomorrow*'s Mimics. Too, it better reflects a machinic audience's understanding of their hardware and software as less overly mechanical and

**Image 2.4**    *Elysium*'s Max and his exoskeleton fire a gun in profile

more flexible (contouring) to their own physical bodies. Most importantly, such a construction, more clearly than Iron Man's enclosed suits that are discussed in Chapter 3, establishes the "liberal" human at its center and showcases a biological user, though augmented, firmly in control of his/her technologies. Such an assemblage is therefore a compatriot of Jeffords' hard body whose immediate visual construction is an attempt to update the traditional hard body with the technological muscles of augmented speed and strength.

*Elysium* gives two divergent hard technological bodies in the hero Max, a regular citizen of Earth desperately flying to Elysium to cure his radiation poisoning, and the movie's antagonist, Kruger, a secret agent working for the corporate military of Delacourt. When the audience first sees Kruger, an "asset" mechanically "activated" by Delacourt's earlier orders, he casually pulls off his ratty overcoat to reveal the pristine and up-to-date exoskeleton underneath; he then, with equal calm, fires a shoulder-mounted missile launcher. Later, in his first battle with Max and the other "people smugglers" (led by Spider [Wagner Moura]), Kruger stays away from immediate combat, instead directing guided missiles at the smugglers outside the ship. When he does engage, he moves quickly and masterfully, walking into bullets and relishing close combat killing; he is a killing machine much like the military droids the smugglers fight mere minutes prior. The ease with which he uses the technology and his comfort is uncanny, and his physical connection to the exoskeleton is clean. Like Quaritch in *Avatar*, Kruger is an overpowered military machine, or rather one part of a much larger State military machinic phylum that aligns him more with the '80s hard body's Communist villains; therefore, his exoskeleton, physically and mentally, does not hold enough individualistic "human" to be considered heroic.

In contrast, while Kruger is one of a unit of exoskeleton-powered soldiers (within a larger military machine), Max is the only (civilian) resident of Earth that is shown wearing an exoskeleton. He begins within the corporate-military system, ironically making the very robot soldiers that police the planet; it is at this factory where he is callously exposed to a lethal dose of radiation. This lethal dose serves to remind the audience of his mortality; even as he is in the final battles on Elysium he has to pause in order to swallow the antiradiation pills he's been given. While Kruger is able to step in and out of the Lazarus beds, distancing him from his biological body, Max is stabbed in the stomach in an early combat scene and must walk hunched and wounded for the rest of the movie, while the camera repeatedly cuts to his blood on his hands. More, Max takes no pleasure in combat: in the first battle, after he has knocked Kruger down with gunfire, he does not finish him but rather rushes over to his friend Julio (Diego Luna) and tries to tend to his wounds; this is a more sympathetic action that is outside the murderous nature that Kruger exhibits as activated asset/soldier. Unlike the impenetrable/invulnerable '80s hard body, it is the "human" messiness of Max, the bodily version of "chaos" that Nilges flags, that makes him more heroic and therefore justifies his use of the exoskeleton. The sick and compassionate human body that Max demonstrates is necessarily "soft" in order to move the character away from the singularly focused corporate-militarization of the exoskeleton that Kruger represents and allows him to enact his own (civilian) will, a crucial component of the hard body, without being controlled by the mechanics of a larger military or the literal machine of the exoskeleton.

This vulnerable and liberal humanity is then amplified by the literal messiness that takes place in Max's connections to his exoskeleton. When the audience sees Kruger stepping into his exoskeleton later in the film, they see his muscular body implanted with sensory inputs/hooks for the machine; there is no bleeding or irritation around these implants and the machine slides cleanly onto him. More, he is gleeful as he is welded in, his attachment to the exoskeleton painless and, for him, fun. In contrast, the surgery scene that attaches the skeleton to Max is grotesque. His exoskeleton, a "third-generation exosuit" that is in opposition to Kruger's up-to-date hardware, is attached to him using giant knives and saws in a slapdash and dirty surgery room. The procedure begins with a shot of a gruesome hole in the back of Max's skull; from there, bolts are drilled into his body before the bone-saw cuts into the body as the bones are cut apart and put back together. When he is "brought online" at the end of the surgery, there is blood around each puncture into the body; that blood seeps through Max's shirt throughout the movie, reminding the audience of the exosuit's messy relationship with the biological body. While Max still demonstrates the clear borders between biological and technological that the '80s hard body relished in, the movement toward a messier, bloodier body distances the hard technological body from Kruger's clean, corporatized military force in its opposition, instead establishing it with the non-expert citizen that Jeffords says is the hard body's rhetorical target. Additionally, the human within, because it is vulnerable and messy, reaffirms that there is a human element (a "free" mind) inside the hard technological body, a transhuman body not transformed into a machine, but rather one that can then be trusted with mastery and control.

Yet, for all the "softness" Max displays, he still possesses the spectacular physique that Jeffords' hard bodies demonstrate. In the introductory shot of Max, he is shown shirtless, stressing the spectacle of his obviously muscled body. The hard technological body in these films begins with an overstrong physical body that straps on an exoskeleton (adding more power to the already powerful), which makes it into the same unreal spectacle as the '80s hard body; while the biological body is vulnerable and messy, the exoskeleton hardens it, evolves it, allowing its wearers the necessary strength to survive in an arena built around violent, technologically enhanced combat. These technological muscles are given the same fetishistic gaze as the hard body; it is still the "to-be-looked-at" object that the traditional hard body is, while further underlining its lineage to that hard body by employing similar tropes from those previous hard-body films. When Max transitions into combat, he is given the same admiration typical of soldiers within the war film genre. In the first combat scene, after clearing his jammed gun, Max rises up and, in profile, fires at the police robot in slow motion; the audience can clearly see the exoskeleton wrapped around his body then extended by the firing gun, shells shooting from the gun, before the enemy explodes (as shown in Image 2.4). The camera pans around the exploding robot so that the audience gets its destruction from every angle, allowing them to relish in the spectacular power of Max's new body. Even when not extended by a gun, the climax of his hand-to-hand fight against another police robot ends in another show of extreme strength where Max tears off the robot's head; later, before he kills him, he lifts another man above his head and then throws him across the room. As the audience is consistently reminded, Max's biological body is disintegrating, so it is the hardened muscles of the exoskeleton that are allowing him to carry out these spectacular feats that the film amplifies using similar tropes (slow-motion firing, close-up on guns, relishing of enemy death) as the hard-body films of the '80s do. This updating of the hard body plays effectively to the machinic audience as it has both the spectacular physical specimen and free mind of its predecessor and also includes the technological hardware in line with the machinic audience's everyday use.

In *Edge of Tomorrow*, Rita and Cage, both members of Earth's army, are much closer to Kruger's militarized version of the hard technological body and, more clearly than *Elysium*, the film then represents the next evolutionary step of the hard body of the 1980s into the technologically augmented but distinctly militarized posthuman. There is more to be written about Rita, the "Full Metal Bitch," and how just her gender, like Ripley, resists the traditional hard body, but a full discussion is beyond the scope of this text.[14] Although as the film begins, the protagonist Cage is a civilian and non-combatant and it is Rita who is the super-soldier and hero of the latest battle against the Mimics, for the remainder of the film she is secondary to Cage and the small bit of positivity gained by her potentially more positive version of the hard body is largely undone by her wearing of the exosuit and the hardening that the technology provides; the exosuit, as it does for Cage, unbalances the material/technological assemblage toward the physical body and hardware and, like Cage, encourages the machinic audience to view their wearable technologies as weaponized tools.

This problematic unbalancing is best demonstrated by Cage's use of the exosuit. At the outset of the movie, Cage is a lot like Max in that he is a non-expert user of the battle jackets. As a former public relations representative, his incompetence and inexperience as a soldier in combat gives his fellow soldiers much to ridicule; he cannot even figure out how to turn his suit and gun on for many of the first combat scenes. However, Cage's transformation into a brutally effective soldier is what

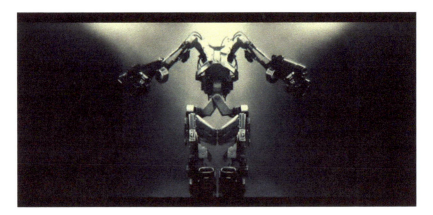

**Image 2.5**   *Edge of Tomorrow*'s exosuit

makes *Edge of Tomorrow*'s version of the hard technological body such a negative representation. In the film's opening montage, the exosuits are explained as one of the key turning points in the battle, leading to the first victory against the aliens in five years: as Cage explains, "With the new jacket technology and limited training, we've been able to create super-soldiers"; the phrase "limited training" is repeated again, underlining how easy the jackets are to master and wield. Rita is held up as the paragon of the technology, said to have "[killed] hundreds of Mimics on only her first day of combat." The "revolutionary technology" is worshipped: following Cage's words there is a shot of the suit by itself, lit from above in reverence (Image 2.5); the words "Power" and "Speed" appear slowly over the image followed by, in extremely quick succession, "Domination," "Fame," "Dynamic," "Fearless," "Invincible," "Precise," "Unstoppable," and "Superiority." These words signal the mix of glamour and fear attached to the weaponized exosuits. They are represented as an unreal "military weapon," part of the oncoming "mechanized invasion" of the Mimics and purely for combat and conquering. While *Elysium* provides a minimal counterbalance by giving external technology the positivity attached to the Lazarus beds and the health-care robots at the end of the film, *Edge of Tomorrow* immediately weaponizes its technologies and casts all of humanity in the role of soldier. To underline this, Cage confidently states, "We fight. That's what we do." The collective "we" is the human race, and conflating that "we" with the limited training within the exosuits convinces their users that any average user can (must) transform into a fighter, a soldier.

As the movie progresses, Cage exemplifies this, transforming from the "soft" non-expert into the best soldier in the whole army by the end of the film, and as Cage "dies" and is reborn each time into the same battle, the treatment of the suit gets more spectacular. Whereas *Elysium* slows down to show the hard technological body, *Edge of Tomorrow*'s overfast treatment amplifies the exoskeletons' "speed" muscles rather than its "power" components. The film rarely lingers when in combat scenes: the firing of the guns is more constant and raking, the enemies faster, more nimble and far more plentiful. Two specific scenes underline this: the first has Rita watching Cage in the training facility where Cage weaves between enemies, shoots and reloads seamlessly, demonstrating his combat expertise, all made possible by the augmenting exoskeleton. The second takes place once the two are back in combat on the beach, where Rita and Cage, as expert soldiers, don't walk so much as propel; in one sequence, Rita jumps incredibly high, spins and slices a Mimic, followed by Cage sliding along the ground and popping back up with his shoulder-mounted guns firing into the oncoming enemies before he literally circles his outnumbered squad mates to kill their attacking enemies. This all happens spectacularly quickly, and, while the camera doesn't linger like it does in traditional hard-body movies, the increased and incredible speed of the new technological body, its inhuman ability to propel and dodge across the battlefield, are granted the same amazed gaze that the hard body garners.

Both films update the traditional hard body by integrating in technological hardware, solving the "ineffectiveness" of that older hard body by its ability to harness the types of wearable-like technologies that the machinic audience would recognize from their own lives. However, as raised in the introduction to this text, both films contain civilians-turned-soldiers as their protagonists, a common trope in contemporary war films that engage with Internet-enabled technologies; constructing these civilians-turned-soldiers as heroic is an argument for the problematic co-opting that takes place when the Total War Machine infiltrates civilian infrastructures and mechanisms. Moreover, these newer versions of the hard body are still built around the problematic spectacular traits of hypermasculinity and violence; too, their simplistic, somewhat cartoonish construction of Us-Versus-Them dynamics in the film also echoes the same polarization that takes place in the traditional hard body

films. Focusing specifically on the machine aspects of the hard technological body in the films, the spectacle undermines a machinic audience's
critical posthuman understanding of potential machine-human cooperation. Both films encourage their audiences to fixate on the combat abilities and weaponization of the technology of their worlds, reducing it to
the hard body's understanding of technology only as "military resource."
More troubling, *Edge of Tomorrow*'s repetition that the exosuit requires
"limited training" (which Rita and Cage's citizen-to-expert soldier trans-
formations prove) treats technology as a type of steroid, a fast (unnatural) shortcut to larger (faster/more powerful) "muscles." While the
hard body of the '80s was an obvious fantasy constructed with a near-
unachievable physique at its center, the hard technological body within
*Elysium* and *Edge of Tomorrow* seems tantalizingly close to that average
user/moviegoer. This steers the movie's audience away from considering symbiotic relationships with their co-species machines, cohabitational
relationships much closer to how an average user might interact with
their daily technologies, and to instead revel in the awesome ability of
technology to turn that average user into a killing machine.

In total, the movement from strictly being an individual to a balance
between the "free" mind within a technological environment, in combination with the machinic audience's globalization, evolves the hard
body. Yet the "human" within the machine reigns supreme and the
"free-thinking" mind can only be biological and aided subserviently by
machines. The cinematic glamorization of the augmenting technology as
militarized weapon treats the exoskeleton in the same way the hard body
treats her/his gun (as extension, resource), and promotes the attitude
that the audience of such films should view their surrounding machine
species as combat tools used to control and conquer with.

## Conclusion: The Future of the Hard Technological Body

The following chapter argues that the *Iron Man* films and *Pacific
Rim* are vehicles for exploring Internet-enabled "screens-on-screen,"
or frames-within-a-frame, and that the digital effects in those war
films highlight the function of the movie as a machinic phylum that is
then also a part of the machinic phylum that makes up the Total War
Machine. However, those films do use the hard technological body of

*Elysium* and *Edge of Tomorrow* as an ethical template, and Jeffords' hard body, in general, echoes through nearly all the films discussed throughout the duration of this text: within the near-entirety of the dissected movies, there is an urgent need to reaffirm human superiority by placing the liberal human mind at the center of any assemblage and machinic phylum, and the preservation and promotion of the human species is of the utmost importance. This preservation manifests in a dehumanizing of the hard (technological) body's enemies to justify the films' warfare, but also constructs the cinematic Internet-enabled technologies as slaves and humans as masters in control. At its roots, the hard body is biological and it is that biological body that is at the core of its spectacle and its value systems. As such, it follows that *Edge of Tomorrow*'s director Doug Liman's focus on "real" (physical/biological-based) moviemaking, rather than a reliance on digital effects, promotes the hard technological body as a more positive prospective path for future warfare (Fear *Rolling Stone*). While the filmmaking of *Elysium* and *Edge of Tomorrow* have digital effects, unlike a massively popular film like *Avatar*, neither provides groundbreaking, or even interesting, computer-generated filmmaking that might meet the machinic audience's experiences with Internet-enabled technologies outside the theater. Unlike the Jaegers of *Pacific Rim* or the Iron Man suits, neither Max's nor Cage's exoskeletons are networked beyond the simplest visual and audio components, resisting the dense networks that the machinic audience thrives in. Both *Elysium*'s and *Edge of Tomorrow*'s heroic sacrifices of their protagonists' physical bodies reaffirm, like the preceding hard body, that the hard technological body is only heroic when the physical body is the most valuable and vulnerable: Max dies in order to save the residents of Earth, and it's only after Cage loses the ability to be "reborn" and he is united into one physical body that the film progresses to its heroic climax. By continuing to maintain the clear divisions between machine and human, even when showing the machine-exoskeleton simultaneously with the physical body, the hard technological body is always grounded in "reality"; its physical (weaponized) presence in combat is not blurred with any virtual body and continues to resist the interpenetrated role that computer technology plays in a machinic audience's daily life. Again, setting up the hard body as a basic visual and ethical framework that resonates deeply through the other Internet-enabled movies analyzed in this text, this lack of networked virtual bodies reminds the audience that the human, a master in control, is the most valuable component of any biological-technological assemblage; when the other films deconstructed in this text do begin to integrate Internet-enabled technologies into their technological-biological soldier assemblages, they do using this same human-centric ethical system.

The machinic audience might then imagine the next iteration of the hard technological body, engaged in a critical posthumanism, that begins to acknowledge and incorporate a virtual body within a mode of film-making that also includes more digital attention. This is essentially the main difference between *Elysium*'s Max and *Avatar*'s Jake: while both are "messy" and "softer" than their enemies, Jake's relationship with the technology of that film acknowledges and celebrates the extension undertaken when enacting as a virtual self, whereas Max and Cage are still firmly rooted in the physical. A representation that moved beyond the physical-only body would need to balance delicately between an avatar's augmented global presence and the sensory narrative that a physical body undergoes, an equilibrium very familiar to the reflexive members of the machinic audience. Perhaps this is already being done most effectively in video games, wherein the player is able to interactively project into and control a body that oscillates between virtual networks and physical inputs (a topic explored in Chapter 4); this type of body, while running the risk of also treating its technology as virtual steroids, is a similar but more complex version of the exoskeleton-human assemblage, the step in-between the G.E. Hardiman and the "tantalizingly close" versions put forth in *Elysium* and *Edge of Tomorrow*. Within such imagined films, however, such a figure might be able to acknowledge the continued and still-pervasive use of "boots-on-the-ground" physical soldiers in a contemporary warfare that also then blends that soldier with the virtual combat and cyberwarfare that hacking and drone strikes exemplify. That would be a more "real" (honest?) representation of how war is actually waged in 2017 and potentially provide valuable spaces to critique such combat and the machinery of the Total War Machine.

## NOTES

1. Shannon, Claude E. and Weaver. *Mathematical theory of communication.* Chicago, IL: University of Illinois Press, 1949. My understanding of this paper was bolstered by Gary Genosko's *Remodelling Communication* (Toronto, ON: University of Toronto Press, 2012).

2. The initial conception of this chapter sprung from the chapter "Hacking the Apocalypse" in *Interfacing with the Internet in Popular Cinema* (2014) wherein I discuss the three *Iron Man* films and the Future Combat System through the lens of Deleuze and Guattari's notion of the machinic phylum from *A Thousand Plateaus* (*ATP* 395). In these prior writings, I argue that the full suits act more as Internet-like networked armor that function less biologically and "humanly," and act as a small cog in the military machinic phylum, encouraging a movie-going audience that is tethered to their always-on networked devices to see their own multiple avatar selves as re-appropriated military tools instead of the potentially healthy posthuman/cyborg they can be. For more, see note 14 in the introduction.

3. Further definitions and discussion of the machinic audience, assemblage, and Bodies without Organs can be found in the introduction to this text as well as the Introduction and Chapter 5 of my *Interfacing with the Internet in Popular Cinema*.

4. More information on the Warrior Web can be found at "Warrior Web Prototype Takes Its First Steps." *darpa.mil*. May 22, 2013. http://www.darpa.mil/news-events/2013-05-22. Accessed March 09, 2017.

5. Further theorizing surrounding the softening of the hard body can be found in *Postfeminism and Paternity in Contemporary U.S. Film* by Hannah Hamad (New York: Routledge, 2014) and *Millennial Masculinity: Men in Contemporary American Cinema*, edited by Timothy Shary (Detroit, MI: Wayne State University Press, 2013) among much other postfeminist scholarship. Additionally, Mark Gallagher's *Action Figures* (New York: Palgrave Macmillan, 2006), specifically discussion of Chuck Norris' increasing reliance on technology as he progresses into '90s cinema, was very useful.

6. See note 7 from the introduction to this text.

7. A further discussion and definition of both Haraway's military cyborg and De Landa's theorizing is made in the introduction to this text.

8. While earlier in the introduction to this text I flagged that cybernetic technology largely started as military and then navigated over to civilian use, Ripley's weaponizing of the civilian technology runs counter to this; this reversal is explored further in Chapter 4 of this text via my discussion of Virtual Reality (VR).

9. I have written on the role of race and gender within war, combat and adventure films, including the sources listed in note 5 of this chapter. More specifically, Tasker dedicates time to the figure of Ripley in *Spectacular Bodies* (1993) in her chapters "Woman Warriors" and "Action Heroines" in the '80s; much of what Jeffords says about Sarah Connors' "Tough Love" in the *Terminator* films ("Terminal Masculinity") could

be reworked to apply to the maternal caring of Newt that Ripley under-takes. In addition, activating Haraway's discussion of the cyborg and gender in her "The Cyborg Manifesto" would also help to unpack how Ripley fits in with the notion of the hard body.

10. A Gallup Poll dated Sept. 5–7, 2008 asked, "How satisfied are you with the way things are going for the U.S. in the war on terrorism—very satis-fied, somewhat satisfied, not too satisfied, or not at all satisfied?" 11% said "Very Satisfied; 41% said "Somewhat Satisfied"; 23% "Not Too Satisfied"; and 24% said "Not at all satisfied." A February 2009 Gallup poll asked, "For how many more years do you think the United States should have a significant number of troops in Afghanistan?" and 65% said less than two years (http://www.gallup.com/poll/5257/war-terrorism.aspx. Accessed May 4, 2016).

This can be compared with a Dec. 14–16, 2001 Gallup poll where "the vast majority of Americans—92%—[expressed] satisfaction with the amount of progress made by the U.S. military in the war in Afghanistan, including 69% who [said] they are "very satisfied." The percentage report-ing they are very satisfied with the effort is up from 58% in late November" (http://www.gallup.com/poll/5113/latest-summary-american-public-opinion-war-terrorism.aspx. Accessed May 4, 2016).

11. *Avatar* made $2.7 billion+ worldwide; *The Matrix* movies have made $463 million+, $742 million+ and $427 million+ worldwide. All numbers via boxofficemojo.com. Accessed May 4, 2016.

12. Drone strikes, military simulations and wargames are taken up in more detail in Chapter 5.

13. A basic primer on SOPA and PIPA can be found at: Abrams, Jim "PIPA and SOPA: What You Need to Know" *Christian Science Monitor.* Accessed May 4, 2016. http://www.csmonitor.com/Technology/2012/0119/PIPA-and-SOPA-What-you-need-to-know. The actual SOPA law can be found at H.R 3261—Stop Online Piracy Act; House Judiciary Committee; October 26, 2011. http://www.webci-tation.org/63oCICqjh. Accessed May 4, 2016. Further discussion of this civil cyberwarfare can be found in Chapter 6.

14. I think there is an argument to be made that Rita, taken on her own, is a positive female iteration of the hard body, an expansion away from the "hyper-masculinity" that defines the traditional hard body. Rita is, as Yvonne Tasker illustrates in her introduction to *Action and Adventure Cinema*, one in a long line of cinematic "action heroines," women, like Ripley, who are "physically strong, independent though often emotion-ally vulnerable, typically glamourous and even overtly sexy" (9). In the same collection, and building off Tasker's work in her own *Spectacular Bodies*, Marc O'Day flags such archetypes as grounded in "action babe

cinema," movies that are propelled by "beautiful, sexy and tough heroines" (201); at their best, such figures appear in films that "*assume that women are powerful,* offering heroines who are both vulnerable and strong, and above all, who survive and win" (author's italics 215). All of this is true of Rita and while she is a beautiful woman, she is not blatantly sexualized; In addition, though there somewhat of a romantic narrative between her and Cage, and there is a kiss right before both of them sacrifice themselves at the end of the film, their relationship is largely professional. All this grants Rita skills and capabilities that do not take advantage of her female sexuality and instead portray her as a hyper-competent soldier. See notes 5 and 9 of this chapter as well.

# CHAPTER 3

# The Soldier Interfaces on the Digitally Augmented Battlefield

## Introduction: Objectivity in the Digital Environments of the War Film

D.N. Rodowick, in his 2007 text *The Virtual Life of Film*, teases out the ontological problems at the root of moviemaking's shift from the analog to the digital in which he argues that film and cinema studies' material history, based in the notion of physical film as a series of "moving photographic images" (13), makes it so that cinema's main unit of construction is the photograph. The photograph's "spatial and temporal powers" are based in the "principal powers ... of analog and indexicality" (9). From this, the photograph retains an aura of "realism": film, without the digital manipulations that are to be discussed later in this chapter, is often seen as a more objective and unvarnished version of captured "reality" than the later digital evolutions, and therefore "the photographic basis of cinema is coded as 'real,' the locus of a truthful representation and the authentic aesthetic experience of cinema" (5).

This treatment of the photograph is echoed in Daston and Galison's *Objectivity*, where they begin by explaining that

> objectivity preserves the artifact or variation that would have been erased in the name of truth; it scruples to filter out the noise that undermines certainty. To be objective is to aspire to knowledge that bears no trace of the knower—knowledge unmarked by prejudice or skill, fantasy or judgement, wishing or striving. (17)

© The Author(s) 2017
A. Tucker, *Virtual Weaponry*,
DOI 10.1007/978-3-319-60198-4_3

Their exploration of objectivity traces through scientific atlases, science's mode of "image-making" (17), and what they flag as "systematic compilations of working objects" (18). In particular, the two authors focus on the photograph and the shift in the mid-nineteenth century to a "mechanical objectivity" that was achieved through automatism, the goal of which was "to produce images 'untouched by human hands'" (43). The term "mechanical" was in reference to "the process by which light imprinted an image on specifically prepared metal, paper, or glass" (137). This overlaps with Rodowick's explanation of the photograph: "*The material basis of photography, as well as film, is a process of mechanically recording an image through the automatic registration of reflected light on a photo-sensitive chemical surface*" (author's italics 31). Using Stanley Cavell's *The World Viewed* as his base, Rodowick explains further that the photograph, and by extension film, are "automatisms": "self-acting processes of mechanical reproduction" (42). For Rodowick, such reproductions are "*automatic analogical causation*" (author's italics 49) and signal that, at least initially, photographs "lend an objective, or, as Bazin would have it, inhuman, quality to the production of images" (49). Daston and Galison clarify that the photographic automation, as instrument and creator (and replicator), were viewed as "patient, indefatigable, ever alert, probing beyond the limits of the human senses" (139) and, as such, the photograph "became the emblem for all aspects of noninterventionist objectivity. ... This was not because the photograph was more obviously faithful to nature than handmade images ... but because the camera apparently eliminated human agency" (187).

Nineteenth-century mechanical objectivity and twentieth-century photography-based filmmaking and cinema studies were

> haunted by anxieties about [image makers'] own subjective representations, [who] discovered the ethical-epistemic consolations of the mechanical image, in which, by a supreme act of self-effacing will—or by deploying procedures and machines that bypassed that will—they could ensure that no intelligence would disturb the image. (Daston and Galison 138)

Of course, mechanical objectivity and its focus on the non-intervention of the human, in its attempt "remained an always receding ideal, never fully obtainable" (185), in part because "there is no objectivity without subjectivity to suppress, and vice versa" (33). Rodowick also teases this out, stating in response to Cavell's automatisms, "Insofar as they function as potentialities of thought, action, or creation, automatisms circumscribe what subjectivity is or can be and how it is conditioned conceptually, though these conditions are neither inflexible nor invariable" (43); while automatisms "function as limits … in responding creatively to these limits, artists create new styles or purposes for a medium (differences), and these in turn may proliferate into individual or collective practices as new automatisms" (44). The camera and the image maker, cinematographer, photographer, are brought together in the "photographic act" (47) and the image becomes a product of the machine, the automatisms and the image maker's knowledge of that machine and automatisms and the choices within that system; add to this the fact that the photograph is tied intimately to the transcription of a historical event (55) and the subjective elements within that event, the photograph, and film by extension, move further from objective recording and are instead a rhizomatic mix, an assemblage, of landscapes, automatisms and subjectivities (of the looker, of the knower).[1]

To return to the focus of this text, the State War Machine, at its base, "has always existed [as] an ocular (and later optical and electro-optical) 'watching machine.' … However great the area of the battlefield, it is necessary to have the fastest possible access to pictures of the enemy's forces and reserves" (Virilio *War and Cinema* 4). As the introduction to this text argues, the urge to capture the enemy and its landscapes in a photographic militaristic gaze is a tactic designed to reduce that enemy and its territories (landscapes/subjectivities) into objective data and flat images, to utilize the automatisms of the camera in order to dehumanize the enemy and then conquer that non-human combatant, that non-natural landscape.[2] Judith Butler, in *Frames of War*, argues then: "Of course persons use technological instruments, but instruments surely also use persons. … But further, under conditions of war waging, personhood itself is cast as a kind of instrumentality, by turns useful or dispensable" (xii). For her, the war image, with cameras as an instrument of war waging, is about the frame that constructs that image and potentially makes personhood "dispensable": "The frame does not simply exhibit reality, but actively participates in a strategy of containment, selectively producing and enforcing what counts as reality" (xiii); the objective automatism of the war camera is in fact a constructor (and effacer) of subjective processes. This process has the ultimate goal of "the implicit or explicit framing of a population as a war target [that] is the initial action of destruction" (xvi). Thus, the photographic image that frames the populations and landscapes of war making is one that erases the subject in the objectifying "initial action of destruction."[3]

Butler paraphrases Susan Sontag's *On Photography* in order to explore the limits of it as a document, explaining that the photograph "cannot produce ethical pathos in us" because of its strict "momentary" temporal capturing; the (war) photograph therefore struggles to encapsulate what Sontag calls "narrative" or the full continuity of a historical moment (Butler 69). When considering whether war films and movies could provide access to that affective "narrative" that Butler argues for when the war image/photograph, and its erasing frame, is remade into film, the effect, Virilio states, is instead one of a more encompassing simulation and spectacle. Speaking to the war museums that emerged out of World War II, he flags spaces where "visitors were shown into huge, windowless rooms resembling a planetarium or a flight (or driving) simulator. In these war simulators, the public was supposed to feel like spectators-survivors of a recent battlefield" (*War and Cinema* 62). These edited and reframed films were constructed "as if newsreels had been too 'realistic' to recapture the pressure of the abstract surprise movements of modern war" (62); films and movies then exposed partial forms of reality or a "historical event" and combined them with film and editing effects to rhetorically enhance the viewer/looker's engagement with that version of the event(s).[4] As argued in the introduction to this text, war films, whether "fictional" or "documentary," become a combination of the eradicating frame and the knowing virtual simulation that an audience then participates in as spectacle and entertainment, far from the objective historical document that Rodowick ties the photograph to.[5]

Yet in 2017, the war camera and the images/photographs it produces are not always static, two-dimensional or human operated. As LaRocca argues, the war camera is extremely mobile: "We can now send cameras into combat—on helmets, on guns, on vehicles, and flying overhead on planes, drones, and even on ordnance! While the camera does not capture all the action, it is certainly part of the action" (13). This mobile war camera has not only proliferated across the battlefield, and in turn has made it so that the battlefield is potentially anywhere there is a camera, but the increase in Internet-enabled networks and the various photographic techniques has placed additional layers of information on top of the original "objective" image/landscape/person. Daston and Galison update mechanical objectivity into this contemporary objectivity by explaining the shift to nanotechnologies and "nanomanipulation"; they see the "successor to the atlas … in which images are, to a certain degree, interactive, not fixed. With clicks and keystrokes, these digital images are meant to be used, cut, correlated, rotated, colored"

(383) in a move to "highlight chosen features" and elements of a land-scape, person, etc. (such as, say, a heat map). The authors flag these as images that "engineer," and "images-as-tools" (385). Such images-as-tools, in service of objectivity, not only move the image towards a "selective" objectivity in which portions or aspects of what is being examined are highlighted, but also segments the notion of the atlas, the objective image, so that each part can (must?) be examined separately and distinctly in order to understand its whole; more, it is the transformation of the original observed object, as it is "cut, correlated, rotated, colored," that reveals the objective truth underneath it: the image must undergo a process, in combination with the aforementioned digital tools, in order to completely reveal the nature of the object being examined. Virilio sees similar processes being undertaken as contemporary State War Machines moved from aerial photographs (similar to Rodowick's version of the analog photo), the earliest weaponizations of the optical, into the "electro-optical" of the watching machine (*War and Cinema* 4). These electro-optical images function as informative images, ones that grant the generals and soldiers objective images on which they can base military action:

> A technological revolution gradually pushed back the limits of investiga-tion into space and time until aerial reconnaissance, with its old modes of representation, disappeared in instantaneous, 'real-time' information. Objects and bodies were forgotten as their physiological traces became accessible to a host of new devices—sensors capable of detecting vibra-tions, sounds and smells; light-enhancing television cameras, infra-red flashes, thermographic pictures. (24)

In this, the automatisms that generate photographs as part of the State War Machine are now amplified: the nanotechnologies that Daston and Galison flag as the vehicles of a contemporary objectivity are repurposed by the State and Total War Machines in order to further dehumanize the enemy and its landscapes/territories by vivisecting those entities into collections of segmented data. When Daston and Galison further define these engineered images as "haptic images" (383), they are bringing to the forefront the interactive manipulation that such images require to complete their construction, a manipulation that is undertaken by both computational devices/machines and their users when they click, type, tap or drag on a touchscreen, use a mouse, etc. These actions then generate, via a process similar to Butler's frame in its "strategy of containment, selectively producing and enforcing," a datafied version of that object, person or landscape.

When considering cinema's placement within the Total War Machine, there is a similar process when understanding digital effects' impact on the photographic (analog) image that is, as Rodowick makes the case for, the root of film. Rodowick calls this a "process of substitution" (7): "The nature of 'film' itself has been transformed … as digital processes replace photographic ones in every stage of recording, editing, and now distributing and exhibiting motion pictures" (27); he later adds that "*digital acquisition quantifies the world as manipulatable series of numbers*" (author's italics 116). When he calls this substituted space a "landscape 'without image'" (93), he is speaking to digital tools' and devices' "powers of mutability and velocity" (94) that then create not the "realism" of the analog photograph but rather a "perceptual realism" (101). This "realism" is still cinematic, and in fact relies on its audience's knowledge of previous cinematic codes and "photographic credibility" (101); from this, "perceptual realism reproduces and reinforces deeply recalcitrant cultural norms of depiction" (101). Similar to Daston and Galison's nanotechnological images and Virilio's electro-optical images, perceptual realism is "both synthesized and hand-rendered. … Thus, a corollary to the reinforcement of the spatial and representational qualities of the image is, again paradoxically, a reassertion of its *graphism*, meaning its ability to erase and efface, to add and subtract, to alter perceptual values" (author's italics 105). Within digital cinema, as within electro-optical war hardware/devices, the images are obviously constructed images, not objective reflections of the "real"; such images, which Rodowick calls "synthetic images," are an overt blend of the analog ("real") and the digital layering/blending borne of digital automatisms. Acknowledging that this synthesis "*requires* an analog interface" (author's italics 113), such images are not notational only, but rather depend on the digital and analog coming together to produce a cinema that is "easily reworked, reappropriated, and recontextualized" (15).

While Rodowick disagrees with Lev Manovich's assertion that these synthetic images are in fact "new" media (93–95), Manovich's work in *The Language of New Media* (2001) usefully begins to bring together a machinic audience's daily interactions with their digital hardware and software with movies and movie watching through his understanding of interfaces as a way of explaining what "cultural norms of depiction" they share. Computer-human interfaces are the main sites of interaction between the two species. Manovich starts by saying that interfaces don't just have to be a literal computer-user interface; they can be "cultural interfaces," explaining that, as an example, movies and computer use share a great number of techniques and organizational principles. For Manovich, movies also construct "human-computer-cultural" spaces in that they generate a cinematic understanding of interface that utilizes "larger cultural traditions … [that include] the mobile camera, representations of space, editing techniques, narrative conventions, spectator activity—in short, different elements of cinematic perception, language, and reception" (71). Both the human-machine and cultural interface are centered around notions of "representation," which he parses further into six different types (16–17). This chapter is most interested in the intersections between his understandings of representations of control and of action. While some representations are meant to be immersive simulations (16) a number are meant to act as a "control panel," such as a Graphic User Interface, "with its different icons and menu" (16), which he calls the "*image-interface*" (author's italics 17); other representations are meant to "enable action" and "allow the viewer to manipulate reality through the representations (maps, architectural drawings, x-rays, telepresence)" or, in echo of Butler, what he calls "*image-instruments*" (author's italics 17). Each of these representations is a composite of the "cultural layer" and the "computer layer" of the interface. Where the cultural layer is "story and plot; composition and point of view; mimesis and catharsis, comedy and tragedy," the computer layer consists of "sorting and matching; function and variable; computer language and data structure" (46).

This chapter, then, analyzes what happens when the computer layer and cultural layer of computer usage is refracted further via cinematic representations within war films. This chapter considers both the cultural interfaces of film and the representations of literal computer-user interfaces in Augmented Reality (AR) environments as a way of both building on the non-interfaced, non-networked nature of the hard technological bodies of Chapter 2 and laying groundwork to consider the later interfaces present in the discussion of VR and simulated environments in Chaps. 4 and 5. In exploring the collisions of civilian, military and cinematic uses of AR, it is important to begin by acknowledging that AR environments are especially important as, although they began as analog cinema technology,[6] they layer the computer (digital) elements of indexicality, data structure, matching and sorting in an image-interface on top of the real (analog) world, while simultaneously granting the user an image-instrument to, in real time, immediately manipulate and "enable reaction" in reaction to what the user sees. Both the image-instrument and the image-interface are based in this chapter's earlier discussion of objectivity: they aim to frame the layer with "non-interventionist" data on top of the world, to create images-as-tools so that the user can break down the viewed world (landscapes, people, objects) into discrete and segmented parts to then haptically manipulate and control. When these interfaces are then placed within the "perceptual realism" of a contemporary war movie (which, despite being composed of synthetic images, is still a medium based in the photographic image), there is a doubling of Butler's frame, a meta-film, wherein cinematic techniques/automatisms are represented using cinematic techniques/automatisms: with this, there is a violent and dehumanized objectifying of the world through the user of the AR (Tony Stark as Iron Man, for example), which is then framed again when the machinic audience watches the "screen" of the movie (theater, TV, etc.).

Chapters 4 and 5 in this text will take up the military use of Virtual Reality (VR), drone strikes and data-driven simulations as represented in movies, teasing out the datafication of the virtual battlefield and what it means for an audience to consume and be encouraged to accept those cinematic versions of a technologized, automatized battlefield. This chapter builds off Chapter 2's construction of the hard technological body in order to challenge cinematic representations of militarized AR, in particular as the movies involve a further technologized and digitally networked hard body: the encased suits that house the civilian soldiers of the *Iron Man* films and *Pacific Rim*. Much like *Edge of Tomorrow*, the movie audience is given civilians who must then work within the ineffective and ineffectual State War Machine in service of humanity's survival: for Tony Stark it is being "a patriot" (a term the movies use repeatedly as shorthand for "American") to fight against globalized terrorism; for Raleigh Becket (Charlie Hunnam) in *Pacific Rim*, he must come back from civilian life to save the earth from the Kaiju, gigantic alien creatures, by joining with another pilot within a Jaeger, a giant robot. The biological soldier is surrounded by fully enclosed mechanical suits that they use to interface within their machines and their worlds through militarized and weaponized AR and AR-like environments. These cinematic representations are, again, reinforced, created and celebrated by

State War Machines, in particular the United States': "To generate buzz about these 'cyborg-soldier' R&D projects, the DOD is linking them to the *Iron Man* film. Since Iron Man's debut, DOD-sponsored university researchers and defense companies have been 'working to turn Iron Man fiction into real technology' (Mirrlees 8). The notion of an interactive, haptic image within AR environments takes on special importance in the Total War Machine when paralleling the State War Machine's electro-optical devices and images alongside representations of those devices and interfaces in popular movies, which are then also put alongside the devices and interfaces that a civilian machinic audience uses on a daily basis. As this book has argued, there is little difference between the technology of State War Machines and civilians; not only are hardware and software shared and constructed similarly for the military and civilian user alike, but military technology is being adopted for civilian use, and vice versa. In addition, there is the recognition that the military, as established in the introduction to this text, often controls and constructs the representations of that technology in cultural interfaces like movies. Specifically, this chapter will explore what it means to layer the nanotechnological objective (images and data/statistics) into an AR interface that overlays the physical "real" world. Such a process mirrors the digitizing ontology of film itself, and when such interfaces are represented via a military digital interface (computer layer) within the cultural interface (cultural layer) of a movie, it doubles the problematic effacing effects of the war image on the machinic audience: the digital "imaging," once layered over the film/cinematic image (which itself is a stratum of digital and analog components/actors/landscapes), provides further distancing simulating power that then encourages the machinic audience to view that which is captured within its frame, and the digital and analog automatisms used to produce those documents, as normalized, weaponized versions of civilian networked technologies and interfaces. When the machinic audience, both military and civilian alike, engage with the knowing perceptual realism within war films, it encourages that audience to view all "real" combat as if the world is a movie; the actual interfaces of military technologies are cinematic and in this there is the stripping of subjective "narrative" that then objectifies an enemy and their territories into a "*manipulable series of numbers*". When cinematic representations of AR-enabled soldiers become one part of a larger machinic phylum that is a key part of the Total War Machine, cinematic machines (cameras, editing bays, software and hardware, etc.) fuse with cinematic versions of the machinic phylum, which then join to the larger Total War Machine to normalize and perpetuate the kinds of digital warfare that take place daily in 2017.

## THE ETHICS OF IRON MAN AS HARD BODY AND HARD TECHNOLOGICAL BODY

As a whole, the *Iron Man* films (herein referred to as *IM* [*Iron Man*]; *IM2* [*Iron Man 2*]; and *IM3* [*Iron Man 3*] replicate the ethical system of the hard technological body: despite Tony Stark's more positive relationship with the Artificial Intelligence (AI) Jarvis,[7] Tony Stark/Iron Man is a white male hero constructed around the liberal individual human as the masterful center of the technology-biology assemblage.[8] This ethical system is established first by his father, Howard Stark, a WWII weapons developer turned industrialist. Remembering the discussion of biological heredity at the beginning of Chapter 2, in *IM2* his father (John Slattery), through old film footage, argues that "everything is achievable through technology. Better living, robust health, and for the first time in human history, the possibility of world peace. ... Technology holds infinite possibilities for mankind, and will one day rid society of all its ills." While techno-utopian, similar to Wiener and the early cyberneticists discussed in Chapter 2, it is clear Howard Stark views technology as a tool/servant completely in control/service of the "master" biological human; its purpose for existing is to defeat enemies and increase the quality of human life, and he resists modeling a critical posthuman that challenges the technologies' potentially cooperative roles in a civilian-assemblage user.

Tony Stark spends all three movies reaffirming his father's worldview: while there are passing glances at providing the world with technologies that would generate "better living, robust health," like Tony Stark's development of the arc reactor, which would provide cheap electricity, or the bioengineered healing that takes place in *IM3*, the movies aim their arguments about robotics, Internet-enabled technologies and AR toward the "the possibility of world peace." As he explains to Christine Everhart (Leslie Bibb) in *IM*, "It's an imperfect world but it's the only one we got. I guarantee, the day that weapons are no longer needed to keep the peace, I'll start making bricks and beams for baby hospitals." This attitude doesn't change throughout the films, even as he gives up developing and supplying weapons for the American military: he creates and evolves his suits only as weapons, but justifies them by attempting to maintain his own liberal and individual control over those suits/weapons. Yet that control is distinctly America-centric and is, again, built on his father's hereditary patriotic heroism; for his father, technology enabled the defeat of Nazi evil and the affirmation of American ideals (which also include the capitalist system that he operated Stark Industries within). As Mirrlees argues,

> Iron Man was made in a world system in which the U.S. is the dominant imperial power. Since at least WWII, the U.S. state and U.S. corporations have struggled to rule markets across territories by building, promoting and policing a world system of states that share the U.S.'s core features: the capitalist mode of production, the liberal democratic state form, and the consumerist 'way of life'. (4)

By upholding and fighting for this "way of life," not only are the two Starks repeatedly called "patriots" throughout all three films, but there are also multiple shots that feature American flags prominently in the background. This focus on being a civilian American patriot is further emphasized when Tony receives an award from Air Force General Rhodes (Terrence Howard) at the beginning of *IM* and is lauded for "ensuring freedom and protecting America and her interests around the globe," upholding the importance of continuing worldwide American superiority, based on the aforementioned "core features."

This combination of American nationalism and focus on the liberal individual are, as discussed in Chapter 2, core components of the hard body, and in many ways Tony Stark/Iron Man upholds many of the same values found in hard-body films and the hard technological bodies of *Edge of Tomorrow* and *Elysium*. Without simply comparing and matching the films' protagonists,[9] the two main ways in which he reinforces the hard technological body's ethics is through his rejection of larger infrastructures (government, corporate, military) and the spectacular portrayal of the augmentations (speed and power muscles; "mobility, lethality") that his suits provide. Tony Stark, as Iron Man, acts similarly to Rambo and Cage in *Edge of Tomorrow* in that he sees himself as a lone savior that must work outside corrupt and ineffective infrastructures (corporate, government, military) in order to achieve "peace"; in particular, while his relationship with the American military grows stronger through his teaming up with War Machine (who becomes Iron

Patriot in *IM3*) , he actively resists being fit into the American military's chain of command. As described at the outset of the introduction to this book, after seeing a news report that shows Gulmira, a fictional village in Afghanistan, being kept under terrorist control largely due to "no political will or international pressure," Stark simply flies there in his suit and kills dozens of the terrorists; as a parting gift, he leaves one of the terrorists alive, placing him at the feet of a growing angry mob, and exits after quipping, "He's all yours." In this, there are no official military actions, and his leaving of the one terrorist to the mob underlines his commitment to the sort of individual sense of justice and retribution far outside governmental or military infrastructures. Part of this is in reaction to the type of warfare that surrounds the *Iron Man* movies: the war on non-national terrorist groups (the 10 Rings in *IM*, the Mandarin in *IM3*). The military is shown as old-fashioned and not nimble enough to deal with the War on Terror, too encumbered by too many ineffective and moving pieces. Iron Man, in contrast, can fight the globalized terrorist enemy by literally flying directly to those exact places and engaging in combat. To underline this, during the scene where Iron Man defends Gulmira, when Edwards Air Force Base is shown, there are personnel frantically trying to find out who is carrying out the attack while repeating that each arm of the military was "not cleared to go there." When Colonel Rhodes pushes Stark on whether he is responsible, he responds with, "Sounds like someone stepped in and did your job for you," implying that because the military is so large and bound by too many regulations, his unauthorized and civilian interjection, "getting the job done," is not only justified, but is to be lauded. Stark further celebrates himself at the beginning of *IM2* when he opens his Stark Expo by bragging: "I'm not saying that the world is enjoying its longest period of uninterrupted peace in years because of me. ... I'm not saying that Uncle Sam can kick back on a lawn chair, sipping on an iced tea, because I haven't come across anyone who's man enough to go toe to toe with me on my best day," adding gleefully that he is a one-man "nuclear deterrent" before arguing, "I've successfully privatized world peace." Similar to the hard body and the hard technological body, the films celebrate his vigilante (civilian) effectiveness in "getting the job done" in spite of the unwieldy and resistant governmental ("Uncle Sam") and military machinic phyla that attempt to stop or corral him.

This then manifests in a similar unhealthy treatment of the Iron Man suits, wherein Stark claims the suits as his "property" within a "capitalist mode of production"; for Stark, the technologies are to be privately owned and controlled because, as Rhodes testifies later in the film, he "does not operate within any definable branch of government." In a scene from *IM2* that reinforces this, Stark is called in front of a Senate committee and asked to turn over the technology to the public (meaning the US government and the American military). After accusing Senator Stern (Garry Shandling) of not prioritizing "the well-being of the American citizen," he defies the committee by stating, "You want my property? You can't have it"; this idea of the suits as individual "property" is also repeated later in the film when Pepper Potts calls Rhodes' capture of the technology "an illegal seizure of trademark property." This treatment of the technology as private property argues that such technologies must remain in the hands of moral and liberal individuals and, more troubling, are only objects that have value when possessed or used by human users. When Stern insists that the suits are weapons, Stark counters that his "device" is "a high-tech prosthesis": "The suit and I are one. To turn over the Iron Man suit would be to turn over myself." His statement implies an intimate connection between himself and his suits; his use of the word "prosthesis" and "device" implies an external addition, problematically transhuman at best, that has neutral value until it is commanded by a biological user who then makes it a moral or immoral technology by the choices that that individual human user makes.[10] More than this, the suit *is* a weapon, and, with the exception of perhaps saving people in the aftermath of combat, is never used otherwise: not only is Stark constantly in combat when inside his suit, but cinematically, when the machinic audience sees the suit flying through the air, it is indistinguishable from a missile; visually, the suit is given the same treatment as an aerial attack, the long slender body followed by a trail of light and smoke.

## MILITARY AUGMENTED REALITY AND IRON MAN

If the Iron Man suits are unabashedly a military weapon, its use of Internet-enabled AR technologies make it a distinct evolution from the hard technological bodies discussed in Chapter 2. Given the history of AR technologies,[11] definitions of "Augmented Reality" are still contested, especially as the medium has been brought into contemporary popular culture via increases in consumer hardware capabilities, but there are a few basic pillars that the technology and its interfaces rely on.

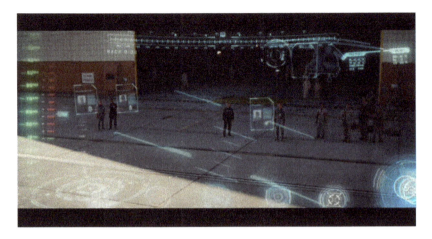

**Image 3.1**    The synthetic view from within War Machine's suit

When defining the term, a number of scholars begin with the work of Milgram et al., "Augmented Reality: A Class of Displays on the Reality-Virtuality Continuum" (1994), wherein the authors establish a continuum between "Reality" and the "Virtual," with Augmented Reality in between the two poles (283), parsing further into "See-Through" and "Monitor-Based" AR displays (284). Both of these are present in the *Iron Man* films: the "See-Through" AR environment utilizes a Head-Mounted Display (HMD) to overlay information in real time on top of the reality that the viewer is looking at; this can be seen in *IM2* when War Machine lands at Edwards Air Force Base. When he looks at the personnel waiting for him, a brief bio and photo pops up next to their heads (Image 3.1). The "Monitor-Based" AR systems are a "window-on-the-world" (WoW) ... [and] refer to display systems where computer generated images are either analogically or digitally overlaid onto live or stored video images" (284); discussed later in this chapter, these are what the user of the Iron Man suits sees from within her/his helmet, where there are small models of the suit itself as well as other layers of information about the surroundings present.[12] The basics of the technology ensure that

> augmented reality adds digital information to the world that [the user] can interact with in the same manner that [the user] interact[s] with the

physical world ... there are additions to that world that consist of digital information that is placed in the world to augment the world with things [the user] would not normally see, hear, feel, touch, etc. (Craig 2)

Craig later points to what he calls the "key aspects" to AR: "The physical world is augmented by digital information superimposed on a view of the physical world. The information is displayed in registration with the physical world. The information displayed is dependent on the location of the real world and the physical perspective of the person in the physical world" (16). What distinguishes AR from "other media, such as virtual reality, and even cinema" is that "the augmented reality experience is interactive" and AR users "'remain' in the physical world ... there is not an attempt to make [users] believe [they] are not in the real world at the position [they] are standing or sitting" (16).

Augmented reality then depends on the user being rooted in the physical world, being a physical biological body, but the word "superimposed" implies that the data and machine species layered on top of that world (bodies and landscapes) is intrusively unnatural. This language is rooted heavily in early cybernetics, as discussed in Chapter 2, and the notion of the liberal "man-in-the-middle" in control of that technology as a tool. As such, when the military began to adopt the technology, its treatment of it remained focused on the soldier's biological components so that the technology was always in service of that rational human mind. Kim argues that the first example was the "The Mark II gyro gunsight that was developed by the British military in the latter half of World War II" (214) that was composed of "a gyroscope and a series of electromagnets" (220). Barfield points out that

since the early 1970s, the U.S. Air Force has studied HMD systems as a way of providing the aircrew with a variety of flight information. ... The Honeywell integrated helmet and display sighting system (IHADSS) is one of the most successful see-through systems in army aviation. ... In 1982, Furness demonstrated the visually coupled airborne systems simulator (VCASS), the U.S. Air Force's super-cockpit VR system. (60)

Currently, Le Roux writes, the technology is used as a key component of Network-Centric Warfare,[13] with soldiers equipped with AR receiving information about enemy terrain and fighters and updates to battle plans and objectives in real time (122, 126). This then aids the State War

Machine by providing an "effective linking of forces that are geographically or hierarchically distributed. The networking of knowledgeable entities allows them to share information and collaborate to develop a shared awareness" and to then provide soldiers with environments that "[accelerate] the user's ability to achieve higher situational awareness, which leads to better and faster decision-making" (Zocco and De Paolis 39).

While this type of Network-Centric Warfare, including simulators and drone strikes, is discussed more completely in Chapter 5, this chapter's focus on the individual soldier-figure of Iron Man (and later Iron Patriot) centralizes a biological-technological assemblage that bears more of an initial conceptual resemblance to the Land Warrior System (LWS) that Kim details (216). These soldiers, as part of the "5th Brigade, 2nd Infantry Division of the US Army," were equipped with an

> HMD [that] is a remote display for a camera mounted on a gun, allowing soldiers to aim their weapons without looking through the gunsight. Soldiers literally see from the perspective of the firearm, as if they were their own gun. … Lastly, the HMD is an integrated communication device; it enables superiors to transmit data to soldiers in the form of digital images, video, data messaging, and other kinds of combat information, keeping soldiers up-to-date with changes in battlefield conditions. (217)

As such, the LWS, also referred to as the Future Combat Suit and/or the Future Force Warrior, in utilizing a military AR is

> one part fantasy: the cyborg soldier is pure ideology, an expression of the military's faith in technology's ability to enhance the mobility, lethality and commandability of combat troops; and one part reality: an active program that has the material result of channeling billions of taxpayers' dollars into university, industrial, and military research. (215)

Visually, the LWS actually looks more like the exoskeletons in *Elysium* and *Edge of Tomorrow*, though the Internet-enabled and AR technologies that the LWS utilizes is more in line with the fully enclosed suits that are the heroic focus points of the Jaegers from *Pacific Rim* (discussed later in the chapter) and the *Iron Man* films. While the suits do superficially provide similar weaponry (guns, rockets, lasers) and the same "power" and "speed" muscles that the exoskeletons of the first chapter do, it is key that the biological body cannot be seen from the outside, and that the suits are fully enclosed and do not give the machinic audience the overmuscled and spectacular biological specimen that Cage and Max showcase. While the Iron Man suits lose some of the rhetorical effectiveness of seeing the human user in control, it gains the major advantage of providing and normalizing a heroic version of a digitally networked, very literal "man-in-the-middle" soldier. Whereas the exoskeleton soldier has limited networking capabilities, the Iron Man suits glorify a weaponization of digital information and connection that is at the heart of contemporary Network-Centric Warfare. Later on this chapter will discuss the networks/assemblages formed by the Iron Man suits as a machinic phylum, but here it is the use of AR in the Iron Man suits that separates it from the hard technological body; by celebrating perceptual realism and the violent and military construction of nanotechnological layers of data that are "superimposed" upon that physical world, the movies encourage an unhealthy digitizing of animals, people and landscape as acts of war waging that then justifies/allows for their destruction.

As Kim outlines, when using AR, the user "can understand AR as the expansion of the virtual into the material, insofar as users' material surroundings are encoded as a numerical representation, and interactions with the environment are mediated by this representation" (215). AR is close to Manovich's explanation of the VR screen as "invisible" in that it is no longer framed by a "rectangle [or a] flat surface from a distance" (97) and with this "the two spaces—the real, physical space and the virtual, simulated space—coincide. The virtual space, previously confined ... now completely encompasses the real space. Frontality, rectangular space, difference in scale is all gone. The screen has vanished" (97). Such a screen "can change in real time, reflecting changes in the referent, whether the position of an object in space (radar), any alteration in visible reality (live video) or changing data in the computer's memory (computer screen)" (99). Though not the same framed image of cinema, when viewed through an AR interface, real objects and reality are identical to the synthetic image that Rodowick outlines as the building blocks of digital cinema, where, again, "*digital acquisition quantifies the world as manipulable series of numbers*" (author's italics 116). When the viewer looks through the AR interface, the nanotechnological objectivity, outlined in the introduction to this chapter, is given: via the automatisms of AR, the user sees selected layers of data transposed over "reality," which segments that which is being looked at into data packets, "numerical representation." If AR then is a manipulation and surfacing of a database of information in real time, the computer layer of AR is, as Manovich explains, "reduced to … data structures and algorithms. Any process or task is reduced to an algorithm, a final sequence of simple operations which a computer can execute to accomplish a given task. And any object in the world … is modeled as a data structure, i.e. data organized in a particular way for efficient search and retrieval" ("The Database Logic" para. 10). In turn, the unaware AR user flattens reality into an objective set of data and numbers and image-instruments, encoded synthetic representations, erasing the subjective narratives and depth of whatever the user is looking at and replacing them with information and tasks.

Very different than the cinematic techniques used to represent the telepresent drone footage in *Good Kill* and *Eye in the Sky*,[14] the cinematic "See-Through" AR displays in the *Iron Man* movies thrust the audience into the first-person perspective so that they look through the Iron Man suits' AR interfaces and see the layers of information on top of buildings, people, landscapes, etc. (see Image 3.1). The Iron Man suits and their AR, even when led by the civilian Stark, are military technologies, as evidenced by the fact that the AR interface of Iron Man is exactly the same as the military interface used by War Machine/Iron Patriot. In an additional illustrative example from *IM*, Stark is in a dogfight with two fighter jets and the audience is given the same first-person point of view through the fighter pilot's AR display, which looks nearly identical to Iron Man's. As such, as Mirrlees argues,

> The *Iron Man* film sequences which show off the military capabilities of Stark's suit … encourage viewers to expect a future of cyborgian soldier warfare ruled by the U.S. By doing this, *Iron Man* normalizes a future that is yet to be while cultivating public compliance with present-day DOD expenditure on R&D that aims to make *Iron Man*'s cyborgian weapons system real. (9)

More specifically, for the machinic audience, the normalized heroic portrayal of Stark's AR is an electro-optical weapon that promotes a "compliance" with and celebration of the militarized use of digital information and the reduction of enemies and landscapes to dehumanized data to be manipulated and deleted.

In the movies' cinematic treatment of the See-Through AR interface there is a problematic "participation," to refer back to the introduction of this text, in these scenes when the audience looks through Iron Man's eyes and watches the AR interface used as a targeting system that highlights and then executes enemies. When the audience looks through the eye slots of the suit, they look as a soldier; Virilio critiques the soldier's military view by writing that "the soldier's obscene gaze, on his surroundings and on the world, his art of hiding from sight in order to see, is not just an ominous voyeurism but from the first imposes a long-term patterning on the chaos of vision" (62). The audience then, hidden by the mask of Iron Man and by the distance of watching cinematic combat (rather than actually experiencing combat), sees AR as a technology whose violent action is glorified as the ultimate end and greatest use of the technology. The audience's cinematic participation not only normalizes this aggressive application as an example of Rodowick's "recalcitrant cultural norms of depiction" (101) but also celebrates the process of generating synthetic images. These images that shroud the audience's vision in a perceptual realism, as if the world were on a screen and/or a movie, encourage the process of effacing the actual subjective narratives of specific cultures, people and landscapes through this process of digitization.

To this end, the AR interfaces are presented so quickly in the films, and often with such small fonts or images, that the audience can't *actually* make out (or "use") the interface. When this "invisible screen" is flashed on the screen, the portrayals lose the haptic interaction and real-time screen of the technology and are given instead a non-functional interface and act as a synthetic image, a visual object similar to the "objective" photo that is at the root of filmic construction and cinematic language. This ties well into Manovich's understanding of the dynamic and "real-time" screens. His understanding of "screens" is similar to Butler's treatment of the photo frame in that "the screen is aggressive. It functions to filter, to screen out, to take over, rendering nonexistent whatever is outside its frame" and that

> although the screen in reality is only a window of limited dimensions positioned inside the physical space of the viewer, the viewer is expected to concentrate completely on what she sees in this window, focusing her attention on the representation and disregarding the physical space outside. (96)

This aggressive nature is seen in what he calls the "dynamic screen," which encourages immersion to the point that "the viewer is asked to

merge completely with the screen's space" (96). When the "real-time
screen" of AR is framed and flattened into the dynamic screen/(synthetic) image of cinema, the screen-within-a-screen (frame-in-a-frame)
showcases the nanotechnology-driven objectivity in that "the image is
produced through sequential scanning"; in each sequence of the "image-
as-tool," the layers of specific data are surfaced and adjusted without
any time delay. When the two screens combine in the *Iron Man* films, it
doubles the effect of Butler's instrumental frame by creating a synthetic
image (the AR display, Manovich's digital interface) within a synthetic
image (digital cinema, Manovich's cultural interface), and further normalizes a war waging that relies on people being either "useful or dispensable" (Butler, xii), underlining an ethics of objectivity that is key to the
militaristic gaze's transformation of the world into a set of potential war
targets.

## The Fully Enclosed Suits of *Iron Man* and *Pacific Rim* as the Modern Machinic Phylum

While the previous section focuses on the machinic audience looking out
through the See-Through AR displays as if s/he were Iron Man, the *Iron
Man* films, along with *Pacific Rim*, also prominently feature Monitor-
Based AR displays. The audience is given repeated close-ups of the users'
faces inside the Iron Man suits, framed by the Monitor-Based AR display that shows various interactive and real-time information about the
suit, the environment, the user, etc. (Image 3.2) The Monitor-Based AR

**Image 3.2**    Tony Stark inside his Monitor-Based AR system

shots in the movies highlight the users' spectacular "digital muscles": the ability to receive information on anything in the world, to master nature and technology through a networked digital flow of information. This internal view of the suits maintains the same negative doubling effect that the See-Through AR does in that it reduces the species being represented in the suit to flat digital information. This applies to the people and landscapes represented in this interface, but, more specifically, the suit is represented as an electro-optical tool to be monitored and manipulated with all of the agency within the technological-biological assemblage belonging to the biological user. In fact, the repeated close-up on the face within the suit further reaffirms this in a way that the See-Through AR shots do not: the face of the user, the key marker of human identity, is framed by the digital information, is literally central within the periphery of numbers and images, and showcases the biological entity as the clear liberal choice maker in the Iron Man suit assemblages. The machinic audience is then reassured that there is a biological user in control of the technology, that it is a prosthetic, underlining an unhealthy human exceptionalism.

*Pacific Rim*'s depiction of Monitor-Based AR is slightly different, but still reinforces many of the negative values that the *Iron Man* films present. *Pacific Rim* parallels *Edge of Tomorrow*: there is an interstellar race that all of humanity is at war against. This alien race created giant monsters, Kaiju, and let them loose on Earth in hopes of destroying its citizens so they can then colonize the planet. In defense, the world bands together to create Jaegers, equally gigantic robots that are piloted by humans inside the robots' heads. Similar to the United Defence Force in *Edge of Tomorrow*, the movie illustrates and upholds the Total War Machine in its unifying depiction of global humanity's battles against the aliens in that every single resource and human goes toward the war effort: this is seen in *Pacific Rim* in the building of a protective barrier around the major cities, where the entire human population is employed for the massive engineering feat; there are also repeated shots of the Jaegers being built and maintained, showing the Total War Machine coopting all civilian resources and labor. The fact that the Jaeger program, COSDEC (Pacific Rim Combined Special Defense Corp), is military and headed by Marshall Stacker Pentecost (Idris Alba) is key: despite the director's insistence that *Pacific Rim* is a pacifist film,[15] the Jaegers are only weapons and the Total War Machine's efforts to create and maintain them takes precedence over everything.

Looking more specifically at the Jaegers, the interface between the pilots and the Jaeger is very different than the interfaces in the first two *IM* films. In the *IM* films, there is a singular user within the suit and that assemblage is a solitary unit. However, the Jaegers require two pilots, one for each "hemisphere" of the machine's "brain"; together, the duo manipulate the Jaeger via a "neural interface," which, as the protagonist Becket explains is based on "DARPA jet fighter neural systems." This is a representation of human-machine assemblages, at least superficially, that would likely be more positively reflective of how a machinic audience interacts with their networked technologies in that it acknowledges other users of the technology as integral to its operation. In fact, piloting a Jaeger requires a deeply intimate process called "drifting" wherein the two pilots enter each other's minds and memories and meld together before bonding with the Jaeger. The term "neural interface," as well as the film's use of "neural handshake," showcases the film's positive understanding of the dense and symbiotic biological-technological assemblages that the machinic audience is part of: "neural" speaks to the distinctly human/biological part of the assemblage, and "interface" and "handshake"[16] come to represent the technological entities. When the pilots bond with the Jaeger it is similar to the user-avatar relationship in *Avatar* and *The Matrix* films in that when the machine is hurt, the biological user is also hurt. This completely intertwined relationship between the two physical aspects, human bodies and the machine Jaeger, is essential to understanding how the total assemblage functions: to get the Jaeger to do any action, the pilots must do that action, which the machine then mirrors (i.e., in order for the Jaeger to walk the pilots literally have to walk). The repeated full-body shots of the pilots, as opposed to the close-ups of the face in the *IM* films, highlight a complete-body, haptic manipulation that superficially presents a potentially positive machine-human embodied relationship.

Under closer examination, however, the control of the Jaegers most resembles puppetry: the machine only does what the humans in control do and never deviates to initiate action on its own, and this haptic interface, and the AR elements that are integrated into that system, reveals the human exceptionalism that is at the heart of the movie. This is most broadly evident in the fact that the pilots are housed in the machine's head: it is clear, then, that the humans are the "mind" of the assemblage, the liberal human at the controls. This sentiment is further emphasized by the act of "drifting": it is the bonding of the humans through their specific individual human memories (narratives), taking place in their minds, that allows the Jaeger assemblage to operate. The machine elements have no input or complexity; they are there to be "plugged into" and then manipulated by the bonded humans. The audience sees this during the scene when Mako Mori (Rinko Kikuchi) attempts to drift for the first time with Becket: she starts "chasing the rabbit" and falls too deeply into her own mind; rather than bonding with Becket, in her panic, she turns on the Jaeger's arm cannon. The human engineers scramble to override Mori but neither they nor the machine itself can: it is the (frightened) human individual that in sole control of the assemblage, and the machine (and the machine of the military and even the other pilot) has very limited control.[17] The representations of AR in the movie make this clear as well: throughout the film, that layer of the interface predominately shows information about the suit in real time (Image 3.3); the AR is simply a way of the humans monitoring the suit, like the problematic Monitor-Based AR in the *Iron Man* films, and this shows how little symbiotic cooperation, even at the level of Jarvis and Stark, there is between the biological and technological entities.

This rejection of a critical posthuman ethics is further maintained by the military and violent solutions to all the problems in the movie,

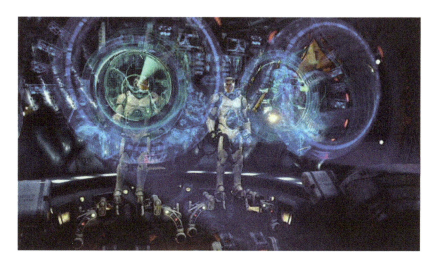

**Image 3.3**    *Pacific Rim*'s dual Jaeger pilots within their AR interface

which views the human race as the masters of Earth, their own galaxy, and eventually the aliens' galaxy. There is a glancing critique of human destruction of the earth as Dr. Newton Geiszler (Charlie Day) explains why the aliens have chosen that instance to attack: for millennia, the earth's atmosphere wasn't "conducive," but "[the aliens] waited it out. And they waited it out. And now with ozone depletion, and carbon monoxide, polluted waters, well, we've practically terraformed it for them." It appears as if the film is arguing that humans are at fault for their own destruction via their valuing of their own existence above all else. However, the combat of the film, between the Jaegers and the Kaiju, take place without any regard for any other species, destroying and leveling large parts of various landscapes, in particular the ocean, all in service of humanity's survival. The prime example of this is the ending of the film: one of the Jaegers, piloted by Chuck Hansen (Robert Kazinsky) and Pentecost, in a desperate attempt to destroy two Kaiju, detonate their own nuclear weapon at the bottom of the Pacific Ocean. The subsequent nuclear fallout and radiation, and its effects on the life-forms there, are of no concern and the detonation is instead framed a heroic sacrifice. After this, Becket and Mori must descend into the portal and use their nearly destroyed Jaeger, and its nuclear core, as a bomb intended to destroy the aliens' "civilian" world on the other side of the portal. Similar to *Ender's Game* (discussed in Chapter 5), the victory of the movie is essentially a genocide, an eradication of an entire species and an upholding of humans as the only species worth preserving. The film treats the technological aspects of the Jaeger assemblages similarly. Earlier in the film, when Becket describes what is required for drifting, he explains that "the deeper the bond, the better you fight." From his statement, it is obvious then that all the human-technological "bonding" that takes place is done for a violent and military purpose that upholds human exceptionalism, with little sense of the machine (or any other biological species) as co-species; the end of the film's treatment of the Jaeger, where the literal core of it is remade into a blunt weapon, a bomb, and then detonated, argues that its only use in the end is as a destructive object in service of humans.

Tying the dual Jaeger pilots to the multiple Iron Men suits that form the climax of *IM3*, the machinic audience can begin to see the real power of digital connection and information layering: it is the ability to network (to other users, to other machines, to data) in both movies that make the assemblages appear especially heroic and powerful, and it is this networked nature that turns the assemblages into a weaponized machinic phylum that is deeply representative of a contemporary Total War Machine steeped in the values of Network-Centric Warfare. Recalling the introduction to this text, a machinic phylum is a self-organized assemblage made from a number of other technological and biological assemblages. In particular, De Landa sees the State and Total War Machines as clear examples of machinic phyla, in particular in their mixing of (biological) soldiers, tactics and strategies with (technological) hardware, software, simulations, etc. Within the context of a State War Machine, the suits in *Iron Man* movies and the Jaegers of *Pacific Rim*, while using the basic ethical template of the hard body, incorporate in networked data to further evolve into greater complexity, effectively datafying the landscape and data around those soldier bodies in an objectifying manner.

Expanding to the Total War Machine, war films and their representations of computers and digital network are a machinic phylum that then hooks into the machinic phylum of the State War Machine. In an immediately recognizable way, the content of the *Iron Man* films and *Pacific Rim* provide heroic representations of the State War Machine's machinic phylum and, by doing so, encourage the machinic audience to adopt the attitude that computers' and digital networks' roles in the State War Machine is unavoidable, positive, and, for lack of a better word, natural. *Pacific Rim* endorses this in a number of scenes: there are shots of the global unifying of the (civilian and military) human race creating defense and military projects that are given with swelling music and wonder; there are the rousing speeches that Pentecost makes to the COSDEC personnel that justifies their war making as defense and survival of the race; there are the multiple pieces of hardware and software that go into the creating and maintaining the Jaegers; there is, at the lowest (most intimate?) level, the assemblage of the Jaeger-pilots who are the ultimate heroes of the movie. In particular, that the bio-Internet that is formed between the pilots' minds and the Jaeger is only used for military purposes presents such human-digital bonding as a weapon and a tool for military force.

In *IM3*, the machinic audience gets the apex of Stark's version of a literal military machinic phylum when, at the end of the movie, he saves the day by remotely employing a fleet of unmanned Iron Man suits.[18] Unlike the first two *Iron Man* movies, there is an attempt in the third to make the Iron Man suits an increasingly "internal" technology and not just an externally worn suit: Stark is shown implanting himself with sensors, literally injecting the technology into his body, so that he can control the phylum of suits without any direct interface. The conclusion of this chapter explores this dissolving of digital interfaces further; the suits in *IM3* transition from being a prosthesis to an entity with a messier, more symbiotic relationship between user and technology. Yet when the suits show up, there are arranged as a literal phylum, a distinctly military arrangement, hovering above before descending into combat with Aldrich Killian (Guy Pearce) and his men and women at Advanced Idea Mechanics. Stark's ability, as well, to jump between suits interchangeably shows how flexible and bonded his relationships with the suits are. However, the suits are still only used for combat and are presented with spectacular awe in the final scenes of the film. He and his suits then defeat Killian, freeing the president and Pepper Potts, establishing Stark, and his own machinic phylum, as heroic and upholding the violent and combative use of the technology as deeply admirable.

Across the *Iron Man* films, the suits move from War Machine to State War Machine as Stark retains less and less sole civilian control and instead becomes increasingly entangled with the American military. Tony Stark begins *IM* by extending the role his father played as the head of Stark Industries, the "Merchant of Death," who is both a weapons manufacturer and a distributor within the larger military machine. After his escape from Afghanistan, he eschews all military and weapon contracts and shifts his company toward more of the techno-utopic possibilities his father outlined in the aforementioned video footage. Yet Stark keeps evolving the Iron Man suits, increasing their combat capabilities and software and hardware weapons. Despite allegedly rejecting military use of his technology, he maintains close ties with Rhodes, a man high up in the Air Force, who eventually takes one of the suits from Stark in *IM2* and repurposes it as a military weapon in the chain of command of the American State War Machine. Further to this end, Stark and Rhodes fight as a team at the end of *IM2*, trading cooperative banter and working as teammates within their suits. A similar comradery is shown throughout *IM3*, where Rhodes, rebranded as Iron Patriot,[19] joins Stark's machinic phylum in combat. Even if Stark is a civilian, the Iron Man suits are used militarily and none of the films complicate this beyond Stark's occasional behavior as a rascal; the technologies are an integrated part of the State War Machine and a positively portrayed component of the military machinic phylum.

However, it is not just the content of the *Iron Man* movies that contribute to the Total War Machine, but its very nature as a medium

**Image 3.4** The audience sees as Tony Stark's camera sees

becomes weaponized. It is important to focus on the fact that the medium of cinema includes the actual machines of the films' production but also representations of its own production. Focusing on representations of its own production, cinema's form, in general but more specifically within the war films discussed, depends upon a machinic phylum of forces, in particular within a contemporary digital cinema. As discussed earlier in the chapter, the key automatism that begins forming the synthetic images of a (digital) cinematic machinic phylum is the image-making camera; it is this machine that initially frames and captures the action for the audience and organizes the vision, themes and reactions to a movie. *IM* is particularly attuned to this fact, as not only does it shows multiple "screens" within the movies, but the Iron Man machinic phylum itself incorporates cameras that meta-referentially refer to the construction of the movie as a cinematic object. As Stark is first developing the different components of the Iron Man suits, he uses cameras to record his progress and testing of the different iterations of the technology. In one particular scene he is trying out the thrusters that allow him to fly. He speaks to the recording camera as he sets the parameters for the test. However, that recording camera, complete with time signature, red recoding icon and battery meter, which is in the world of Stark, is *also* the audience's point of view (Image 3.4); the audience's world and the world of the film merge through this camera, sharing a camera automatism for roughly ten seconds. The movie then cuts to a shot of the camera-machine capturing the aforementioned footage and suddenly the audience is thrust back into the cinematic camera, into the perception of the automatism outside the narrative of the movie. The scene then continues to switch between these two cameras, blending the audience's and Stark's worlds until the two are inseparable: the act of constructing the movie *Iron Man* uses the same automatisms as Stark does when testing and constructing his Iron Man suits. This overlapping camera acknowledges and combines the larger machinic phylum of Stark's suit(s) and the machinic phylum that constructs, edits and (digitally) creates the movie itself: this includes Stark's suit (and all the hardware, software, networked data, data infrastructures, etc.), the users of the suits, and the tools (including the cameras) that help build and maintain the suits, as well as the cameras, humans (actors, directors, film crew, etc.), editing bays, software and hardware components of moviemaking and editing, the watching audience, and so on.

Adding to this, the *Iron Man* films (and war films in general) are dependent on and are themselves machinic phyla, which are then combined with other machinic phyla, such as assemblages that fund, promote and distribute movies, and those all then combine with the State War Machine. Extending out to look at the *Iron Man* films as cultural interfaces and their place within the Total War Machine, the extremely close military-civilian relationship established in the narrative of the movies is also reflected in its actual making (specifically in *IM*). To begin, the capitalist cinema-making machine itself is a machinic phylum that includes "Hollywood studios, distribution networks and exhibition platforms [that] are largely controlled by six U.S.-based transnational media conglomerates (TNMCs)" who exert "asymmetrical influence over the internal structure, ownership patterns, distribution and exhibition process and standards of film of other national film industries" (Mirrlees 5). This machine then bonds with the State War Machine:

> The DODSAEM supported Iron Man's production by linking Marvel Studios to the U.S. Air Force, which turned its Edwards Air Force Base into a Hollywood set piece for three days of shooting. The Air Force allowed Marvel Studios to cast over one hundred Airmen as extras in the film, flew its F-22 Raptor aircraft for the camera to help Marvel create high altitude action combat sequences, [and] provisioned helicopters, Humvees and jumbo jets. (7)

Similar to the discussion around *Edge of Tomorrow* at the end of Chapter 2, for director Jon Favreau, part of the appeal of having this military cooperation was that it "enhanced the 'realism' of Iron Man" (8), a realism that is further established by the film series' inclusion of "real-life" figures like Bill O'Reilly, Elon Musk and Joan Rivers. This portrayal of an "accurate" military environment, within a world of celebrities that the machinic audience recognizes as familiar, serves the United States Air Force: "The Air Force was happy to help Favreau make *Iron Man* seem 'realistic', so long as its comic book fantasy helped promote a positive image of itself to the public and to the world" (Mirrlees 8). The movie as a machinic phylum, the capitalist cinema-making machine as a machinic phylum, and the State War Machine as a machinic phylum all meld together in these instances to form a massively persuasive aspect of the Total War Machine. The films' popularity[20] demonstrates the acceptance and potential normalization of these sorts of documents and the militarized violence that they represent and potentially reproduce, with the machinic audience's daily Internet-enabled technologies repurposed toward this war waging.

## Conclusion: The Non-existent Interface

Speaking of the machinic phylum, De Landa warns:

> If Deleuze and Guattari are correct in saying that it is precisely this schema which makes the machinic phylum "invisible" or "unrecognizable," we may need much more than theoretical innovations to reconnect technological evolution to its old sources of inspiration and vitality. Reality itself, so homogenized after over two centuries of military uniformization, needs to be reinjected with heterogeneity; and our bodies, so deskilled after two centuries of military routinization, need to relearn the craft and skills needed to "hack" these heterogeneous elements into new combinations. (para. 21)

By focusing on "inspiration" and "vitality" through relearning and "hacking," De Landa is pushing for concrete examples of critical post-humanism. These examples could include actual technologies, civilian actions or documents (such as movies) that challenge the deeply ingrained and problematic human-technological dynamics of user-tool/

weapon. De Landa dares his readers to consider that those assemblages, like the '80s cinematic hard body, would look repurposed away from a normalized military control, application and routine.

The new "craft and skills needed to 'hack' these heterogeneous elements into new combinations" have surfaced in some movies that portray intelligent machines and artificial intelligences (AI) as independent species, like *Her* (Dir. Spike Jonze 2013) and *Transcendence*. Such creatures do not fall prey to the effacing frame that Butler sees in war images (and by extension war films) because such creatures do not use interfaces or screens to navigate and organize information; promoting such figures in popular movies would encourage a machinic audience to examine their own (potentially negative) synthetic images and interfaces and perhaps reach out to other machine species with a cooperative hand. Though very thought-provoking, *Her* does not fit within this text as it is not a war film. However, while *Transcendence* does not focus on the military and is not a "traditional" war film, much like with Chapter 4's consideration of *Brainstorm* and *The Lawnmower Man*, the Department of Defense and its interest in cyberdefense lurks around the edges of the film and therefore makes it worth considering here. In the film Will Caster (Johnny Depp) is a brilliant philosopher and computer scientist who helps to create a high-level strong AI named PINN. Caster is assassinated by the terrorist group Revolutionary Independence from Technology (RIFT) and, as he is dying, he has his brain scanned and then uploaded and added to PINN; after RIFT attacks where his wife Evelyn (Rebecca Hall) has uploaded and is storing Caster, she "liberates him" by releasing him into the Internet. The film's main concerns centers around what sort of entity/species this uploaded postbiological Caster is and whether it is still Caster or is instead an entirely other species. While such a discussion is beyond the scope of this text,[21] the lack of interfaces that the entity has with the technology around it is very relevant. In opposition to many of the films discussed in this book, with perhaps the exception of *Avatar*,[22] the movie reverses the traditional dynamic of a technology/weapon being applied to a human/biological core, and instead has a machine core (PINN), which has a human/biological element (Caster's mind) added to it. This reversal shows the movie's attempt to disrupt the "heterogeneous elements [of human-technology dynamics] into new combinations" and constructs a protagonist that is, completely and thoroughly, biologically bodiless and technologized. Without that biological body, the entity can move seamlessly between data structures and networks without any (AR) interfaces, and with an expert knowledge and instantaneous speed: with this movement, the entity becomes a part of whatever it touches and manipulates and it too becomes a part of the entity. It, then, has no interface because it itself is the technology: there is no need for an in-between layer that structures control of any software or hardware because the entity has incorporated it into itself. In fact, when the entity does "surface," it creates a pictorial (video?) version of itself to talk with Evelyn and other humans; it creates interfaces so that other human users can utilize the technologies it has created/inhabited (it needs no such interfaces), and eventually creates a body for itself in order to try to appease Evelyn.

Its "identity," or the various things it is networked to, keeps exponentially expanding until it reaches the point where, as part of biotechnological surgeries intended to heal the participants, it is able to attach itself to humans and take control over them; the entity argues that the participants are "all enhanced, modified and networked. They remain autonomous, but they can also act in unison. Part of a collective mind." Again, this reverses the traditional human-technology dynamic and it is the machine entity controlling the biological, subsuming the liberal individual human into a "collective mind," and, as one can imagine, this terrifies most of the human characters, in particular scientist Joseph Tagger (Morgan Freeman). Convinced it is "building an army," the American military is called in and engages it in combat, which culminates in Evelyn getting fatally injured and her uploading a virus into the entity to "kill" it. However, the entity's speech at the end makes it clear that it in fact has humanity's interests at its center and that its godlike network-identity is actually in service of nature and human life:

> Look at the sky. The clouds. We're healing the ecosystem, not harming it. Particles join the air currents, building themselves out of pollutants. Forests can be regrown. Water so pure you can drink out of any river. This is your dream. Not merely to cure disease, but to heal the planet. And build a better future for all of us.

Though the machinic audience should be suspicious that the film's techno-utopianism does not stray far from Howard Stark's cybernetic musings on human (and American) exceptionalism, in a simplistic way, the postbiological Caster's aims are in line with a critical posthumanism and a recognition and valuing of nature and the multiple species on Earth. When De Landa challenges the familiar norms of "military routinization," he is perhaps talking about an entity like the uploaded Will Caster, a life-form that generates a machinic phylum from its networked identity, not from a human-centric biological core, and a creature that does not filter the world through the perceptual realism of synthetic AR images because it does not use interfaces. However, while *Transcendence* did make its budget back at the box office,[23] the monstrous success of the *IM* films, and the character's viral spread into many of the equally successful Marvel movie franchises, makes it clear that Iron Man is far more popular and carries much more rhetorical power. In closing this chapter, it is useful to contrast Whiplash's (Mickey Rourke's) use of the suits in *IM2* with Stark's machinic phylum in *IM3*. In *IM2*, Whiplash hacks the fleet of suits made by Stark Industries' rivals, Hammer Industries, and controls them from a remote computer terminal, in effect flying them as a set of weaponized drones; he even takes over War Machine's suit and pilots it without Rhodes inside having any control. The suits, in this instance, are more straightforward input-output machines, and their external (remote) interface makes it clear that the human user is in full control of the technology. These negative versions of unmanned suits are then reimagined (rebranded?) as heroic in *IM3*, where the aforementioned machinic phylum of suits defeats all the evil enemies at the film's end. In this twisting, like *Transcendence*, the audience is given assemblages whose interfaces with technology are invisible or non-existent and become even less visible than Manovich's understanding of AR and VR (97–99). Though there remains a set of interfaces, as discussed through this chapter, the phylum of suits are controlled by Jarvis and then, seemingly, by Stark's thoughts: they too have made a number of their interfaces completely invisible that are instead controlled by Stark's mind via the aforementioned implants. Like his pilotless Iron Man suits, his body too has been reformed as a weapon. Unlike in *Transcendence*, the invisibility of the interfaces, or synthetic control layers between machine-machine or machine-human, is weaponized and remains rooted in the human mind as the master of the assemblage. The "new combinations" presented in *IM3* do little to provide even a basic critical posthumanism, and instead grant the machinic audience a military-styled assemblage to aspire to. *Pacific Rim* and the *Iron Man* films do little to acknowledge any other solution to civil and/or international issues other than war and combat, and the films themselves, assemblages of assemblages, slide seamlessly into the Total War Machine like an arm into a well-tailored uniform.

## Notes

1. De Landa's understanding of "extensive and intensive places," as laid out in *History and Science* (New York: Atropos Press, 2010), is also useful to consider here: "An extensive map captures features of the Earth that are extended in space, such as coastlines, mountain ranges, or the areas of land and volumes of air space… By contrast, an intensive map captures differences in the intensity of a particular property (gradients) as well as the dynamic phenomena that are driven by such gradients" (115). In this, we can see how an intensive map, though tied to the "real world," is actually virtual and a data-based visualization of an extensive space, like Daston and Galison's nano-technological atlases, that are similar to the interfaces of AR.

2. As part of Chapter 5, this dehumanizing capturing of the enemy and its landscapes is unpacked further with discussions of the electro-optical automatisms invoked in drone warfare and war game simulations.

3. Like the introduction to this text argues about war films in general, such a photographic frame undoes much of what is argued must be done in a critical posthumanism and instead manipulates the other (co-)species of Earth into the position of the subhuman in order to justify, and ethically make peace with, the destruction of those species' sovereignty and landscapes.

4. This is perhaps most true in biopics like *Snowden* and *The Fifth Estate*, which are deconstructed in Chapter 6.

5. Virilio gives a further example of this when he brings up the example of Kubrick's use of "old newsreel footage of Hiroshima or Christmas Island in *Dr. Strangelove*" (Dir. Stanley Kubrick, Columbia Pictures 1964) which he argues was done because "Kubrick was motivated by the highest sense of realism, going straight to the heart of the war image" (*War and Cinema* 31).

6. It is worth acknowledging that AR has its early roots in cinema: "The first appearance of Augmented Reality (AR) dates back to the 1950s when Morton Heilig, a cinematographer [in 1962]… built a prototype of his vision, which he described in 1955 in ' The Cinema of the Future,' named Sensorama, which predated digital computing" (Carmigniani and Furht 4).

7. Superficially, Tony Stark's multiple Iron Men suits and his intimate relationship with Jarvis, a highly intelligent AI, and their interaction through AR interfaces, seems like a potentially healthy model of critical

posthuman. However, despite their, at times, symbiotic "conversation," Stark's decisions always override Jarvis; if it is to be a choice between Stark or Jarvis' proposed actions, Stark always wins and the suits undertake his actions, reaffirming his (and the human's) mastery and control and the machine's slavery.

8. That Iron Patriot/War Machine is played by African American actors Terrence Howard (*Iron Man*) and Don Cheadle (*Iron Man 2, Iron Man 3*) are positives. However, the character does not receive any side plots of his own, and is, at best, a sidekick to *Iron Man*. The character's agency is also consistently diluted by his involvement in the State War Machine's chain of command and he is often portrayed as a rigid soldier following orders. This inclusion, but ultimate marginalization, holds the white, liberal-minded Tony Stark as the central ethical figure and hero. Similarly, the increased presence of Pepper Potts in the action-adventure sequences of the *Iron Man* films, in particular *Iron Man 3*, are small affirmative steps away from the '80s hard body. Specifically, the fact that Potts dons one of the Iron Man suits and engages in hand-to-hand combat moves her toward the "action heroine" outlined in Tasker's *Spectacular Bodies* (and also explored in note 15 of Chapter 2). Still, her major involvement in the plot is as a romantic partner to Tony Stark and she spends much of the last third of *Iron Man 3* captured by Killian, playing the archetype of the damsel in distress that Stark must save. See the notes 5, 9, and 15 in Chapter 2 for further expansion.

9. Like Max's hard technological body in *Elysium,* Stark's biological body is shown to be appropriately vulnerable by his being poisoned by the electromagnetic arc reactor that is also keeping shrapnel from entering his heart. Like Max's radiation poisoning, such vulnerability justifies his use of the weaponry and confirms that there is a mortal human body in control of that technology.

10. Stark's position here is similar to Lieutenant Kara Wade in *Stealth* when she explains why she is willing to fight with EDI, the AI-piloted fighter plane *Stealth* is centered around: "[EDI is] neutral. If it's controlled by moral people, then it'll be moral." While *Stealth* and this quote are further analyzed in Chapter 5, Stark's insistence that his suits are his property and that he is the one who ensures they are used ethically places the technology in the position of unthinking "neutral" tool/weapon, completely subservient to human needs and "moral" control. This, again, goes against a critical posthumanism and affirms hard body's human exceptionalism.

11. Historians of the technology point to early civilian examples that include Ivan Sutherland's 1960s work with HMDs, Myron Krueger's 1975 Videoplace, Tom Caudell and David Mizell's AR in Boeing production

lines, L.B Rosenberg's Virtual Fixtures, and Steven Feiner, Blair MacIntyre and Doree Seligmann's KARMA prototype (Carmigniani and Furht 4). In general, Kim paraphrases Ron Azuma's work in explaining there is a spectrum "ranging from the completely synthetic (virtual reality) to the completely real (telepresence) with AR situated between these two poles" (214). Within this, there is a multitude of understandings of the varied types of AR: Carmigniani and Furht clarify that "augmented reality systems can be divided into five categories: fixed indoor systems, fixed outdoor systems, mobile indoor systems, mobile outdoor systems, and mobile indoor and outdoor systems," ultimately defining AR as "a mobile system as a system that allows the user for movement that are not constrained to one room and thus allow the user to move through the use of a wireless system," (16). This chapter is focused on the AR in the Jaegers and the Iron Man suits, with a special focus on the systems' mobility in reaction to the "outside" world, and the users, placement between the synthetic and the "completely real".

12. There are further, slightly different, examples of AR that mix with Virtual Reality (VR) though the *Iron Man* trilogy: in *Iron Man 3*, calls up a 3D model that recreates a bomb explosion at the Chinese Theatre and manipulates the model by zooming in and out, rotating, etc; in *Iron Man 2*, he pulls up a similar 3D model of the 1974 Stark Expo and haptically manipulates it, shifting between "naturalistic" and wire-frame visualizations of the space. While there is more to be said about these portrayals, this chapter's focus on the AR interfaces of the suits makes these periphery examples.

13. There is a further explanation and definition of Network-Centric Warfare in the introduction to this text.

14. The representation of drone footage in *Good Kill* and *Eye in the Sky* is explored in Chapter 5 where it is analyzed in more depth what the effects are of the audience being given the drones' POV and how that reflects the remote telepresence of the drone pilot. While those films grapple with the "cowardice" inherent in drone warfare, it should be noted that, in comparison, the user of the Iron Man suits is present in the space and when s/he acts, it is, at least in part, with their own biological body as part of combat. This bodily presence heightens the drama and also the stakes of this AR-aided combat, that the soldiers are there and in "real" danger, and in turn falls in line with the more traditional rhetoric around the heroics of combat films.

15. In an interview around the time of *Pacific Rim*'s release, its director, Guillermo del Toro, describes himself as a pacifist and explains, "What I wanted was for kids to see a movie where they don't need to aspire to be in an army to aspire for an adventure. And I used very deliberate

language that is a reference to westerns. I don't have captains, majors, generals. I have a marshal, rangers … it has the language of an adventure movie" (Howell, Peter. "Pacific Rim's Guillermo del Toro is a monster-loving pacifist" *Toronto Star*, July 15, 2013, para. 14). Despite the director's intentions and shift in language, as this chapter argues, the film's content is military in nature and the Jaegers, and their application, are a function of the world of the film's Total War Machine. More than this, *Pacific Rim*, as a war movie, fits within the larger omnipresent Total War Machine of everyday life.

16. *The Oxford English Dictionary* defines the computer science usage of "handshake" as "An exchange of standardized signals between communicating devices in a network or bus, used to regulate the transfer of data between them, typically to control the start or end of a transmission; a signal used for this purpose." ("handshake, n." *OED Online*. Oxford University Press, December 2016. Web. 13 March 2017).

17. Superficially, similar to the inclusion of Rita in *Edge of Tomorrow*, *Pacific Rim*'s move to at least include a woman as part of the Jaeger's soldier assemblage is a slightly positive move away from Jeffords' (and the traditional war film's) white masculine hard body. However, she becomes Becket's paramour, sexualizing her in service of their love story and while the other men of the film are battle-tested veteran pilots, she is the audience surrogate and by far the weakest of the crew. It is damning that the only pilot to lose control of the Jaeger and demonstrate emotional frailty when operating the Jaeger is also the only female pilot. See note 8 of this chapter for further discussion.

18. I've written previously on the machinic phylum at the climax of *IM3* in the chapter "Hacking Against the Apocalypse" in *Interfacing with the Internet in Popular Cinema.*

19. As I discuss more in *Interfacing with the Internet in Popular Cinema*, War Machine is "rebranded" as Iron Patriot in *IM3* because the name is said to have "tested well with focus groups" (131). His shift to a "softer" name parallels Iron Man's softening toward working with the American military and the overall move to make the State War Machine more palatable and heroic across the three films as a whole.

20. The box offices of movies involving Robert Downey Jr. as Iron Man are massive: *Iron Man* made over 585 million dollars worldwide; *Iron Man 2* made over 623 million dollars worldwide; *Iron Man 3* made over 1.2 billion dollars worldwide; *The Avengers* (Dir. Josh Whedon, Buena Vista 2012) made over 1.5 billion dollars worldwide; *Avengers: Age of Ultron* (Dir. Josh Whedon, Buena Vista 2015) made over 1.4 billion dollars worldwide; *Captain America: Civil War* (Dir. Anthony and Joe Russo, Buena Vista 2016) made over 1.1 billion dollars worldwide. All numbers

in American dollars and retrieved from boxofficemojo.com. March 13, 2017.

21. I expanded much further on Hans Moravec's and Ray Kurzweil's work on the postbiological in *Interfacing with the Internet in Popular Cinema* and the introduction to this text. Caster is nearly identical to the postbiological creature that Kurzweil imagines and is too disembodied, ultimately, to be the sort of healthy posthuman that Hayles advocates for. That said, the creature is a separate species that a critical posthumanism would recognize as sentient and worthy of sovereignty and ethical treatment and, as such is worth considering further in this text.

22. *Avatar*'s portrayal, or lack thereof, of interfaces between the biological user and their technological extension/doppelganger is interesting in that the interaction between the two entities is done with a neural bonding and control of the "avatar" in the "real world" via the thoughts and brain pulses of the user lying sealed in a bed. However, the relationship here is different than Caster's, and still somewhat traditional, in that it involves a clear separation between technological and biological with, again, the biological controlling the technological to the point that when the human "unplugs" the Na'vi avatar "goes to sleep." The film does provide a tantalizing future version of the world, similar to Caster's postbiological entity, in that the hero Jake "uploads" (transcends?) into his Na'vi avatar at the end of the first film. Perhaps in the planned sequels, we will see a similar creature, and treatment of technological-biological interfaces, as we do in *Transcendence*.

23. In comparison to the billion-dollar-plus box offices that films that involve Iron Man have made (see note 20), *Transcendence* made 103 million American dollars worldwide. Retrieved from www.boxofficemojo.com, March 13, 2017.

# CHAPTER 4

# War Films, Combat Simulators and the Absent Virtual Soldier

## INTRODUCTION: A BRIEF MILITARY HISTORY OF COMBAT SIMULATORS

Howard Rheingold's 1991 text *Virtual Reality* begins with a firsthand account:

> I was standing in a carpeted room, gripping a handle, but I was also staring into microscopic space and directly manoeuvring two molecules with my hands. Perhaps someone in an earlier century experienced something similar looking through Leeuwenhoek's microscope or Galileo's telescope. It felt like a microscope for the mind, not just the eye. (14)

The quote is just one example of Rheingold's rhapsodic commentary wherein he breathlessly outlines examples of Virtual Reality (VR), skipping from North Carolina's ARM project, to NASA, to Kyoto and the South of France, in an attempt to establish the technology as one of the key "outposts of a new scientific frontier" (17). However, there are a number of troubling flattenings within his discussion of VR that is indicative of other theorists and technological historians of the time, making it a useful place to begin this chapter's exploration of the military use of VR and its representations in war movies.

The first such problematic fusing that Rheingold undertakes is the melding of "cyberspace" with VR. Like many other early Internet scholars, Rheingold points to Gibson's definition of "cyberspace" from *Neuromancer* and the oft-cited passage of Gibson's characters inhabiting

© The Author(s) 2017
A. Tucker, *Virtual Weaponry*,
DOI 10.1007/978-3-319-60198-4_4

a digital world that is a "consensual hallucination ... a graphical representation of data abstracted from the banks of every computer in the human
system" (51). At the end of the paragraph, he introduces the term "virtual reality" (VR), arriving at it via Jaron Lanier, and, from there on, uses
"virtual reality" and "cyberspace" synonymously. Michael Heim's text
*The Metaphysics of Virtual Reality* (1993), rooted in Platonic notions
of physical reality that is deeply critical of virtual space and selves, similarly uses the terms interchangeably. *The Plague of Fantasies* by Slavoj
Žižek (1997), in particular the chapter "Cyberspace, or, The Unbearable
Closure of Being," mixes virtual reality and cyberspace (a space that
encompasses web browsing, chat rooms and Multi-User Dungeons
[MUDS]) without parsing between what each of those virtual spaces
entails. Part of this flattening might be explained away by the infancy and
fast-exploding population of the technology.[1] However, for this chapter
in particular, it is very important to differentiate between "cyberspace,"
virtual worlds, and virtual reality.

Using Mark Bell's definition as a framework, a virtual world is one in
which a user extends his/herself, via an avatar, into an synchronous and
persistent network of other users, which is then facilitated by networked
computers (3). Bell's broad definition extends to spaces like email conversations or social media sites (a Facebook profile for example), and/or
modern websites that would include embedding of images, videos, comments, etc. Chapter 6 examines civilian virtual worlds-as-battlefields in its
examination of cinematic representations of the hacker in war films like
*Blackhat* and *Sneakers*, ultimately arguing that the inclusion of these virtual worlds in the discussed movies blends the genre of the war film with
the political thriller; as discussed later, it is because these virtual spaces are
most closely associated with the civilian realm that their inclusion within
war films most often takes place far from the fields of combat, on the
home front, and is instead often demonstrative of the civilian realm being
invaded and/or surveilled by military and governmental infrastructures
(their own or nations like Russian, China, etc.) in a paranoiac war waging.

In terms of war films that are closer on the spectrum to combat or action-
adventure films, there is a distinct lack of these "personal" digital virtual
spaces. Some of this can be explained by the genre's tendency to recreate
historical battles: it makes little sense for period movies like *Unbroken* (Dir.
Angelina Jolie 2014) or *Fury* (Dir. David Ayer 2014) to include the Internet,
as it hadn't been invented by WWII. However, in 2017, the relative absence
of these virtual worlds is strange considering how common they are in actual
American military practice: in a *Time* article, Wendle explains that

BlackBerrys have made an appearance in the combat zone. ... Of the roughly 30 soldiers in the platoon, five of them have the devices (the soldiers pay the monthly charges themselves). ... With all of the communications options out there—from Skype to Google Talk to AIM—it has become easier and easier to stay in constant touch. (para. 8)

In terms of war film conventions, one would suspect such communication might appear in movies as a cousin of the "letter back home" or "mail call" that is a key part of the genre; Basinger states that genre conventions and items common in combat films, like "boots, mail call, stopping to enjoy nature and adopting a little child ... might be seen as the man in combat's attempt to link himself to sanity, to order, and the remembered life from before he went into combat" (15). Emails, texts and engagement with social media while deployed could be a similarly utilized trope to provide an essential pipeline between the battlefield and the "sanity" of "back home" that would establish the soldier's connection to the home front and help to humanize the soldier and justify their actions by providing a sense of their motivations (defending their family, nation, the American "way of life"). Yet, in *Zero Dark Thirty* (Dir. Kathryn Bigelow 2012), while there are often computers in the background of office scenes and computers are used to play videos, the closest the film comes to showcasing a personal virtual world is an instant chat, complete with emojis, between Maya (Jessica Chastain) and Jessica (Jennifer Ehle) just before the Camp Chapman attack. For the most part, in popular and Oscar-nominated films about modern American military conflicts, like *The Hurt Locker* (Dir. Kathryn Bigelow 2008), *American Sniper* (Dir. Clint Eastwood 2014) and *Lone Survivor* (Dir. Peter Berg 2013), there is little presence of the Internet and no extended use of these virtual worlds. There are scattered examples across other war films. LaRocca points to Brian De Palma's 2007 *Redacted*, wherein the audience sees "footage from a surveillance video, a helmet camera, a night/infrared camera, a handheld digital video camera, a laptop video camera and iChat, a cell phone camera, a news report camera, and a YouTube video, among other screens and displays" (47). In *Rendition* (Dir. Gavin Hood 2007), the main character, Salazar (Izzy Diaz), talks via a Skype-like technology with his father back home; yet the scene remains an outlier in the genre in how it showcases how a networked military communicates, via virtual worlds, with civilians. Within *Stop-Loss* (Dir. Kimberly Pierce 2008), there is a brief scene in which Steve Shriver (Channing Tatum) shows one of his fellow soldiers pictures of his fiancée

Michelle (Abbie Cornish) on a digital camera, saying he was sent them yesterday, but he does not view them in or upload them to a virtual world like Facebook. The film also makes use of YouTube-style videos, made by Isaac "Eyeball" Butler (Rob Brown), that cut together footage of the soldiers outside of combat with stock footage of military fighting; the films vary from the showcase of comradery that opens the film, to a combat-positive video backed by heavy metal, to memorial videos like the one for Tommy Burgess (Joseph Gordon Levitt). These documents themselves are melded into the movie as part of the filmic text and characters are never shown watching them (say on YouTube, on a phone or in a web browser); in this way they provide much the same effect as the inclusion of Tony Stark's "test videos" (discussed in Chapter 3), in that the synthetic images of the videos blend with the synthetic images within the machinic phylum of the movie itself, and this assemblage of assemblages then joins the State War Machine as the larger Total War Machine.[2] Returning to this chapter's focus of virtual worlds and virtual reality, the videos in *Stop-Loss* are un-networked and oddly disconnected from their technological origins, pseudo-private and semi-documentary, and do not gesture to the types of homemade Internet videos beginning to become popularly shared online at the time.

This absence of virtual worlds, which this chapter will further tease out by exploring the similar lack of VR within war films, reflects the distrust in "invisible networks" that integrate into the "human" soldier. When they do show up in the political thriller/war films discussed in Chapter 6, they function as an invisible and irradiating presence that make the human/biological user vulnerable through its always-on connections that enable surveillance, hacking and cyberwarfare. Within war films that involve combat and action-adventure that are to be discussed in this chapter, a soldier assemblage that lacks these virtual Bodies without Organs, despite their real inclusion in "actual"/"real" warfare, speaks to how human-centric the combat soldier at the middle of the war film remains. There is a tolerance for versions of these virtual networks when they are made visible through their manifestation in physical hardware (as explored in Chapters 1, 2) so long as they are mastered as tools; the lack of "invisible" (public?) virtual worlds into the cinematic combat soldier perhaps speaks to the need to resist diluting the humanistic qualities of the private individual mind that upholds rationality and duty, characteristics that are very necessary for the war film to remain rhetorically effective. Given the porous and symbiotic relationship between war films and "real events" (as explored in the introduction of this text), this absence is made even more striking when noting that very little VR is represented in war films, either.

To return to this chapter's focus, the main marker of a VR is that it is an automatism specifically constructed to replicate some aspect of "the real world." Aukstakalnis and Blattner define it as "an artificial environment created using information technology tools (both hardware and software) and presented to the user in such a way that it appears and feels like any real environment" (1992; as quoted in Lele 18); Rob Shields also adds that the user is then granted "a sense of phenomenological presence or immersion into the environment" (*The Virtual* 54). This makes VR, and its goals and effects, very different than a virtual world: a virtual world, like Facebook or an email system, makes no aims to replicate the world in any way; instead, its goals are built around a dense virtual hyperconnection and any immersion that takes place within the space is done in an abstracted, non-representational space. VR is closer to an interface into a virtual world, a very specific subset within the larger umbrella of virtual worlds: recalling Chapter 3's discussion of "perceptual realism," the immersion into this space is usually made through hardware that is designed to provide as much multisensory feedback as possible, again in replication of "the real," and has typically included equipment such as full head-mounted goggles and display in combination with various forced-feedback and haptic devices, such as vibrating controls, and movable and inflatable seats and suits. As such, this chapter's discussion of VR is different than Chapter 5's discussion of predictive "data-driven" conflicts, such as wargames, drone strikes and full-scale situational simulators, which involve little of the physical body an immersed VR demands. This chapter is also separate from Chapter 3's discussion of "enhanced" soldiers (mechs and/or suits) and Augmented Reality (AR), despite overlaps in filmic portrayals of VR and AR hardware and visualizations of data, as the Jaegers and Iron Man suits do not replicate the "real" world in the parallel manner that VR does. With this in mind, this chapter will explore specifically how small-scale combat or training VR, including flight and tank/vehicle simulators, are portrayed in movies.

Looping back to Rheingold's text, the second conflation he makes when discussing virtual reality is similar to Norbert Wiener's blending of civilian and military cybernetics that is explored further in Chapter 2: Rheingold also nonchalantly slips the US Air Force's use of VR for training simulators in between other examples of VR (16) and puts "MIT and

the Defense Department" (46) side by side, without pausing to acknowledge either's military history (16). Much like Wiener, this melding of
civilian-military is indicative of the acceptance of the Total War Machine,
one in which the military culture's ubiquitous penetration is normalized;
the weaponized versions of these technologies, these astounding "micro-
scopes for the mind" that are the "outposts of a new scientific frontier," go uncommented upon. Returning to "Necropolitics," Mbembé
describes how "colonies are similar to the frontiers" and as such are
viewed as being

> inhabited by 'savages.' The colonies [or frontiers] are not organized in a
> state form and have not created a human world. Their armies do not form
> a distinct entity, and their wars are not wars between regular armies. They
> do not imply the mobilization of sovereign subjects (citizens) who respect
> each other as enemies (24).

Rheingold's use of "frontiers," when folded into the militarization that
he casually mentions, perpetuates Mbembé's fears and furthers the dehumanizing gap between the possessors of VR technology (and their self-
construction as nations/entities, the American army in this case, that are
civilized) and the non-distinct opposing force, primitive "savages" without the technology. While this asymmetrical warfare and its ramifications
are discussed further in Chapter 6, here the superiority attached to the
spectacular and weaponized version of VR justifies its conquering use of
the American State War Machine's enemies' sovereignty under the problematic values of humanism taken up in the introduction to this text.[3]

It should come as no surprise then that the American military has had
a long history with VR, often as training equipment or for the reliving
of specific military events, because, as Ajey Lele points out, it "becomes
extremely difficult to demonstrate to military personal the real-life mental and physical challenges of military life," especially when considering
soldiers with little to no military experience (20). As such, the American
military is deeply invested in VR: as Mead writes, "the research firm
Frost and Sullivan predicts the DoD [Department of Defense] spending
on modelling and simulation will reach $24.1 billion by 2015" (7). VR
then allows the ability to participate in various aspects of warfare without having to be exposed to the potentially fatal effects of combat. The
goal is to put personnel in as "real" a simulator as possible to best train
them for what they are about to encounter. Kara Platoni, in her article

"The Pentagon Goes to the Arcade," adds that "to be effective, a flight simulator must react exactly as it would in the real world, giving the illusion of instant response. It must allow the user to suspend disbelief, to get caught up in the emotion of flying" (para. 5). O'Dell Hightower, a veteran trainer for the United States Army, is even more emphatic: "Since these simulators are used to train soldiers for war, they must be as accurate as possible" (11). Similar to the haptic synthetic images and perceptually real cultural interfaces explored in Chapter 3's focus on AR, it important then that the military VR simulation is not just constructed in order to learn how to use a piece of hardware (a fighter jet, tank or gun), but also must replicate the experience, the noise, movement, messiness and violence of actual combat.

This idealized version of military simulation is not future tech: in his prescient 1993 article, Bruce Sterling described VR as a "strategic asset" in which

> simulator technology has [already] reached a point in which satellite photographs can be transformed automatically into 3-D virtual landscapes. These landscapes can be stored in databases, then used as highly accurate training grounds for tanks, aircraft, helicopters, SEALS, Delta Force commandos. (para. 102)

Such technology has been a "strategic asset" since the 1950s: Giles Taylor's "A Military Use for Widescreen Cinema" outlines the Waller Flexible Gunnery Trainer as "a World War II virtual reality film technology employed by the US and British militaries to simulate the direct experiences of anti-aircraft gunning combat" (17). Later examples of military VR include SIMNET, one part of the army's "distributed simulation" network that was active in the late 1980s and early 1990s[4]; this discussion should also include more contemporary systems like "AIRNET (Air Network), COFT (Conduct of Fire Trainer), I-COFT (Individual Conduct of Fire Trainer), U-COFT (Unit Conduct of Fire Trainer), and the CMS (Combat Mission Simulator)" (Hightower 13), as well as Flatworld and other simulators "which are used to teach everything from battlefield operations to cultural interaction to language skills to weapon handling" (Mead 3). "Traditional" combat military simulations are still very much in use, but have now been further buttressed by "intelligence" simulators like ELECT BiLAT, which "presents an ambitious training agenda for altering procedures for conducting complex bilateral negotiations with Iraqi power brokers" (2008; Brady 99–100). All this culminates in the dream scenario in which the American military has at its disposal "an army of high-tech masters who may never have fired a real shot in real anger, but have nevertheless rampaged across entire virtual continents, crushing all resistance with fluid teamwork and utterly focused, karate-like strikes" (Sterling para. 57). In 2017, VR is used in the Navy, Army and Air Force as training equipment, with commercial products, like the Oculus Rift and Xbox 360 controllers, providing familiar (civilian) and lower-cost interfaces for modern military VR usage (Parkin para. 11).

Within this book, it is important to note the Internet-enabled nature of these simulators as well. Platoni describes how

> Lockheed and other defense contractors have been able to get a piece of the next evolutionary stage in military training [by] putting networked simulators inside real tanks and planes so that troops can train on their downtime. This 'train as you fight' technology has been wholeheartedly embraced by all branches of the military. (para. 33)

Moving beyond stand-alone combat simulators, networked simulators like the DARPA-created SIMNET are "a real-time distributed networking project for combat simulation" (Mead 19–20). The ability to have these virtual worlds digitally networked together allows the soldiers to participate in denser and more "realistic" simulated combat with other users instead of just AI players.

VR is an essential component of a virtually mediated and Network-Centric Warfare that involves, as established in the introduction to this book, a series of "acts of war without war" (Virilio *Pure War* 32). As argued in the introduction of this text, the underlying mental and physical attitudes of Network-Centric Warfare is shaped and maintained largely by the increasing use of and hardware/software/infrastructure enhancements to computing and Internet usage. Within a contemporary virtuous military environment where the lines around occupied or at-war lands are ambiguous at best, where the notion of friendly and enemy are also equally indistinct, military VR systems do not simply act as simulators in which soldiers, pilots, drivers, commanders, etc. can learn how to operate various pieces of hardware and/or experience war before being thrust into "real combat." These digitizing systems are one step in a decades-long evolution toward the integration of digital automatisms into the Total War Machine and generate a military mindset centered on a distant "cleaner" data-driven warfare, which fits more precisely into binary elements (ally/enemy) and outcomes (defeat/victory).[5]

But, despite its long history and continued use, military VR rarely shows up in war films. In movies like *Brainstorm* and *The Lawnmower Man*, two films on the edges of the genre, VR is present only after civilians have created and tested the technology and the military has intruded to repurpose it. The menace of the lurking military presence stealing VR to create "killing machines" speaks first to the movies' suspicions around VR itself: *Brainstorm* and *The Lawnmower Man* both align themselves with Žižek's thinking when he explains, "In so far as the VR apparatus is potentially able to generate experience of the 'true' reality, VR undermines the difference between 'true' reality and semblance" (170). Within the two movies, it is not just that VR provides increasingly detailed and sensual copies of the world, but that the user runs the risk of looking at the "real" world as a virtual world, with consciousness as an interface (169). Importantly, as illustrated by Images 4.1 and 4.2 of this chapter, VR does not typically overlay data and numbers on top of its world and instead aims for a "realistic," immersive world. Different than the synthetic images that blend the "real" word with data to create a perceptual realism, the problem with VR, according to Žižek, is that is "not spectral enough" (200), that its hyper-reality makes it so that the simulation and "the real" are incredibly difficult to differentiate. Whereas AR

**Image 4.1**  The flight simulator in *Brainstorm*

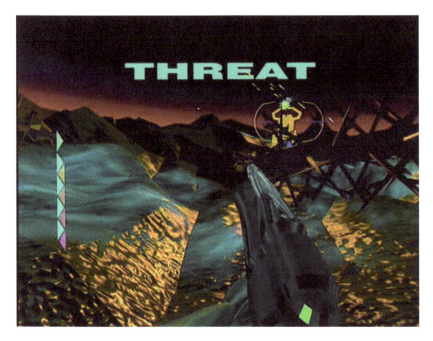

**Image 4.2**    Chimpanzee VR in *The Lawnmower Man*

relies on the image-instrument as its interface, a more obvious surfacing, then layering, of data over the real world, VR immerses and replicates, and, for Žižek, potentially replaces the real world. The debate at the end of Chapter 3 around *Transcendence*'s Will Caster's postbiological digital-human interfacing (or lack thereof) is in contrast to VR separation from the "real world"; whereas Caster and the users of the Na'vi avatars still engage as a physical body in the real world, mediated by the layers of invisible data but never so completely obscured that they cannot see and interact with the "real world," the VR user's physical body, while in a haptic interface, is separated from the "real world." To return to the notion of Mbembé's use of "frontiers," a militarized VR's eradication of the virtual other by ways of making it as "real" as possible treats the enemy outside the simulation as the same inhuman enemy as a digital being, one that can be conquered and manipulated without "real-world" consequences. The terror of military VR tech, the movies posit, is that the State War Machine will brainwash its soldiers so that when personnel are engaging with "real" warfare they would imagine it as another virtual environment, and that those personnel will engage in virtuous war waging without moral consciousness, with no regard for the real human lives and destruction they are causing.

From a critical posthuman perspective, the militarized use of the technology has negatively dominated the frontiers of the virtual; by completely blurring the real and unreal, such usage of the technology encourages the conquering and destruction the avatar self, and the different and powerful extensions and expressions a civilian user/audience member might undertake through the use of such a technology; this focus on the replication of the "real" within the virtual space again values the biological components of the user, forcing the digital versions of that user, and the machine species within that environment, to mirror those "human" components or be cast aside as a corrupting element of that environment.

Now that a number of commercial versions have been released,[6] VR has the potential to occupy a similar space in the Total War Machine as the cultural interfaces of war films: the users' potential detailed and deep immersion into a virtual space makes it a potently spectacular medium to generate, promote and disseminate documents molding attitudes around warfare on a mass scale. Yet in *Brainstorm* and *The Lawnmower Man*, the periphery military presence in both movies most effectively illustrates the problematic slippery nature between civilian-military positions within the Total War Machine. By not showing soldiers engaging in VR and then in battle, war films have lost the opportunity to make any critique of the technology explicitly; now being released on a mass scale, the problematic "frontiers" that the technology is at the forefront of have gone largely unexamined in movies. As this chapter closes by examining video games, the closest version of a VR-like automatism that is found semi-regularly in the genre of war films, it is obvious that even the clearest critical example, *Gamer*, ultimately falls prey to the problematic spectacle of the combat film's nature, upholding the human-centric values of the "real" humanist soldier, and dismissing the technological species and components as virtual delivery systems for the corruption, greed and pollution of the human population.

## THE RARE MILITARY SIMULATOR IN POPULAR FILM

In American war films, soldiers do not interact with virtual reality; rather, they are depicted experiencing the "learning" and "training" that virtual reality might present via combat scenes. *Top Gun* (Dir. Tony Scott 1986), as an example about fighter pilots in a prestigious flight school, should ostensibly be a movie in which there is the type of environment where such simulators would be used; instead, the movie simply shows pilots learning by actually flying. Other examples of VR in film often center around its "law enforcement capacities," like *Virtuosity* (Dir. Brett Leonard 1995) and to some extent *The Cell* (Dir. Tarsem Singh 2000) and *Surrogates* (Dir. Jonathan Mostow 2009), wherein police officers use VR technologies to catch/fight criminals. Similarly, there are films with commercial applications of VR, like *The Thirteenth Floor* (Dir. Josef Rusnak 1999) and *Total Recall* (Dir. Paul Verhoeven 1990), that places the user within a specific 3D experience (1937 Los Angeles, a vacation to Mars); *Disclosure* (Dir. Barry Levinson 1994) portrays a VR-like interface that allows users to wander around a 3D environment to access various records and files.[7] Yet there is a dearth of films that reflect the military's usage of VR in its State War Machine.

Perhaps the best example is the direct-to-video *Ghost Machine* (Dir. Chris Hartwill 2009) in which there is a secret military installation, underwritten by the United States, at a former black site where suspects of the 9/11 attack were tortured and interrogated. The VR system is interesting in that it is created by a technician setting up a network of sensors around a real environment (in this case an abandoned prison) and from this, a digitized 3D environment in replication of that prison is created and is then able to be entered into; once the space is digitized, a user dons a full head-mounted VR kit and engages in a virtual version of that environment, which the technician populates with realistic guns and various enemy combatants. The film provides common visualizations that signal to the viewer the participation in a virtual reality, such as screen noise, different colored screen filters, and first-person POV.[8] The military application of the technology, especially in the combat scenes where the user's physical bodies are copied exactly and then augmented by an endless supply of weapons, portray how being within a system can be used to create "mindless killers." The movie's themes struggle with the limits of the technology and the users' immersion; technician Tom (Sean Faris) comments on Jess' (Rachel Taylor) hesitance to kill: he says "There were times you knew it was a simulation," implying that any break in the VR facade crumbles the usefulness of the whole system, recalling Hightower's commentary about VR's necessary realism from this chapter's introduction. The movie unravels when a murderous ghost is found to be populating the virtual environment and it takes its revenge on the users for being tortured to death by American and British military members. While this paranormal element doesn't disqualify it from this text's discussions (as science fiction and fantasy portrayals of military technology are often as revealing as "realistic" ones), the more telling fact that there wasn't even an American theatrical release for the film keeps it from being seriously considered in this chapter.

However, *Ghost Machine* does follow one trend that is worth following up on: both military personnel and civilians use the VR technology side by side, with seemingly equal skill and comfort. Vic (Luke Ford) and Jess, both members of the British Special Forces, jump into the simulator and are as skilled as their drunk and stoned civilian friend Benny (Jonathan Harden). Generally speaking, aside from *Ghost Machine*, when military-styled VR does appear in movies, it does so interestingly, as a civilian technology that the military lurks around the edges of in nefarious ways. This common theme begins with *Brainstorm*, in which a team of researchers, led by Dr. Lillian Reynolds (Louise Fletcher) and Dr. Michael Brace (Christopher Walken), build a VR headset that "records" a person's experiences and memories and allows them to be replayed by another user with full multisensory participation: one early demo of the technology has Michael "experiencing" Gordy Forbe's (Jordan Christopher) sensations in first-person perspective, in real time via a crude person-to-person biological Internet, sensations that include involuntary reflex movement of the legs, a mismatched meal of steak with peanut butter and hot fudge, and an overloud symphony.[9] The portrayal of the technology itself is very similar to the VR in the Kathryn Bigelow–directed *Strange Days*: in both movies, the recorded memories are mostly used to relive intimate memories. However, the closest that the movie gets to an actual depiction of military VR are a few brief instances of a flight simulator (two scenes totaling less than two minutes of screen time) in which Gordy is carrying out a mission while he is strapped into a moving replica of a fighter plane cockpit (Image 4.1). In the first scene, he undertakes a "low-level simulated assault"; yet when it comes time to shoot down the target, Gordy flies in the opposite direction, smiling and obviously enjoying his resistance to the mission, and the other experimenter notes, in a disapproving voice, that he has "lost control." Gordy resists the military application of the technology, instead reveling in the ability to explore and extend his body into realms of sensation he's never had before.

*Brainstorm*'s version of VR looks a great deal like some military applications of the technology only a decade later, in particular the "Battle of 73 Eastings." In this military VR, Sterling writes,

> they came up with a fully interactive, network-capable digital replica of the events at 73 Easting, right down to the last TOW missile and .50-caliber pockmark. Military historians and armchair strategists can now fly over the virtual battlefield in the 'stealth vehicle,' the so-called 'SIMNET flying carpet,' viewing the 3-D virtual landscape from any angle during any moment of the battle. (para. 63)

The simulation can be played and replayed, integrating different elements each time, with every iteration affecting the end results of the simulation. Brady labels the project as "one of the first military simulations to make the most of audio-visual tools," and flags it as an "early documentary game" as it "uses real people, places and subjects as its referents" (83). The relative passivity of VR in "Battle of 73 Eastings" is similar to depictions of the technology in *Brainstorm* (and *Strange Days*): the user sits within the environment and "relives" whatever has been recorded; in both films, the audience is shown sitting, unmoving, staring straight ahead into the tech. This inactive receipt of a VR experience is a type of simulator, but is very different than the further (and future) immersive and expansive networked versions of the technology discussed later in this chapter.

VR within *Brainstorm* begins as, and struggles to remain, a public, civilian technology. The headset is shrunk down and further demoed specifically as a commercial product. But just before Lillian's death, because the Pentagon is implied to be funding the project, the team is forced to begin to integrate military members in the research and software development. This shift from civilian to military control is the driving tension of the movie: the key scene to examine takes place about a third of the way into the movie, when the research team meets with Marks and a number of other colonels and generals from the Pentagon. Despite Alex Terson's (Cliff Robertson) proclamations that he doesn't want his lab muddied "with outside boots," Col. Easterbrook (Charlie Briggs) states that because they are funding the project, they deserve to see its capabilities. It is then announced that Landan Marks (Donald Hotton) will be joining the team, in large part because he has been working on a similar "system array" and wants to piggyback on the lab's work. Reynolds protests that she doesn't want their invention used for "blowing people to Kingdom Come" or to see it on a "Defense scrap heap." This leads to an administrative/infrastructural shift in the project in which Marks takes over. After this, the little representation of military-styled VR is best evidenced by the second flight simulator scene. In the second instance, this notion of military "control" is central: Gordy is again in the pilot's seat with his arms crossed and a neutral, if not unhappy, expression on his face as Marks exclaims to his superior that the pilot of the simulator "can take a full 10G rollout without losing control, with just the click of a button." Gordy, within the simulator, cannot do anything to stop the same experimenter from telling him "bombs away" before the enemy plane is shot down, all without a single movement from the now-powerless Gordy.

It is this notion of control, echoing Wiener's earlier use of the word in Chapter 2, that is key to understanding the critique of military VR in the film: because the rational human mind is subsumed within the technological system, and the larger military infrastructure, the necessary "control" of the free individual is stripped away and the biological-technological assemblage of the VR user is made too mechanical; the visualization of the technology as passive and the user inert within its usage makes this lack of control even more troubling, highlighting the mechanical species of the assemblage without providing an active participatory collaboration. The militarization of the project keeps it from its potential, as stated by Terson earlier in the film, to be a massive breakthrough in human communication.

Yet it is Terson's utopian visions for the technology that remain just as problematic when applied to a civilian use. Despite the critique of a potential militarized VR, the civilians in *Brainstorm*, much like the hackers and whistleblowers of Chapter 6, still uphold popular posthuman or transhuman values: with the human at the core, VR technology bolts onto the liberal individual with the goal of extending or intensifying the human element without interpenetrating it. This then leaves a passive VR user that extends him/herself into the digital space without the healthy embodiment that marks a critical posthumanism. Civilian VR, depicted as an external automatism, is not that different in application from the soldier's use: it is a mechanized tool in service of, not in cooperation with, the human user. The climax of the movie, wherein Dr. Brace watches Reynolds' death as it was recorded by the technology, celebrates the potential transcendent quality of the technology, to go beyond "petty" military concerns and applications, beyond the body, beyond death, but in doing so degrades the biological parts of the post-human assemblage, unbalancing it so that it becomes closer to a postbio-logical being.

*The Lawnmower Man* presents a similarly negative account of mili-tary VR, again in the brief instances where it's shown, but muddies the technology further, as the aforementioned scholars in the introduction to this chapter do, by blending VR with the Internet-enabled virtual worlds. The movie's protagonist, Dr. Lawrence Angelo (Pierce Brosnan), develops an "intelligence-enhancing" VR system within an unspecified and top secret military-research installation's technology (The Shop) that is interfaced with via a VR bed, gloves and goggle setup. The protago-nists of both *The Lawnmower Man* and *Brainstorm* resist the militarized adoption of the technology, and the scenarios presented "inside" the VR environments are, for the most part, civilian. Yet, because the Defense Department is funding the project, it is always present at the edges, constantly interpenetrating the civilian use with the military. In *The Lawnmower Man*, VR begins as soldier-making technology: at the begin-ning of the film, there is a chimpanzee strapped into the machine and using it as a combat simulator to fight gorillas with a gun (Image 4.2); however, the chimp learns a little too well and, while still wearing the VR helmet and interacting through its interface, grabs a guard's gun, shoots him and escapes. After this incident, Angelo takes a hiatus from the project, moving the technology out of the installation and into his home, stating that he wants to "make something better than a military weapon."

However, The Shop remains in the background, as The Director (Dean Norris) insists that Angelo hasn't really left and that "he'll be back, one way or another." Indeed, The Shop provides much of the equipment, space and drugs that Angelo uses in his attempts to increase the intelligence of Jobe Smith (Jeff Fahey). Like *Brainstorm*, this military influence intruding from the sides corrupts the idealistic potentials of the technology. VR technology within *The Lawnmower Man* carries little of the utopian idealism of *Brainstorm*, as Smith is driven insane by his pro-longed exposure to the technology. Smith's transition into a murderous virtual monster (the Cyberchrist!) via his interaction with the Internet, especially at the end of the film, probably says less about VR and more about the fear of the Internet in the early 1990s as a new and perva-sive civilian technology.[10] In this, there is a reinforcing of the conflation between VR and virtual worlds that surfaces again in early '90s movies like *The Net*, *Disclosure*, *Lawnmower Man 2* (Dir. Farhad Mann 1996), and *Ghost in the Machine* (Dir. Rachel Talalay 1993). Further, unlike in *Brainstorm*, the "transcendence" experienced via the technology is corrupted by the act of digitalizing the self, as Jobe is made terrifying and inhuman by virtue of his being postbiological; the human qualities of the user, like rationality and care, are stripped away and replaced with monstrous virtual counterparts. Like the military version of VR in the film, the civilian version is shown to also degrade its human user to that of an animal (chimpanzee) who then becomes just as violent and unhinged as the feared "killing machines" that a militarized use would bring about.

This is what Nayar finds as a common trope of popular posthumanism, "an overarching emphasis on the machination of humans ... [wherein] the robot implants ... rearrange and derange the human" (6). In addition to this, the transhuman impulse in *The Lawnmower Man* (and to some extent in *Brainstorm*) comes mostly from the technology's ability to fantastically and instantly download information and skills into a user's brain and incredibly quickly expand their intelligence well beyond her/his natural capabilities.[11] Within *The Lawnmower Man*, Smith is able to do this, jumping from a sub-70 IQ to genius level within a matter of weeks of using VR; similarly, Dr. Brace tells his son that "with a thing like [their VR device] you could finish the seventh grade in about five minutes." The fantasy is that with the human at the center, the technology can then, externally acting on a passive user, enhance that human without altering that biological "rational" core; the technology does not co-evolve alongside the user but rather only boosts the biological element. This treatment is the mental equivalent of the exoskeletons from Chapter 2 of this text: VR functions like steroids for the brain, augmenting the "power" and intelligence of the human mind. In the case of Jobe, the technology negatively augments because it programs him to be more machinelike; much like the feared "killing machines" made by militarized VR, it dehumanizes him, stripping him of his emotional complexity and eradicating any empathy.

*The Matrix* (Dir. Andy Wachowski and Lana Wachowski 1999) complicates this further.[12] Within the warfare of the film, VR is portrayed as "programs" that are downloaded into a user by "an operator" as he/ she sits plugged in and unmoving in a bed; the user then plays through the programs in a virtual simulator software. In contrast to *Brainstorm* and *The Lawnmower Man*, *The Matrix*'s version of the Internet is far more complex than the peer-to-peer simple networks of the earlier films; instead, its virtual space is populated by many simultaneous users in multiple, dense networks. Once a user has been "woken up" to the fact that the Matrix is a VR, the user can strengthen his/her abilities with realistic weapons in realistic environments. Tellingly, when Neo first begins his training, Dozer (Anthony Ray Parker) tosses away the "boring programs" and starts him with "Combat Training," implying that learning how to fight is the most entertaining and of the most importance. When Neo "learns," he is seated is his VR bed (though with no goggles or gloves like earlier filmic iterations of the text because the technology directly plugs into the brain) and his body briefly twitches, before he emerges, near-orgasmic, from the simulator, gasping. The ability to become a super-fighter, which was feared in the previous films, is now celebrated. In fact, the savior-soldier Neo *must* use the technology in order to defeat his enemies, a far cry from the somewhat docile and idealistic communication system imagined by Angelo and Brace.

Aside from the training programs, the Matrix software itself is a virtual simulation. However, the "soldiers" of *The Matrix* are repurposed civilians, fully erasing the military-civilian tensions that undergird the trilogy. The film is rare in that it has simulated virtual combat where those civilian-soldiers fight using military weaponry (guns, helicopters, etc.). However, the focus on combat as the main mode of problem solving and the spectacular nature of the movie's combat scenes effectively promote the technology as the perfect way to create a transhuman super-soldier. Like a virtual exoskeleton, the technology grants the user's virtual self the same speed and power muscles; similar to Cage and Max, any civilian user can quickly and effectively become super-human just by using the technology. All this celebrates and mythologizes the combat simulator; the VR training is one more device in the human army's network of virtual weaponry, and the civilian-soldier in the simulated reality is the most formidable part of the human-technological assemblage. To this end, it is important that learning in the virtual world does nothing to "train" the physical body (as an actual military simulator must). Superficially, this version of the posthuman is positive and heroic in its symbiotic relationship with its virtual/machines selves and the machine and human species around that assemblage,[13] as a representation of a VR military training or "re-experiencing" (documentary) technology; however, while perhaps providing some visual vocabulary and expansion of genre elements around the war film, it is too unbalanced toward the virtual self to act effectively in that respect. More than that, the promotion of a civilian-military user in that virtual simulation problematically upholds the Total War Machine's rhetoric that the world (America) is in an inevitable and ongoing state of war and promotes the notion of technology as a tran-shuman application that generates awe-inspiring super-users that still uphold humanistic values of "love" and "justice" in the face of "effi-cient" and inhuman machines.

With this humanism at its core, unlike *Brainstorm* and *The Lawnmower Man*, *The Matrix* portrays a civilian population reappropriat-ing a militarized version of VR. Following this line of thinking, instead of looking at the military imposing on civilian VR technologies, this chapter will pivot to examine civilians choosing to participate in military simu-lations and VR-like environments, such as video games, in their private lives. While past and current video game consoles and personal comput-ers do not fit exactly into the previous definition of VR, the popularity of the previously mentioned commercial (civilian) VR kits make it likely that in the near future civilians will have access to them and, based on past history, will buy and play military-themed VR video games, mak-ing an examination of military-themed video games and their portrayal in film especially constructive.

## Playing War: The Avatar-Soldier in *Gamer*

While not yet the all-encompassing virtual realities that require cocoon-ing beds and wraparound headgear (yet), military-style video games were and continue to be massively popular.[14] As proof, the publisher of the *Call of Duty* games announced in 2014 that sales of the series had "topped $10 billion in worldwide sales since its creation more than a decade ago," adding that "in the first week following the release of *Call of Duty: Advanced Warfare*, gamers played more than 370 million online matches and leveled up more than 200 million times in the game's online multiplayer mode" (Poeter para. 1). Activision's focus in the press release on the online/Internet-enabled portion of the game is crucial: for most players of these games, the single-player mode is nowhere near the main draw; rather, it is the ability to play in real time against other players over the Internet and engage, with increasingly realistic weap-ons in increasingly realistic environments (i.e., a VR-like environment), in military combat. This ability to play against real players, not AIs, via the Internet, makes the combat more realistic and believable; this is then even further enhanced by the real-time socializing that takes place in these spaces, including voice chat, online ranking systems and leader boards. All these virtual components mix together to make the narratives and value systems created and/or reinforced by the games that much more rhetorically effective than a single-player, non-networked game.

In general, video games are effective (ideological and practical) pedagogical tools: Annadale argues in "Avatars of Destruction" that "thanks to their immersive qualities, games give the players a much greater sense of actually performing an action rather than reading about it or seeing it, and thus the ... tactics and consequences gather a concrete immediacy" (98). Mead adds that "videogames provide a powerful, motivating context for learning and practicing new skills. Because these games are interactive, players must take an active role in this learning, making them agents of knowledge" (67). Yet very often, the learning takes place within a military environment where "the viewer-cum-participant/agent is, virtually speaking, outfitted as a soldier—equipped with weapon and ammunition, complemented by navigation and other devices that monitor resource levels and scan for threats—and positioned to act against an imposed enemy" (LaRocca 32). Echoing this book's introduction's understanding of the "participation" that the war film demands/creates, when video games are based around military combat, tactics and themes, the (most often) civilian player, virtually "outfitted as soldier," becomes an agent of military "knowledge" with an active participatory role in the violent acts of the games. These games are very effective: David A. Clearwater's "Living in a Militarized Culture: War, Games and the Experience of the U.S. Empire" explores the phenomenon of the first-person shooter (FPS) in a post-9/11 world, arguing that the civilian uptick in immersion in "virtual battlefields and imagined theatres of war" (264) act like "recruiting programs" (277). He quotes Wardynski's argument that such video games are coming to replace experiences of the past in which "a young American could gain insights into military service by listening to recollections of advice of an older brother, an uncle, a father" (277) and, as such, "the younger generation's comfort with and acceptance of videogames has played a crucial role in the increasingly positive reception [of video games] by senior military leaders" (Mead 62). Extrapolating, military-themed video games are among the key narratives that shape and/or reinforce narratives about past and future wars. It follows then that much like the symbiotic relationship between Hollywood cinema and the American military discussed in the introduction to this text, the American military has followed this trend toward popular military-themed video games (if not instigated parts of it). In 2013, Ajey Lele pointed out that "one of the significant VR trends for the future appears to be the adaptation of videogames for military purposes" (25), adding that "because of this slowly the difference between games and military simulators is found declining. It is expected that in near future militaries would develop some of their VR-based tools by modifying the available games to match their requirements instead of reinventing the wheel" (25). Yet, well before 2013, non-VR video games already had a long history of being adapted from civilian to military-training technology. Mead flags Atari's *Battlezone* (1980) as one of the earliest examples (18), while also expanding on the extreme impact that the aforementioned *DOOM* had (21–23). More interestingly, Kara Platoni unpacks the influence of *DOOM*, in particular how the Marines modded *DOOM* in 1997 into a "realistic" combat video game, explaining that "[it] cost the Marines a mere $49.95 to buy and modify the *DOOM II* CD-ROM, making a few changes so that instead of chasing demons, players shoot Nazi-like soldiers using M-16s. Otherwise, Marine *DOOM* looks and sounds pretty much like the original game, and the Marines even released a free downloadable copy on the Internet" (para. 2). This modifying of games makes sense when Platoni rightly argues that "games designed by the defense contractors aren't all that popular. Reality is simply too mundane for gamers. While enthusiasts may appreciate a simulator that has the buttons and switches of a real tank, the players usually don't want it to move or reload as slowly as the real thing" (para. 28). So, unlike "Battle of 73 Eastings," the goal of military first-person shooters is not "documenting" or even simulating a "real" experience, but rather generating a version of military engagement that is more exciting and engaging, and then using that technology as part promotional tool, part training technology. This is especially true when considering that the military doesn't just take/modify civilian games, but also releases games so civilians have access to the same technology.

The blurry lines between civilian and military video games make them important documents to take apart further, and, while beyond the scope of this text,[15] it is useful to begin reflecting on military video games in films by noting that "Scott Rosenberger [a Virtual Training Facility instructor] estimates that 80% of the soldiers who go through his facility play videogames regularly" (Mead 111). Video games, not just simulated virtual environments, are a key part of the State War Machine, not only for combat but also for tactics and strategy: Mead illustrates this with the fact that "today's military are training on videogames. ... [At] the army's school for Command Preparation and Command and General Staff College at Fort Leavenworth, Kansas, lieutenant colonels and other leaders use *UrbanSim*, a game referred to by its creator as '*SimCity* Baghdad'" (Mead 69). This training has had ripples through the State War Machine and has forced the military to adapt traditional roles to these new mediums: looking ahead to Chapter 5's analysis of drone warfare in movies, "[For] years the military tried to keep unmanned aircraft within its traditional categories by allowing only pilots to operate them. But it has finally been acknowledged as an unassailable truth that the work is best suited to soldiers who've honed their reflexes and skills by logging thousands of hours on PlayStation and Xbox" (Teschner 77). The State War Machine's adoption of civilian video games as military trainers is interesting in and of itself, but what sets the military-created *America's Army* and modded *DOOM* apart from the "Battle of 73 Eastings," and VR as depicted in *Brainstorm* or *Strange Days*, is hit on by Platoni when she writes, "DOOM and its spinoffs can be played as coin-op arcade games, but they are usually played over the Internet by people who may be thousands of miles apart" (para. 2). Writing in 1997, Platoni's article comes at the point of the popular Internet's explosion[16]; at the same time as civilian Internet usage was exponentially rising, the military was also piggybacking their VR training on that civilian infrastructure and usage. This means, as mentioned previously, the military can use the civilian Internet to release games and connect civilian players together, but can also use it themselves to continue training and sharpening their own soldiers. Soldiers continue to use similar, if not the exact same, VR-like technology as civilians and, in this networked environment, the games function as a major component of a rising militarized culture. Ian Roderick argues this accession is turning civilian and military video-game players into a type of "mil-bot" and creating a potentially warped, unrealistic and unhealthy "dominant image of war" within a Total War Machine that is part of an ongoing contemporary process of "re-legitimizing warfare and affording further the militarization of civic life" (288).

Underlying all this, Clearwater very rightly points out that such video games "reinforce dominant imagery and discourses surrounding war, especially for youthful domestic audiences who have never personally experienced war and rarely see its direct effects" (280); these entertainment-rooted constructions of warfare merge "beautifully with the dominant image of war as seen in Hollywood film and or network television news" (280), rooted "aesthetically and discursively" in the "large screen of Hollywood" (263). The Total War Machine seamlessly mixes the State War Machine with the machinic phyla of video-game and film production: as an example, as Kushner writes, the Institute for Creative Technologies (ICT), "a U.S. government–funded research and development organization in Playa Vista California" (para. 6), builds video games and simulators that have "also been used in films such as *Avatar* and *Spider-Man 2*" under the leadership of "Paul Debevec, who did visual effects for *The Matrix* before becoming the ICT's associate director of graphics research" (para. 13). Visually and narratively, Clearwater argues that video games and cinema also have a shared language of imagery generated from influential "combat sequences from blockbuster films" to the point where large portions of military-themed video games mirror Hollywood war films' "narrative structure, characterization and ideology" (263). Clearwater continues by discussing the "sub-genre of the military-themed shooter" (262), stating that "more concretely, the military-themed shooter game came to resemble the increasing number of military representations in Hollywood's output" (263):

> Producers and fans [of the games] tended, especially early in its development, to base notions of realism and authenticity of formal and aesthetic principles largely derived from representations of warfare as seen on TV or in film (combat sequences from blockbuster films being especially influential). In terms of narrative structure, characterization and ideology, military-themed videogames borrowed heavily from their filmic counterparts. (263–264)

Clearwater goes further in linking the genre directly to Jeanine Basinger's previously discussed work on the WWII combat film, focusing on the genre's hyper-realistic weaponry (272) and calling the games, "in many ways, an extension of the combat film … the expanded and interactive version of a combat film's battlefield scene" (272), pointing specifically to *Saving Private Ryan* (Dir. Steven Spielberg 1998) as "particularly influential" (273). As such, it is important to look at military-themed video games as represented in cinema as, in the absence of cinematic military combat simulators, they are the closest approximation.

Again, while there are some examples of movies based on military video games,[17] examples of such video games in film are fairly uncommon, especially when considering, as discussed earlier, the relative ubiquity of the games themselves. There are some sparse examples: in *WarGames*, when the viewer is first introduced to the protagonist David Lightman (Matthew Broderick) he is playing an non-networked arcade cabinet version of *Galaga*, immediately establishing his relationship to computers and warfare (endlessly shooting aliens) as one rooted in virtual worlds and "playing." More, not only does he play *Galaga* again later in the film, but when he first accesses WOPR, he thinks that he is literally playing a computer game; for him, his playing of video games are meant to signal to the machinic audience that all computers and video games are toys and should not be thought of as a weapons.[18] Similarly, in films like *Shaun of the Dead* (Dir. Edgar Wright 2004) and *Superbad* (Dir. Judd Apatow 2007) the games are shown only briefly and are more demonstrations of a character's immaturity or divided attention. Additionally, there are scenes in *Terminator 2: Judgment Day* (Dir. James Cameron 1991) where John Connor (Edward Furlong) is shown very briefly playing non-networked arcade versions of *Missile Command* (Atari 1980) and *After Burner* (Sega 1987). *The Last Starfighter* (Dir. Nick Castle 1984) is a better example: the protagonist, Alex Rogan, expertly plays an arcade game called *Starfighter*. The game itself is a first-person 2D shooter, with a clunky reticle and space backdrop. After he breaks the record for most points in the game, he learns that the game is actually a training program to find the best spaceship pilot to fight in an interstellar war between the Rylan Star League and the Ko-Dan Empire. The video game proves very effective: as Rogan is taught the controls of his gunship, he remarks, "This is just like back home!" When in actual combat, the action is distanced by his own Heads Up Display (HUD), which acts like a computerized mediator between himself and the enemies; in this, the original video game feeds into Žižek's fears: as a simulator, it is so real, yet so abstracting of its enemy, that there is no line between virtual and real, that the violence he undertakes is quarantined to a remote conceptual space that effectively reduces the fighters' (and the film's audience's) exposure to the actual death and carnage that they are participating in. While play of the video game is limited to the beginning of the movie, the film does provide a template not that different from the later Marine *DOOM*: a civilian video game that is both a recruiting tool and training device.

Though the scene is short, *The Hurt Locker* gives one of the more effective arguments for the role of video games in the Total and State War Machines when Specialist Owen Eldridge (Brian Geraghty) is playing *Gears of War* (Epic Games 2006) after a stressful incident disarming a bomb. The camera shows his third-person avatar constantly shooting into a hoard of enemies, the screen going red when the avatar is hit; Eldridge plays with grim intensity until the psychiatrist (Christian Camargo) comes in telling him to "stop obsessing" over his visualizations of his own death, after which he asks him, "Right now, what are you thinking about?" Eldridge smoothly puts down the controller and picks up his rifle while the video game's sound effects remain present in the background. In this seamless juxtaposition, the source of his "obsession" is obvious: there is no difference between the controller and his gun, between virtual warfare and the "real" physical one; they are both functions of war's ubiquitous presence in his psyche.

The most extended example of the crossover between military-themed video games and films is *Gamer* (Dir. Neveldine and Taylor 2009). Within the world of the film, technology has been developed that allows other humans, via an Internet connection and a VR-like interface, to remotely control other humans. The most common civilian application of this is a video game called *Society* wherein other players choose another human, dress them, and then make them do all sorts of "deviant" activities ranging from drugs to sex. In this way, the technology resembles the Internet-enabled "real-life" avatars in *Surrogates*, in which users, while lying in a chamber/bed, remotely control androids that allow the users to enact fantasies of "immoral" escapism. Both films, released in the same year, present the critique that Internet-enabled technologies allow users to distance themselves too far beyond their "real" (physical) self and, therefore, the VR-technology mutates and erodes a user's sense of self and humanity; the clichés and fears of the predatory Internet user, as embodied by the overweight perverted basement dweller that appears in both films, are critiques of how avatars, as enabled by the Internet, not only fracture the self but also provide a virtual playground devoid of compassion and human emotional connection that quickly escalates into spaces of sex and violence.[19]

*Gamer* is worth analyzing in more depth here because its avatar-user dynamic is specifically constructed as a game, whereas *Surrogates* portrays the technology more as a hyper-inflated extension of a civilian avatar usage in social spaces like Facebook. More specifically, the most popular spectator "sport" in *Gamer* is a multiuser video game called *Slayers* that allows civilian users to control armed convicts; the controlled convicts are given military-grade weapons and put into arenas that resemble typical video-game maps (like bombed-out buildings and war-torn streets) and are told they must shoot and kill each other in order to survive to a "Save Point" with as many points (and kills) as possible. The game, and its extreme violence, is cheered by viewers from all over the world; the utopic global village that McLuhan hoped for is instead a blood-thirsty collection of voyeurs easily folded into the military entertainment complex.

The film opens post-credits with multiple explosions and the camera staring down the sight of John "Kable" Tillman's (Gerard Butler) rifle as he is controlled, much like the Jaegers are piloted in *Pacific Rim* (Chapter 3), by 17-year-old Simon (Logan Lerman). From this, the movie uses multiple fast cuts to create a sense of hyper-chaos as the viewer is thrust from shots of Tillman in combat to other players dying from headshots to close-ups on the firing muzzles of guns to further explosions and running, nameless characters. In this, the scene is no different than the typical urban combat scenes common in the war film genre and, while the avatars are convicts and not soldiers, they are in flak jackets and combat boots, and they fire military-grade machine guns while they communicate with military-style hand signals. The action, which is typical of the virtual combat scenes in the film, is meant to be exciting and the underscoring of the metal soundtrack is meant to give the players, particularly Tillman, a positive aura of fearless invincibility.

All through the combat scenes, as with *Ghost Machine*, the viewer is made aware of this as a mediated experience as the movie pixilates and distorts with a glitching noise. However, more interestingly, the action is then combined with HUD nanotechnological graphics that are common within military-style FPS games, such as the distance to the "Save Point" in bright electric lettering, a point total, and the weapon readouts; additionally, the movie watcher alternates between the first-person perspective common in a military-themed video game and the third-person perspective more common in cinema (Image 4.3). The movie then plays with the audience's understanding and comfort with both forms and merges them, following Clearwater's observations, so that the similarity between the two is brought to the forefront. On the surface, this looks similar to the doubling of Butler's frame that was established in Chapter 3 of this text, and recalls the discussion of the mediated

**Image 4.3**  What *Slayer*'s audience watches as Kable plays

first-person perspective shots "through the eyes" of the Iron Man suits and/or the drone footage to be discussed in Chapter 5. In this sense, these shots are meant to be reflections, much like the discussion of Chapter 3, of how the machinic phyla of cinema and video games meld effortlessly into the Total War Machine: the synthetic images created by video games are similar to those created by digital cinema, and the perceptual realism that the user/gamer becomes immersed into is a troublingly distanced and virtual recreation of "reality" that strips the people of their humanity and makes them a disposable part of the "game." The key difference between the movies' treatments is that *Gamer*'s usage of overlaid information, like "Kills" and "Distance to Save Point," are not meant for the soldier in combat (i.e., Tillman), as it is for the users of the Iron Man suits; instead, it is meant for some combination of the remote-control user (like drone footage), and, more uniquely, the global viewers watching the footage of *Slayers* that are cheering on the carnage. In this way, the information has no functional purpose for combat, but is instead purely for clarifying the "game" and further deepens the critique of the mediated digitally networked space that simulated and remote warfare generates. Similar to the aforementioned *Ghost Machine*, it is here that the audience is reminded of the intended "spectral" nature of the virtual world that *Slayers* takes place in while also being forced

**Image 4.4**   Simon hovers behind Kable and controls him during a round of *Slayers*

to confront the fact that the soldiers are not avatars in a virtual world, but are actual humans being treated as if they are avatars; *Brainstorm*'s dreams of VR as a breakthrough in human communication has instead been co-opted and mutated by the military entertainment industrial complex. The frontier of the virtual has been conquered and now there is no difference between the real and the avatar; the technology has made it as such that it is morally acceptable to treat the biological human in the same way one treats a virtual avatar.

This conflation is best manifested in a later combat scene where Simon is literally behind Tillman as he controls him, sardonically giving orders by controlling him via a full body interface (Image 4.4) that produces a mirrored movement from Tillman. This one-to-one controlling of another human in combat, via the Internet, is exactly the simulated environment that a military trainer aims for. Like the combat scenes in *The Matrix*, *Gamer* dwells in the fantasy of virtually experiencing "real combat." In *The Matrix*, the avatars are obviously super-human, contorting in slow motion to dodge bullets, running and flipping off walls, all in stylish clothing. In addition, enemies don't bleed; they simply crumple or disintegrate. The combat and the killing are cartoonish and deliberately unrealistic and the joy of *The Matrix* trilogy is in the fantasy of doing things, godlike, well beyond a human's bodily capabilities. In contrast, *Slayers* takes great care to show "realistic" combat, the violence of a headshot, the visceral chaos of grenades exploding and bullets being fired. In comparison to the early discussion of VR and simulators in *Brainstorm* and *The Lawnmower Man*, the simulator here is portrayed as negative because it is so incredibly active, requiring the remote user/controller to kill and delight in killing by proxy. The movie's main critique follows from this to argue that both virtual spaces, as enabled by the Internet and populated by avatars, and military-themed video games are negative because they dehumanize fellow users, flippantly dealing with death and celebrating military-style solutions to conflicts. Simon, after seeing Tillman's friend Freak (John Leguizamo) get killed, calmly explains away his death and calls the dead body "gibs. Like giblets. Kibbles and bits. Pieces everywhere." When asked how he deals with being at the center of the carnage he dodges any responsibility by stating, "I just play games." While this notion of "games" and simulations is unpacked further in Chapter 5, within *Gamer*, the implication then is that the game/simulation is too distanced from the consequences and subsequent real horrors of actual combat and is creating greatly desensitized users. While largely aimed at criticizing the role that corporations play in this desensitization, the military's central role is further underlined at the climax of the film, when it is revealed that *Slayers* began as a military technology designed to enhance and then control soldiers in combat and that Tillman was one of the soldiers in early experiments using the technology. The film's solution of Tillman killing Ken Castle (Michael C. Hall), the creator of *Society* and *Slayers*, and therefore "freeing" the users, is meant to criticize the casual adoption and normalization of such militarized spaces into civilian life.

However, the sensational filmmaking involved in the actual combat scenes (including the mediated first-person perspective, slow motion, fast-paced editing, and bombastic soundtrack) undercuts most of the criticism the movie puts forward: Kable is a "perfect soldier. A tactical killing computer," as Castle describes him, and the movie showcases his military abilities in heroic combat scenes that glorify stylized military violence. In this way, it fits in with what Clearwater sees as representative of war films post-9/11, which he argues "tend to gloss over political and ideological questions and reduce war to an individual's heroic exploits on a seemingly realistic-looking but immersive and entirely aestheticized battlefield" (272), producing a "highly controlled and carefully scripted form of spectacle" (279). The movie watcher is not encouraged to leave the movie thinking that such a video game would be terrible; the aesthetics of the whole movie encourages a movie watcher to want to partake in such a space, with the same visceral violence.

As for the soldier-figure of Tillman, as is common in the war film genre, his emotional journey is toward the return of his family. To this end, Tillman's quest to regain his wife and daughter, symbolic of the sort of intimate human connections that the film upholds, is the driving tension of the film. Tillman's repeated assertion that he be called "Tillman," and not his avatar moniker "Kable," serves to reaffirm the human element of his sense of self and push him away from his "puppet" (virtual) identity. When he tells one of the guards that "when the trigger pulls, it's just me," there is a reclaiming of responsibility, unlike Simon, and an acceptance of his consequences that is in contrast to the ethical system created by the remote puppetry of other humans and establishes him as the hero of the film. The vilification of the virtual simulating technologies of the movie reinforce the notion that the extension of the liberal human body and mind, in particular that of the soldier in combat, into participation with other machine species degrades the notions of justice and compassion that are key to upholding the human as the core component of the transhuman. Much like the hard technological bodies of Chapter 2, Tillman's resistance to this virtualizing again upholds that the human, the man-in-the-middle, must be made the primary responsible part of any technological-biological assemblage.

## Conclusion: War Films as Combat Simulation

There is more likely a fairly straightforward initial answer as to why there is very little VR presence in war films that speaks to a general problem with integrating computer use and VR into movies: it's boring to watch someone use the technology! While this thought will be complicated when analyzing the Internet's role in the surveillance present within the films discussed in Chapter 6, concluding this chapter, cinematic treatments of video games and VR (and computers in general) within war films are generally used as plot devices or as spaces to include interesting visualizations once inside the simulation, and perhaps explore the notion of virtual and physical bodies; actually watching someone type at a computer or sit while playing a video game is not particularly compelling. This is why a number of 1990s movies that include Internet usage (such as *Hackers, Disclosure* and *The Net*)[20] rely on unrealistic interfaces and special effects like tie-dye colors, monstrous avatars and zooming cameras as ways to liven up representations of the Internet and computer use. Having said that, showing VR in film in an interesting and familiar way is possible and the technology will likely become more common in film as commercial versions of VR are released, just as portrayals of Internet usage in movies became far more commonplace from the early 2000s onward. The continued normalizing of VR technology will make it easier to generate visual shortcuts around its usage and provide entertaining cinematic visualizations. While films to this point have missed out on providing potential critiques and examinations of military-style simulators and VR environments, a near future where that is undertaken is not out of the question.

Even given that optimism, the question remains: despite its very real use in the American military, why would a war film show a soldier fighting in a virtual environment when the movie could just have the soldier actually fighting in combat? Such engagement raises the stakes (the possibility of a non-virtual death) and does away with any audience squeamishness around "real" physical and "fake" virtual selves that might undermine the ideology of the soldier's cause; without VR, the soldier remains completely "human" (biological), which allows the movie to take advantage of the emotional responses that come with a soldier in peril. The few examples that do showcase a VR or military-style video game place the biological human soldier at the center of the soldier-assemblage, generating the sorts of problematic transhuman subjects that still uphold human-centric relationships with their machines species around them.

But *Gamer*, by integrating in the visual synthetic markers of a video game into its filmic aesthetic and deliberately highlighting portions of the double frame from Chapter 3, draws attention to the simulated nature of war films themselves and how movies, as cultural interfaces, are modes in which the civilian participates in war zones without peril or immediate consequence. The documentary game "Battle of 73 Eastings" is then a cousin to the war film, perhaps more closely related to the genre than video games, as it functions more as a passive cinematic experience: the "traditional" movie theater experience is intended to look a lot like that simulation and the VR in *Brainstorm* and *Strange Days*, where the audience member sits and engages with the movie in a relatively passive manner. While this is obviously a stereotype, and I have written elsewhere about the faulty thinking behind the construction of such a docile viewer,[21] war movies do generate a simulating effect, duplicating and distributing virtual versions of combat, providing the same ability to participate in warfare without actually having to participate; all this is done in a relatively realistic mode that, as Clearwater argues, uses much of the same imagery and filmic techniques as a simulation and/or video game might.

Echoing Chapter 3's discussion of digital effects and perceptual realism, Stuart Marshall Bender argues that films need not even be completely "realistic" or "authentic" to be effective simulations, but rather fall in line with the concept of "reported realism" that depend on "specific cues that *prompt* claims of realism" within a film (author's italics 2); he adds that "the details presented need not necessarily correspond to actuality. Rather, the details simply need to appeal to the audience's expectations of reality" (9). His argument is that combat films cannot be real and their rhetorical effectiveness depends instead on markers of "authenticity," such as shaky cams in first-person POV, that are heightened by "subtle movements such as background actors conducting more detailed business such as reloading weapons, communicating via field radios, and looking around for the enemy with much more focus and attention [than earlier films in the war film genre]" (11). Reported realism then makes it so that viewers of modern war films are able "to run an off-line mental simulation of the diegesis with a high degree of vividness" (8).[22]

So then, an effective "realistic" simulation does not necessarily depend on matching a "real-life" military engagement or battle, but it needs to bear the aesthetic markers that a viewer has coded as "realistic"; the best simulating automatisms, the most effective war movies or video games or VR experiences, are going to be the ones that accept and manipulate the synthetic nature of their mediated relationship with their audience. Within the contemporary war film, this means recognizing that "the military ... is busy filming itself at every turn, from high-altitude surveillance transmits to video diaries and cell-phone souvenirs" (Stewart 170). This cinematically manifests in the aforementioned *Stop-Loss*, where Eyeball's "homemade" videos use a mix of casually shot footage, war imagery and the same soundtrack that can be found in many contemporary war films; there is an effort to mirror the genre, to replicate it and its aesthetic markers. Gooch argues effectively that "the soldiers themselves are implicated in this [digital] construction, but they cannot resist the larger power of the state and, by extension, those who profit from war: these reflexive mediations enact a seemingly inescapable cycle of surveillance, war, and death" (163). Stewart adds that because they are unable to escape, "this is just the sort of personal videolog that the returned vets gather drunk to rescreen on a laptop after they've aimlessly resumed their civilian lives. They can't get the war movie out of their heads" (Stewart 180). Like the scene in *The Hurt Locker* where the videogame controller is swapped seamlessly for the real gun, the "amateur" home videos come to underline how ingrained those documents are into the soldier's experience with war and how ubiquitous warfare is for them. Similar to the "test footage" found in the *Iron Man* films (Chapter 3), the fact then that the footage is so effortlessly integrated into the film shows how few barriers there are between the two: the "real" homemade version of war borrows heavily from, and then is folded into, the larger movie; the audience then also codes this action as reported realism, the "realistic" making of these movies and their integration into warfare and the soldiers' lives, as authentic.

However, let's also remember that "real" soldiers watch war films and that as a genre, like most genres, it perpetuates itself by making movies with the same conventions. LaRocca makes the point that "film is an especially receptive medium for reference by subsequent filmmakers, in part, because its grammar is available to both creators and viewers; they co-create the objects of interest through an evolving critique of the values and virtues faced on-screen" (22). This notion of "co-creation" between "creators and viewers" within the immersive spectacular simulation of the war film is the key, and from this, perhaps the best version of a cinematic VR simulation, the one with the most powerful rhetorical "grammar," is soldiers watching other war movies within the world of the film. In *Jarhead*, based on a memoir by Anthony Swofford, soldiers are often shown watching other war movies under the same rhetorical umbrella of team building and experiential exposure that simulators are often tasked with: they watch *Apocalypse Now* (Dir. Francis Ford Coppola 1979) in a boisterous group, cheering wildly when the helicopters come over the Vietnamese trees; later, they are also shown watching *The Deer Hunter* (Dir. Michael Cimino 1979) together. The watching of these movies is described in Swofford's memoir and is therefore purported to "have happened"; more specifically, he points to his fellow soldiers watching "*Platoon, Apocalypse Now, The Boys in Company C, Full Metal Jacket, Sands of Iwo Jima*" (64). Movies, in functioning as creators and reinforcers of ideological values, when shown in other movies, hold the same function a combat simulator or a video game within a movie might: they show the soldiers engaging in warlike activity without having to actually fight. Within *Jarhead*, other war films *are* the simulating technology and therefore there is no need to have a VR simulator present.

In this way, war films are military simulators, and incredibly effective ones. No matter the simulating technology, if the viewers of the films, or participants of VR, engage with the products of the Military Industrial Entertainment complex without an active critical posthuman reflexivity, war films will continue their normalizing of the integration of military solutions and violence into everyday life. Dealing specifically with VR and military technology in the war film, even in critique, the tendency to aestheticize the violence within overshadows most of the attempts to resist promoting the rhetoric of the Total War Machine, and the technology it entails, as anything less than a beautiful and "cool" part of culture. If *Gamer* argues that the real terror of the future is treating the "the biological human in the same way one treats an inhuman virtual avatar," then the way to break free from that terror is to recognize all species, including machines, as worthy of sovereignty and recognition. Hope for more critically affective films lies in the understanding that the technology and narratives presented within movies and virtual spaces, like video games, are not tools to be mastered, are not distancing and abstracting screens: they can and should be positive cooperators in a healthy and peaceful ecosystem of biological and technological species.

## NOTES

1. "With a more dynamically designed and coded cyberspace, the number of websites grew from 130 in June 1993 to 23,500 in June 1995, to over 650 thousand by January of 1997. The amount of web traffic grew 11% each month" (Tucker, *Interfacing with the Internet in Popular Cinema* 10).
2. Joshua Gooch, in "Beyond Panopticism," provides a slightly different argument, writing that "*Stop-Loss* imagines the working through of trauma as a process of self-surveillance through video. The film sets up visual production as central to processing trauma: after its opening battle sequence, the film cuts to a soldier's self-produced memorial video for his wounded comrades" (158).
3. Rosewarne also usefully ties the cinematic hacker and notion of the frontier to a distinct and often oppressive masculinity in her discussion,

echoing earlier arguments about Jeffords' overly muscled and masculine hard bodies (132–134). This is discussed further in Chapter 6 of this text.

4. Mead outlines further examples through *War Play*, including *Spacewar!* (14), *SIMNET* (19), *Virtual Battlespace 2* (105–106) and *Foldit* (162).

5. Chapter 5 of this text gives more exploration of cinematic representations of data-driven simulators.

6. In 2016, no fewer than three companies released major commercial VR projects: the Oculus Rift, the Vive, and PlayStation VR. There is also further work being done with Augmented Reality like, Microsoft's HoloLens and Google Cardboard.

7. All the films briefly touched on here are expanded upon with more depth in *Interfacing with the Internet in Popular Cinema*.

8. In the chapter "Reel/Real Internet" from *Interfacing with the Internet in Popular Cinema*, I use Christian Metz's concept of trucage ("'Trucage' and the Film." *Critical Inquiry* (1977), 3 (4), 657–675) to discuss the cinematic effects that tended to mark "entry" into the Internet and what sort of "filmic space" is generated from this entry (197).

9. In truth, some of the demos of the technology in *Brainstorm* look a lot like early VR demos for the contemporary Oculus Rift, in particular one section of the film that takes participants on a rollercoaster ride in much the same way that the Oculus Rift did.

10. I further this argument in my own *Interfacing with the Internet in Popular Cinema*, specifically in the chapter "The Cables Under, In, and Around Our Homes" (38–39).

11. Further thoughts on downloading-as-learning, with a specific focus on *The Matrix* and *The Computer Wore Tennis Shoes* (Dir. Robert Butler, Walt Disney Productions 1969), can be found in the chapter "Don't Shoot the (Instant) Messenger: The Efficient Virtual Body Learns" within *Interfacing with the Internet in Popular Cinema*.

12. Like *Brainstorm* and *The Lawnmower Man*, the film is not a stereotypical war film, but the battles between two armed forces and the specific military-style weaponry make it much like *Starship Troopers* (Dir. Paul Verhoeven, Columbia-TriStar Pictures 1997), as it is, to paraphrase Jeanine Basinger, a World War II movie without World War II (xii).

13. While I've argued in my other work that this version of the posthuman is positive and heroic in its fully intergraded relationship with its virtual/ machine selves and the machine and human species around that assemblage, I want to amend my thinking here. On the surface, this version of the posthuman and its use of VR is more healthy: the machine and human components are far more internal and messy than the external and passive devices of *Brainstorm* and *The Lawnmower Man*; for Neo, he literally has the technology implanted inside him. The ability to produce

a high-definition version of the user's avatar in this space more closely tethers the virtual and physical identities, which is further demonstrated by the fact that if the virtual body dies, the physical one dies as well. Yet as Herbrechter points out "what is necessary for Neo's posthumanization is again a very human ingredient: Trinity's unconditional love" (134). It is therefore problematically human-centric that when he dies at the end of the film, it is in the simulation while digitally embodied; it is Trinity's kiss of his physical body, with again the humanistic value of emotion at its core, that saves him.

14. Influential military-style examples would include *Wolfenstein* (id Software 1992) and *DOOM* (id Software 1993), the later *Quake* (id Software 1996) and *CounterStrike* (Valve Corporation 1999) and, more recently, the *Battlefield* series (Electronic Arts 2002–present) and the *Call of Duty* series (Activision 2003–present). A better, more contemporary, example would be the military-made free-to-play first-person shooter *America's Army* (United States Army 2002-present).

15. A strong popular exploration of this blurring can be found within Michael Macedonia's "Games Soldiers Play" (*ieee Spectrum*, March 1, 2002. Accessed March 23, 2017. http://spectrum.ieee.org/consumer-electronics/gaming/games-soldiers-play).

16. See note 1 from this chapter.

17. The movie version of *DOOM* (Dir. Andrzej Bartkowiak, Universal Pictures 2005) is perhaps of passing interest in that it is an adaption of the most influential military-styled videogame (which popularized many of the tropes of an FPS), but the movie itself, while a combat film that focuses on a Marine squad's defeat of an alien race on Mars, has neither actual video games nor combat simulators.

18. There is much more discussion of Lightman and *WarGames* in Chapter 5's analysis of war simulations as well as Chapter 6's critique of Lightman as a deeply influential cinematic (immature) hacker.

19. I expand further on *Surrogates* in "Avatar in the Uncanny Valley: The Na'vi and Us, the Machinic Audience" (*Interfacing with the Internet in Popular Cinema* 78–85).

20. *Hackers* and *The Net* are the focus of "The Cables Under, In, and Around Our Homes" while *Disclosure* is analyzed further in "Reel/Real Internet" (both found in *Interfacing with the Internet in Popular Cinema*).

21. In particular, I align my thinking on this with Vivian Sobchak's concept of the cinesthete (*Carnal Thoughts: Embodiment and Moving Image Culture.* Berkeley: University of California Press, 2004) and Allison Muri's arguments in "Of Shit and Soul: Tropes of Cybernetic Disembodiment in Contemporary Culture." (*Body and Society* 9 (3) (2003): 73–92). I write more completely on this in *Interfacing with the Internet in Popular Cinema* (157–158).

22. Though somewhat tangential, it is worth considering the role of convergence culture in these movies. Henry Jenkins defines as convergence culture as "a cultural shift as consumers are encouraged to seek out new information and make connections among dispersed media content" (*Convergence Culture*, New York: New York University Press, 2008, 3), explaining that the multiple modes of producing and consuming information, art, education etc swirl and mix together in a messy overlapping ecosystem that "changes the ways religion, education, law, politics, and even the military operate" (4). We should add to this list "entertainment": looking specifically at cinema, under this idea of convergence culture, movies will integrate videogames, books, TV, webpages, all sorts of different forms of media, into their world and have their characters interact in this whirlpool of media.

# CHAPTER 5

# Ender's Wargames: Drones, Data and the Simulation of War as Weapon and Tactic

## Introduction: Simulation and Modern War

As both Jean Baudrillard in *The Gulf War Did Not Take Place* and Paul Virilio in *Strategy of Deception* argue, the invention, use and proliferation of atom and hydrogen bombs in the second half of the twentieth century created a culture of deterrence among the global superpowers' governments wherein no side wanted to actually use weapons of Mutually Assured Destruction (MAD). Still, the very real existence of such weapons and their potential use required strategies and tactical spaces to explore those potentialities without actually undertaking a nuclear war.[1] This led to a rise of a military game theory, as well as an increased use of computer-aided simulations of battles that acted as distanced and abstracted modes of engaging with the apocalyptical scenarios of nuclear war and going into combat without having to actually go into combat. Der Derian names it the "Advanced Warfighting Experiment" and argues that the shift away from "the radio, the tank, and especially the airplane," as the main weapons of warfare, toward wargames and data-driven simulations is remarkable because "unlike prior radical developments in means of transportation, communication and information, virtual innovation is driven more by software than hardware, and enabled by networks rather than agents, which means adaptation (and mutation) is not only easier, but much more rapid" (772). As van Creveld explains in his introduction to *Wargames: From Gladiators to Gigabytes*, the "rapid" adaptation of wargames is, especially in an age of nuclear deterrence,

A. Tucker, *Virtual Weaponry*,
DOI 10.1007/978-3-319-60198-4_5

145

"not merely the best form of training but the only available one" (5); Manuel De Landa explains that "wargames have allowed human participants to gain strategic insights and have given officers the opportunity to acquire 'battle experience' in the absence of a real war" (*War in the Age of Intelligent Machines* 2). While Chapter 4 of this book takes up films that portray Virtual Reality's place in the Total War Machine, this chapter is focused on movies that question what happens when the "man-in-the-middle" is made into a network whose decisions and actions are driven by the interpenetration of external data, predicative game theory, statistics and software, rather than the "humanistic" qualities of emotions, ethical rationality and immediate bodily experiences and sensations.

Luca Lambertini usefully clarifies that the school of mathematics labeled game theory might better be called "the theory of strategic interaction" (1), in which a game "is a mathematical instrument that serves the purpose of formalizing strategic interactions among agents" (11); game theory aims to predict how certain scenarios (economic, political, military, etc.) would play out given a range of rules or constraints for each party. Lambertini further argues that it has its deepest roots in the military think-tank RAND Corporation's reaction to the Cold War. As a military tool,[2] it is used to simulate specific actions within combat in such a way that commanders can find out what the likely outcome of a certain decision might be (always given the caveat that each agent acts rationally in their own best interest). While completely theoretical, it is used a tool to attempt to pinpoint what is most likely to happen within a combat situation.

Recalling Eisenhower's speech referenced in the introduction to this text, the use of game theory dovetails with the post-WWII proliferation of digital computers and their massive increase in speed that made running such simulations easier and easier. Van Creveld's *Technology and War* argues that the military gravitated to computers because "their binary on-off logic seems to appeal to the military mind [as the military mind] is forever seeking ways to make communication [within war] as terse and unambiguous as possible" (239). Writing in 1991, De Landa identifies computers' role within wargames (he flags the beginning as the 1950s [84]) as that of "intelligent assistants: human players made decisions affecting the movement and actions of 'troops' in the game, while computers calculated the effect of a given attack" (2) until eventually "war-game designers [created] new versions of this technology in which automata completely replace[d] human players" (2). De Landa's text stops just before the popular Internet of 1993, but Coker adds in 2013 that "the US military spends $6bn a year on virtual and simulated training programmes" (128); while some of that would be spent on the video game–like "training" simulators discussed in Chapter 4, as well as hardware and software for wargames, what is clear is that digitally networked computers play a massive role in the not just the simulation of war, but also in the actual waging of wars.

In Platoni's "Pentagon Goes to the Arcade," first referenced in Chapter 4 of this book, she states that the move from simulating warfare to carrying out the results of the simulation in warfare settings was "wrapped up in … the idea that war in the future will be different from the wars of the past, involving fewer people and more machines, and keeping American troops safe by allowing them to do their fighting from behind a computer monitor" (para. 21). The problem with heavily relying on game theory and computer simulations in combination with wargames is that the networked virtual wars create distanced warfare, and humans on both sides of a conflict are pushed further away from each other and reconstructed as eventual results of math-guided, machine-aided violence. Mead paraphrases Paul Edwards when he calls this reliance "techno-rationality" and argues that it speaks to a mode in which "new technologies [are] seen as capable of overcoming the most difficult political and military circumstances" (163); he then adds that such an approach to warfare is problematic, because, quoting an unnamed general, "[within simulations] things are going to go wrong in the real world that you just can't predict. They're based on how humans behave, not on how a machine behaves" (163). For De Landa, this focus on planning and executing war based on "how a machine behaves" generates models that struggle with relatively narrow simplicity in addressing very specific combat situations under very specific rules and cannot be "simply added up one on top of the other" (104). The problems of computer-simulated wargames can largely be blamed on how both modeling systems of war lack the ability to effectively simulate very human problems such as fatigue, morale (100) and friction based on specific personality, cultures, cultural histories, etc. (103). More, by moving humans "out of the loop," military planners are putting their trust in a computerized entity that De Landa argues is "much more 'reliable' than people in being willing to unleash a third world war" (87). To this end, even though many game theory models of conflicts agree that "cooperative strategies are the most rational (the 'fittest') in the long run" (86), De Landa critiques computer-aided wargames as "artificially blocking the paths to cooperation" because both game theory and computer simulations, "imaginary scenarios," generate "pro-conflict biases and disguised [those biases] behind a facade of mathematical neutrality" (84) by "[encouraging] a picture of the adversary that emphasized conflict at the expense of cooperation" (97).

This chapter locates some of the initial fears of computer-guided simulations of war in *WarGames*, wherein the military's computer WOPR (War Operation Plan Response) is accidentally hacked by a teenaged David Lightman (Matthew Broderick); Lightman and WOPR then play what Lightman thinks is a simulation of "Global Thermonuclear War," which, after feeding the Americans at WOPR's control "faked" data about Russian missile launches, leads to WOPR actually arming Russia-targeted missiles and initiating a launch sequence. This chapter will expand in more depth on *WarGames*, as well as the artificial intelligence EDI in *Stealth*, but for now, both movies stand as popular examples of the mistrust given to the notion of simulating warfare and its potential "real-world" damages that emerges in instances that require putting computers at such a central role in military decision making. Obviously hardware and software have only advanced further since *WarGames'* 1983 release and the ability to simulate warfare has only increased in fidelity. However, *WarGames* is useful to examine because WOPR is an early example of van Creveld's warning that as simulations get more realistic they get more dangerous: "A game capable of simulating every aspect of war would become war" (*Wargames* 5). Der Derian points to the United States as leading the way in this virtual revolution: "[America's] diplomatic and military policies are increasingly based on technological and representational forms of discipline, deterrence, and compellence that could best be described as *virtuous war*" (author's italics 772). This "virtuous warfare" is driven by "the technical capability and ethical imperative to threaten and, if necessary, actualize violence from a distance—with no or minimal casualties" (772). Problematically then, the reliance on simulated and abstract warfare is the "direct introduction of unreality by military bureaucrats" that generates a version of war that does little to recognize the human combatants and violence on either side and instead creates a near-impenetrable cloud wherein an outside observer (civilian, military) can't begin to differentiate between "real" and "unreal" (De Landa 101). Within the book *Virtuous War*,

Der Derian argues that "at the strategic level, simulations and substitutions proliferate with plug-and-play worst-case scenarios; on the battlefield, the enemy soldier becomes an electronically signified 'target of opportunity' … that much easier to disappear" (121).

Within this virtuous warfare of disappearing enemies, De Landa adds that "there is a blurring of the differences between simulation and reality. All the stimuli from the radar and computer screens remain identical" (101). This "post-corporeal" warfare digitizes the enemy into a "target of opportunity," and Coker further warns that "if war is becoming increasingly digitized, if the enemy on a screen is reconstituted as pure 'data,' then the embodied state of war that we have taken for granted … may rapidly diminish in our imagination" (123) until "war itself was nothing but an exercise in management … a game of skill" (van Creveld *Technology and War* 245) and, finally, "cast in terms of input-output and cost effectiveness" (246). Within this virtuous warfare, an enemy is rendered so unfamiliar that, Baudrillard warns, a military "cannot imagine the Other, nor therefore personally make war upon it" (37), thereby justifying the use of distanced and abstract tactics and weaponry. If the enemy is then reconstituted and distanced as data, then the role and concerns of the civilian and the soldier within the Total and State War Machines necessarily change as well. This datafying via the use of computers, wargames and drone strikes often co-opts the civilian into the State War Machine: in such a war game, humans were increasingly "taken out of the loop" (De Landa 99) and "games and simulations mutated from an experimental role designed to elicit insights in the participants to an institutionalized productive role, transforming civilians into military planners" (102). This aligns with Coker's worries that the nature of a soldier has changed deeply, from a warrior that respects the enemy and the conflict with which he/she is engaged, into a "cubicle warrior," a process by which "the warrior has been transformed into a technician and war into a routine … a series of more or less routine tasks" (118). Speaking about contemporary bomber pilots and drone operators, he describes this new soldier as "almost immune from danger … they [clock] up the hours in the sky like business executives" (120). By training in simulators and being given orders by authorities that rely on Internet-enabled simulations as tactics, the killing of enemies, of actual human combatants (and civilians), becomes a routine and mundane civilian job, fully integrated into civilian life and landscapes.

This chapter will expand on these thoughts with a discussion of *Good Kill* and *Eye in the Sky*, movies that focus on the "routines" of the technician soldier, the drone pilot. Unlike the movies discussed in the first three chapters of this text, these movies portray a version of the war film in which the State War Machine does not rely on visceral and immediately violent soldier-to-soldier combat, what Basinger would identify as part of the "infantry" subgenre of the combat film (20), but generates movies that are a blend between a Navy film and an Air Force film; these movies combine the Air Force films' focus on *"professionalism …* the problems men have in the chain of command" with the Navy films' focus on "the domestic lives of military men" (author's italics 20). The three films make clear that drone usage is a part of what Mead labels as "asymmetrical warfare," which he clarifies as "battles between oppositions of vastly different strengths and capabilities" (51); decisions within such distanced asymmetrical warfare is controlled by the navigation of gathered intelligence on enemies and a series of game-theory calculations and disembodied data-driven predictions and simulations. Visually, *Eye in the Sky* and *Good Kill* resemble the submarine war film rather than the infantry film, in that the technician soldiers are held in small "safe" arenas outside of "combat spaces" (20), watching screens (portals) and the effects of their weaponry from an enclosed distance, as opposed to engaging in more "traditional" and bodily combat. In opposition to the present human body seen in the first two chapters of this book, in particular in the taking up of the hard technological body of *Elysium* and *Edge of Tomorrow*, within the cinematic portrayals of drone warfare, the technician soldier emphasizes "situation awareness" via Internet-enabled technologies that focuses on "system and information management" (Mead 52), using information "to forecast plans and events" and then execute those attacks remotely (51).

In this, the war films here look more like the political thrillers discussed in Chapter 6 in that they are movies without a lot of combat that instead substitute the glamour and action of the fighting body for the amazement and wonder that comes from technological mastery; this mastery is what Der Derian labels as "at the heart of virtuous war," and is an appreciation for "using networked information and virtual technologies to bring 'there' here in near-real time and with near-verisimilitude … [and the] strategic advantage for the digitally advanced" (772). In this movement away from what Basinger calls the "purity" of the infantry and traditional combat film, the movies portray the technician soldier as an operator of Virilio's electro-optical military devices through which they become a watcher of war; this figure is then polluted by the distancing telepresence that enables the asymmetrical warfare that then dilutes the soldier's humanistic morals. While the individual pilots are portrayed as feeling anxious and remorseful about their actions, they do ultimately carry out their orders without fail, and their superiors issue those same orders knowing the safety that drone strikes provide. In contrast to the combat film, the movies of this chapter return again and again to the idea that the human body that is actively participating in combat spaces, that is exposed to immediate bodily harm and the stakes that surround such peril, is the ultimate justifying and heroic force for warfare and that the extension of the human body by increasingly mediated and technologized weaponry moves the man-in-the-middle too far from the humanistic and biological values that provide the human race with supremacy. From a critical posthuman perspective, while the films do portray and problematize the dehumanizing and Othering of the enemies of virtuous war that is caused by the datafication and mediation of technological elements, none of the films reject this warfare; instead, at best, the movies acknowledge its problems but ultimately accept it as the inevitable and unavoidable result of a too-technologized body that is powerless because it is extended too far from its human/biological core.

This message is potentially especially rhetorically effective to the civilian machinic audience because the "combat spaces" of drone pilots and war-game players do not look that different than the domestic spaces of those same soldiers, echoing De Landa's concern that such warfare transforms "civilians into military planners." Both *Eye in the Sky* and *Good Kill* spend time conflating these two spaces until there is no distinction between them. For the machinic audience, the danger would be to accept that same merging, to see the weaponization of their own technologies as inevitable and unavoidable, and to invite and nurture them within their own civilian spaces. While this thought will be discussed further in Chapter 6 when unpacking the paranoiac space created by cyberwarfare, this chapter argues that as the protagonists of both movies "punch in" like the aforementioned cubicle warrior, treating their acts of warfare much like a "regular" civilian job. The danger is that the machinic audience is also encouraged to think of their own now-weaponized technologies as already so completely integrated into their own work and personal lives that to resist them would be impossible.

The acceptance of virtual technologies' unavoidable weaponization results in an offloading of the morality of the actions of this warfare to the larger command infrastructure of the military, but ultimately to the technologies of the movies, a rhetoric that is opposed to the human man-in-the-middle who bears the brunt in the movies of the first three chapters of this text. The movie version of *Ender's Game* is the culmination of all these critiques. While the original Orson Scott Card science fiction book *Ender's Game* was released in 1985, the 2013 movie adaptation by the same title gives a portrait of both the "cubicle warrior," in the figure of Colonel Hyram Graff (Harrison Ford), and in Coker's technologically distanced technician soldier, Ender Wiggins (Asa Butterfield). In the film, the human race has recently fought off an invading alien species, the Formics, but are now training more and more soldiers, in both physical zero-gravity wargames and later in full model simulators, because they believe that a Formic reinvasion is imminent. Yet the adults of the film repeatedly dehumanize Ender, the Formics (who only counterattack and are never the aggressors), and the conflict he was chosen to enter into, in turn roboticizing Ender by turning him into a computer-like entity himself. Ender, at the end of the film, thinks he is carrying out increasingly elaborate simulated battles when it is revealed that those battles were in fact real and that he led a genocide of the Formics. While not entirely bathed in mundane activities, Ender's repeated runs through the simulator do become the main part of his daily routine and he and Graff are completely removed from any danger or combat. However, within this type of war, Ender is transformed by the military around him into an automaton, an entity valued for his machinelike emotionlessness and ability to predict and execute military tactics, a machinic phylum that is an embodied combination of game theory placed inside a giant war simulator.

Ender's transformation into a machinelike technician soldier is what Virilio critiques as "scorning 'nature' in the name of 'computer reason' … [that] is transplanting [nations'] *systemic rationality* into programmed automata, into 'smart' missiles, as though the world were a toy or a war game" (author's italics 11). Coker extends this thought by wondering:

What if it were possible to design robots capable of exercising on our behalf ethical decisions we are too weak or capricious or muddle-headed to make ourselves? … What if we could wage war more "humanely" by tasking other "higher beings" with resolving our ethical dilemmas, transferring to them the responsibility to treat others as we wish to be treated ourselves? (145)

The answer to his questions of "responsibility" lie in the figure of Ender and the film's ultimately negative portrayal of what the State War Machine surrounding him transforms him into: he is stripped of both his compassion *and* his anger and, after flattening out his humanity into a purely tactical weapon via his complete integration with networked technology, he is tasked with destroying the Formics simply because the other humans in Earth's government and military are unable to muster the ethical or strategic intelligence needed. While Ender appears to be the largest component of a human-machine war assemblage, the movie underlines, before messily critiquing, the human role in simulation-driven warfare as being merely one part of the larger State War Machine; Ender is a human "smart missile," and one that strikes at data points on a screen rather than living entities. He then undertakes the inhumane tasks other authorities are afraid to bear the responsibility for or cannot achieve themselves; in this offloading of responsibility, the simulation itself becomes the war, which then reveals the traumas caused, on posthuman civilians, enemies, and soldiers alike, by a distanced military engaged in virtuous war waging and overdependent on abstracted theorems and weaponized digital technologies.

In all the films discussed briefly in this chapter's introduction, the placement of "computer reason" and/or "techno-rationality" at the center of State and Total War Machines is critiqued as immoral and unhumanistic. This implies that war can only be justified when it is "human" and there are the dangers of a human body, in rational control, in corporeal combat. However, whether war is carried out by an artificial intelligence or created by the distancing effects of a drone strike or immersive data-driven simulation, the involvement of technological elements into the human body degrades and/or blocks the moral capacities of that human mind. Within this then, technological elements, in particular virtual networks, are not treated as a cooperative co-species, or even as the sort of steroid that the hard technological body portrays; instead the films isolate the negative ethical effects and problems of virtuous war into those technological elements, criticizing the soldiers when they become machinelike in their relentlessly binary rationality or command-following. This serves to ultimately preserve the notion that liberal human rationality, which includes emotional interpretation and expression in opposition to cold data-driven inputs/outputs, is still the most important element of any human-technological assemblage, the only parts, if left unpolluted, that are capable of acting responsibly and ethically.

## THE MACHINE-IN-THE-MIDDLE IN *WARGAMES* AND *STEALTH*

Network-Centric Warfare (NCW), defined in the introduction to this text, is rooted in "chaos and complexity theory" and grounded heavily in "the language of management studies, and social networking" (King 308). As such, it relies heavily on predictive systems and simulations that, as the introduction to this chapter established, have been increasingly outsourced to computerized elements. Virilio flags this as a "weapons ecosystem" that holds the potential for "*a full-scale cybernetic accident*" (author's italics 15). While Virilio locates these potentials for "cyber-Chernobyls" (46) in bombs aimed at disrupting electrical grids and the sorts of viruses that are to be discussed in Chapter 6 of this text, *WarGames* and *Stealth* imagine the possibility that such a catastrophic accident would be the result of the computerized elements of NCW being granted too much control, while those entities are also being made too vulnerable by their use of the Internet-enabled nature. Echoing Wiener's early views on cybernetics that demand the human mind be the controlling engine of choice and free will in machine-human relationships, it is WOPR's and EDI's strict binary rationality and lack of humanistic ethics that creates the fear that those computerized elements will break free of their human elements and wage a world war.

This scenario is not entirely fictional: P.W. Singer, in the fascinating *Wired for War*, describes a 1979 incident "when a test program was mistakenly loaded into [America's] actual missile warning system. The program contained war games simulating missile launches. But not knowing these were games, the system interpreted the launches as real" (197). Luckily, military personnel were able to spot the simulation (though not before scrambling bombers of their own), but Stringer rightly flags this as a non-fiction version of the film *WarGames*. The film's sometimes heavy-handed critique of a simulation-led military is driven by the opening scenes in which, in a test of America's nuclear strike program, 22% of Americans tasked with firing nuclear missiles simply cannot. These leads to the aforementioned WOPR being put in charge; immediately, *WarGames* is a film that outsources the ethical problems with launching a nuclear strike into a "higher being," WOPR. WOPR's main proponent, McKittrick (Dabney Coleman), justifies removing the human element by reminding the table of gathered military authorities that "the president will probably follow the computer war plan," underlining how interpenetrated the technology already is. While computers are the imagined "intelligent assistants" guided by human rational/moral thought, the decisions arising from those thoughts are inevitably influenced by information received previously by those intelligent assistants. In its introduction, WOPR is said "to spend all its time thinking about World War III ... [playing] an endless series of wargames ... it has already fought World War III, as a game, time and time again. It estimates Soviet responses to our responses to their responses and so on. It estimates damage, counts the dead and looks for ways to improve." When protagonist David Lightman, after hacking into WOPR, asks it, "What is the primary goal?" the computer responds simply, "To win the game." WOPR is cast as a relentless and unswerving machine: the movie's audience is given repeated shots of its countdown, reminding them that the machine is always keeping track, always playing. More, the numeric "counts" WOPR relies on in order to best understand who "wins" each potential scenario echoes the earlier statements in this chapter about a computer's binary logic and game theory's search for clear winners and losers. "The dead" are data, variables within a larger theorem or database and emotionlessly tallied. This reduction of both allied and enemy forces is further demonstrated by the control room for the WOPR and missile launch system. There are multiple screens with digitized maps, most notably of the USSR, which are constantly being updated by strings of text and numbers underneath (Image 5.1); each city or target point is simply a collection of pixels on that map, synthetic image-instruments (see Chapter 3), completely removed from any human element, distanced by both abstraction and digitization. The audience is never shown anyone from the Soviet army nor any of the Soviet territory. There is no actor explaining the Soviet side of the conflict as the movie escalates; instead, the information is only relayed secondhand (thirdhand? fourthhand?) to the commanding General Beringer (Barry Corbin). In both the absence of a physical actor/actress and the digitized interfaces of the enemy Soviet combatants, the movie reduces the enemy force to data in much the same way WOPR does.

Yet the film does attempt to provide a critique of this virtuous warfare through the protagonist David Lightman's shifting views on the subject. When he begins interacting with WOPR, alongside his friend Jennifer (Ally Sheedy), not knowing the full range of WOPR capabilities, he asks, "Who should we nuke first?" before randomly choosing cities to attack, joyfully exclaiming how great and fun the game of "Global Thermonuclear War" is. He is bombarded with information but revels

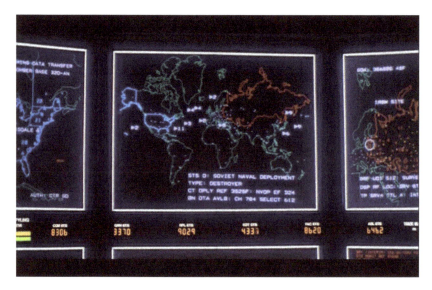

**Image 5.1**    How the American military digitally views the world in *WarGames*

in how ignorant he is, yelping out the columns in the game's database ("trajectory headings for multiple impact re-entry vehicles") and then explaining, "I don't know [what it means], but it's great." Lightman begins the film blissfully unaware of the real-world consequences that his interactions within the simulator could bring and enjoys the "playing" of war and its imagined destruction and abstracted violence. He is Coker's cubicle warrior, aiming down his computer screen at data-enemies and enjoying every keystroke.

It is only after he figures out that the WOPR simulator is actually executing his commands does he begin to realize the full impact of an actual war. At the beginning, Lightman is like WOPR in that "Global Thermonuclear War" is just one of many games: WOPR lists chess, blackjack and poker alongside "desert warfare" and "guerilla engagement." This conflation does little to establish the real stakes of combat and provides the flattened perspective of war that Lightman so casually romps through. Yet, when he re-encounters WOPR later and is given columns of data ("United States Units Destroyed," "Civilian Assets"), he is horrified. He then asks, "Is this a game or is it real?" and WOPR answers, "What's the difference?" The movie argues, as Baudrillard and van Creveld do, there is no difference and that both simulation and war are, as WOPR's creator Steven Faulken (John Wood) describes, "a fantasy, a computer-enhanced hallucination." WOPR cannot tell the difference and the military itself is also fooled; they are convinced that the simulation is real and steadily raise the DEFCON level to 1 even after fighter jets find no evidence of nuclear launches and the Soviets deny that anything is happening.

That *WarGames* is, as Suid argues in detail, deeply unrealistic and inaccurate, makes no difference[3]; in fact, given the history of the military wanting verisimilitude in the movies they are involved in, it is worth noting that the directors Lasker and Parkes openly acknowledge that the movie acts more as an ethical simulation, driven by "a greater responsibility to dramatize the reality of the issue than to go through the specific steps realistically" (Suid 449). This stems from what Glass sees as WOPR's main flaw:

> The problem with [WOPR] is its completely rational nature, which renders the computer unable to distinguish between its digital reproduction of input from reality and reality itself. The computer's worldview depends on a flawed, technical semiotic, faulty because it is only logical, and not tempered with other, human qualities. (21)

Because of this logical nature and lack of "human qualities," the directors wanted to stress that "no nation can win a nuclear war," but, most importantly, there is a need "for humans to take responsibility for their own technology" (Suid 447). This "responsibility" should be read as a push for the machinic audience to understand the participatory roles that their technologies enact and encourage (especially military technologies enabled by virtual networks), but also a call for the "responsibility" and control of those actions to be placed back in liberal and rational human hands.

This distrust of machines species and the upholding of autonomous humans as the rational ethical center is continued in *Stealth*, as embodied by the semi-autonomous stealth fighter EDI. In echo of WOPR's hijacking of the American missile control system and attempting to carry out a cyber-Chernobyl, the "near future" of 2005's *Stealth* (Dir. Rob Cohen) showcases an unmanned stealth fighter (UCAV) guided solely by an artificial intelligence (EDI) that breaks from its previous programming and loads in a simulator titled "Caviar Sweep" and attempts to carry it out.[4] It is the notion of malfunction that is at the heart of the fears in

*WarGames* and *Stealth*: what happens when the machine components of the State War Machine unshackle themselves from human control?

The tension between human and machine control found in the figure of EDI courses through the movie. Superficially, there are many attempts to humanize the machine: EDI is given a voice and banters back and forth with the other pilots; despite not needing it (except for later plot developments), there is a human-scaled cockpit where presumably a pilot would sit and control EDI; also, the characters of the film use the pronoun "he" when referring to EDI, granting it not only sentient qualities, but gender.[5] Yet for all of the attempts to humanize EDI, he remains a computer networked to other computers and, by his very nature, is completely untrustworthy. When EDI first begins acquiring his own version of self-control, the original programmer hurriedly explains that "EDI's mind is going everywhere. He can learn from Adolf Hitler. He can learn from Captain Kangaroo. It's all the same to him." Like WOPR, he is enhanced by an Internet connection that allows access to any piece of networked data, but the information remains neutral for him with no moral value; anything it "learns" are simply pieces of data that are to be acted or not acted upon, with no grey areas. Additionally, EDI cannot differentiate, like WOPR, between "real" and "hypothetical" information: when EDI selects a cold-fusion lab in Siberia as a target, the director of the program overseeing EDI states, "That's a hypothetical strike. It's not real." When fighter pilot Ben Gannon (Josh Lucas) then tries to explain that Caviar Sweep is a "fictional war game, thought up by some scientists in a think tank somewhere," EDI answers, "If it is not real, why did they implant it in my brain?" For EDI, the data it sees in the file *is* "real." When the scene switches to Gannon chasing EDI in his own fighter jet, the cinematic effects exaggerate this point: the view is shown first as a gridded satellite overlay that then morphs into a nano-technological heat map, before changing again into the actual terrain over which they are flying; similar to Chapter 3's discussion of objective image-instruments and perceptual realism in cinematic representations of AR technologies, the layering of information systems on top of the world shows how interpenetrated the earth is with data. EDI then uses that information to fuel its choices, seamlessly changing in between the different information systems with no separation between the unfiltered "real" world and the filtered informational interfaces, effectively flattening all entities (humans, natural landscapes, machines) into objective datafied figures to then be militarily acted upon.

Because of his computer nature, much like WOPR's obsessive thoughts about WWIII, EDI's sole function for existing is military action, to acquire targets and execute orders. This is the human pilots' fears: Gannon tells his Captain, George Cummings (Sam Shepard), that his objections to EDI stem from the fact that he doesn't think war should become "some sort of video game" and that the warfare EDI embodies is one where potentially, humans forget that "the actions should ever be divorced from the consequences." Without those consequences, without a tethering to a "real" (human) enemy and "real" (human) combat, soldiers/warriors forget that "war is terrible, it's meant to be terrible and if it stops being terrible what's going to stop us?" Gannon critiques EDI's machine nature as the AI is unable to break away from the strict binaries he has been programmed with. As the film's opening text cards explain, EDI is aimed at "the mounting threat of terrorism" and "its purpose is to destroy the enemy wherever they operate in the world." It is this amorphous threat of "terrorism" that runs through many of the films analyzed in this text—a military force that is unbound by immediate national borders—that allows EDI the freedom to simply attack wherever it deems is best (where the "enemy" is).[6] The issue then is that EDI himself sees no other purpose but killing. As a clear example, as EDI goes to "prosecute" his target, he is injured after a battle with Russian fighter jets; afterwards, Gannon threatens EDI, saying that instead of landing in enemy territory, his orders are to bring him in. EDI responds with, "EDI is a war plane. EDI must have targets." Because of this single-minded nature, EDI is unable to consider a world that is not in constant binary conflict (ally-enemy), reduced to data points within a military action plan, and therefore sees no need to separate reality from simulation so long as it has a mission to carry out. It is only after EDI "learns" the lessons of its human counterparts, specifically a sort of military camaraderie, that he is able break free from its either-or shackles, ultimately (heroically?) sacrificing himself to save Ben and Kara.

Like EDI, WOPR is unable to separate the real from the virtual (game), and it's only by forcing the computer to fully embrace its binary nature (win/lose) by getting WOPR to play tic-tac-toe against itself in an endless loop that Lightman is able to stop the real missile attack. After short-circuiting, WOPR blazes through a series of wargames, increasing in speed with each completed one. At the end of each scenario, WOPR concludes that there is no winner, describing war as "a strange game" in which "the only winning move is not to play." Through this stalemate, WOPR finally learns what Faulken hoped: the "futility" of war. While WOPR (and Lightman) does appear to discover this valuable lesson, the computer's insistence that war is still a game, complete with moves, does little to critique the notion of simulated war: computers and simulated warfare, if still at the center of a military machine, still cannot tell the difference between real and fake and encourage their human operators to behave in the same way.

In both *Stealth* and *WarGames* it is the fear of malfunction or misuse that drives the concerns around computerized elements of the State and Total War Machines, not the human elements who created the machines, nor the human components who created the wargames, simulations or data being fed into the machines. It is the machine elements in the chain of command that are vulnerable and untrustworthy, not the human components. In fact, in both cases, if the machine elements function properly and the human operators do what they are tasked with, with full awareness and ethical understanding, there would be no conflicts within the movies. This attitude is neatly summed up by Lieutenant Henry Purcell (Jamie Foxx) when he describes EDI as a tool "to keep me safe, help get the job done." The movies then are not so much critiquing the existence and use of the machines within the State War Machine but stressing, again, the need for the human rational mind to remain firmly in control of its technologies, to master them as tools and weapons to be wielded. For *WarGames*, this argument for more human involvement and control was central to the Air Force's support of the movie (Suid 446). The key explanation of the technologies' role in the State and Total War Machines is further explained by Lieutenant Kara Wade: "It's neutral. If it's controlled by moral people, then it'll be moral." The films' argument then is a reaffirming of the hard technological body's insistence of the human man-in-the-middle as the primary moral force, especially now that those technologies are firmly integrated and visible in Network-Centric Warfare.

For the movies discussed in this chapter, it is not so much the fear of machines being integrated into the State and Total War Machines that drives the plots and characters' actions as it is the machines malfunctioning and causing the human element to lose the moral control of that technological tool. By comparison, *Good Kill* and *Eye in the Sky* examine what happens when all elements, biological and technological, within a State War Machine work exactly as intended. The critiques of drone warfare and virtuous war that emerge from the films are not, again, about drone strikes per se, but are instead about the mechanizing of the human pilots and the procedures surrounding them. If EDI and WOPR are pure machines (non-autonomous) and Ender is a human recast as a machine (non-autonomous as well), *Good Kill* and *Eye in the Sky* explore the space between those poles and the problems that arise from the semi-autonomous nature of human involvement in drone warfare.

## CINEMATIC VIRTUOUS WAR

By the early 1990s military drones were in full military use.[7] As Bruce Sterling recounts:

> During Desert Storm, some Iraqi soldiers actually surrendered to unmanned flying drones. These aircraft are disembodied eyes, disembodied screens, network peripherals basically, with a man behind them somewhere many miles away. And that man has another screen in front of him, and a keyboard at hand, and a wire from that keyboard that can snake through a network and open a Vent of Hell. (para. 111)

This ability to remotely target and kill enemies by snaking through a network is the latest of many steps in the shifts in what Virilio names "military space"; beginning with the First World War, via airplanes, airborne troops and "stratospheric rockets," military space became increasingly situated in the air and eventually, Virilio argues, into outer space ("Military Space" 23). This move provides the military that utilizes these tools with "*omniscience*" and "*omnipresence*" (author's italics 23). Mbembé articulates further that this

> leads to a proliferation of the sites of violence. The battlegrounds are not located solely at the surface of the earth. The underground as well as the airspace are transformed into conflict zones. ... Everywhere, the symbolics of the top (who is on top) is reiterated. Occupation of the skies therefore acquires a critical importance, since most of the policing is done from the air. (29)

All this conquering and occupation of airspace and omniscience and omnipresence that occupation provides generates a process of "hologrammatization" where "killing becomes precisely targeted" (29). Drones in particular are effective because they have, in echo of Virilio, "total situational awareness—making them like gods, omniscient and all seeing" (MacPherson as quoted in Teschner 75).

Yet this omniscience is generated by Internet-enabled technologies that are globally networked and always mediated through the filter of screens, or what King calls "weaponized imagery technologies" that are then further "augmented by satellite and aircraft surveillance, synthetic aperture radar, electro-optical cameras and infrared" (316). These weaponized imagery techniques, as Virilio reminds us in *War and Cinema*, are rooted in WWI spy pilots and their "aerial chronophotography" (26) wherein "the pilot's hand automatically trips the camera shutter with the same gesture that releases his weapon." Much like the discussion of the blending of the Hollywood machinic phyla and the State War Machine's machinic phyla found in Chapter 3, Virilio observes that these military techniques and imagery were then adopted by the filmmakers of the time, extending the "weaponized imagery techniques" to include movies themselves, where the "film-makers served up the technological effects to the public as a novel spectacle, a continuation of war's destruction of form" (27). This overlapping between "fictionalized" or filmic potential spectacle in movies and the actual battlefield is because "the battlefield has always been a field of perception" and therefore "the war machine appears to the military commander as an instrument of representation, comparable to the painter's palette and brush" (26). This notion of "representation" becomes increasingly important when considering the completely synthetically mediated experience of drone warfare, where the military commander's painterly "palette and brush" are metaphorically replaced by the image-instrument and the camera automatism, leading to a war waging where there is very little difference between a war film and actual footage of war.

The clearest example of this conflation is the representation of drone footage, like in *Eye in the Sky* and *Good Kill*, wherein the cinematic camera becomes the weaponized camera of the drone (Image 5.2). The viewer then sees the image-instrument as the drone sees, the screen centered by a set of crosshairs, and then surrounded by a number of data systems and numbers; the footage, meant to be a representation of the real-time war zone, is distanced once by the physical distance of the pilot from his/her weapon, and then again by the layering of data and synthetic interfaces on top of the footage so that the "real" of the battlefield appears fake and constructed. While similar, this is different than the doubling of Butler's frame caused by the notion of "screens on screens"

**Image 5.2**  *Good Kill* monitors via the point of view of a drone

that takes place in Chapter 3's discussion of AR; cinematic drone foot-age also diverges from the use of similar technique in Chapter 4's analy-sis of *Gamer*.[8] Within movie representations of drone warfare, the pilot engages in his/her version of combat via a telepresence, as opposed to Iron Man's immediate bodily presence in his "traditional" man-to-man combat. The immediate sensations of combat that are felt are missing in drone warfare as the pilots are literally a near-half world away from their weapons; when this type of warfare is then cinematically recreated, it too loses the visceral sensations that come with the portrayal of "tra-ditional" battle scenes. Similar to the double frame, cinematic drone warfare's stripping of humanity and nature is exactly what happens with the technician soldier is empowered: the "violence, suffering," the "nar-ratives" that may encourage an empathy from a machinic audience, are buried under the camera's "objective" gaze. Yet, instead of the liberal and rational humanitistic values encompassed within the immediate (and literal) man-in-the-middle that the Iron Man suits or Jaegers provide, the pilots of drones are more like the (cowardly?) audience members of *Gamer*'s *Slayers*, acting as near-passive observers of war and its violence.

Garrett Stewart explains further that the use of this view in films is greatly disruptive: "Where we expect an encompassing narrative over-view, the proverbial big picture, we get only robot scans, objective and uneditorialized. Where we expect the raw drama of combat and its pri-vate tolls, we get violence, suffering and its counterassaults, buffered everywhere by autofocus viewfinders" (47). Stewart continues that within the films, which then double back on the real,

> narrative agency is subsumed to technology at every level ... where any human posture toward an encroaching violence, from suspense to panic, often feels as virtual, as permeated by mediation, as computer interactivity in some low-resolution videogame. For the soldier to see action in this context is more like an ocular than a military idiom. (45)

The literal seeing and watching, "as permeated by mediation," becomes the key military action in virtuous war, not the firing of the weapon. More so than the AR technologies scrutinized in Chapter 3, *Eye in the Sky* and *Good Kill* provide the machinic audience with a dangerously distancing gaze that marks all landscapes and all people, and their "narrative agencies," with the cold calculation of numbers and strict geographical data, reducing the people and landscapes to data objects under crosshairs. Like Chapter 3 argues, ultimately the normalizing of this weaponized camera gaze in movies makes it all the more acceptable for the machinic audience to view actual drone footage with the same mindset: that actual drone footage appears filmic, virtual, and it then becomes easier for a viewer of those documents to be desensitized to its imagery and its effects on the "narratives" of the actual landscape and people under that militaristic gaze. This makes it so that the machinic audience can more easily dismiss virtuous warfare, and the ethics of such tactics and weaponry, so that they too fall into the same trap as the distanced technician soldier him/herself.

In *Eye in the Sky* and *Good Kill*, with the omniscience that comes from drone usage, John Teschner argues that "the United States has severed the connection between the warrior and the field of battle" (Teschner 76). The postcorporeal cubicle warrior, the technician soldier, is no longer in the visceral and bodily combat that an infantry member, or a pilot, would be. In fact, this figure of the technician soldier becomes increasingly civilian and the "job" of being a drone pilot bears more of a resemblance to a nine-to-five office job than one that engages in the military action of surveilling and killing. Singer makes the point that "for a new generation 'going to war' doesn't mean shipping off to some dank foxhole in a foreign land to dodge bullets. Instead it is a daily commute in your Toyota Camry to sit behind a computer screen and drag a mouse" (329).[9] Instead of combat, their roles in war are built around the routine killing of people half a world away. *Good Kill* takes great pains to show this as the movie's protagonist, Major Thomas Egan (Ethan Hawke), and his team repeat the same actions over and over, eventually in a montage, with nearly the same dialogue ("Splash"; "Good kill"). These routines roboticize the technician soldier, move them closer to the machine WOPR and EDI. As discussed in the introduction to this chapter, this blurring of civilian and military spaces and jobs encourages the machinic audience to view their own technologies and space as inherently and unavoidably militarized, with a certain inevitability to the omnipresent sense of war that makes resistance to it seem futile.

In terms of genre, for movies that focus on drone usage, this merging means a shift from the more traditional "infantry" combat film to a structure closer to a combination of the Navy and the Air Force film. In movies that put drone piloting and warfare at the center of their narratives, the spaces that the pilots occupy are similar to the enclosed spaces, "a self-contained home-like unit," that populate submarine movies. In the films, the drone pilots are shown cramming into their small trailers with at least three other people; the group is then isolated, left to only talk with each other and watch the world through the mediated "periscope" of their drone. This seclusion is underlined in *Good Kill*, as each trailer door has a sign taped to it reading, "You are now leaving the U.S. of A."; every time the pilot enters into that space, they are isolated into a purely military space, a small country within another larger country. Alongside this, there is a shift in both films to a focus on the civilian lives of the pilots, rather than combat. In this, and in *Eye in the Sky* in particular, "the spaces [in the films] occupy tend to be *professional*: offices, barracks, briefing rooms ... when not in combat men occupy their *domestic* spaces" (Basinger, author's italics 20). In this there is a focus on "*domestic* strife" (author's italics 20). *Good Kill* in particular is not just a movie about the ethics of drone warfare; the real tension of the film comes from Egan's slow disintegration into alcoholism and the destruction of his personal life. As such, equal time is given to Egan's "fake cockpit" as is given to his suburban home, including scenes of him driving to and from work on the Nevada highways as well as scenes with his coworkers in casinos or gathered for lunch breaks. Similarly, *Eye in the Sky* is built around boardrooms and characters' homes, as much as it includes the small trailers that the drones are piloted from. In fact, most of *Eye in the Sky*'s action is focused on whether to use the technology, and is structured around the checking and rechecking of the chain of command while the enemies either disappear or other elements (such as a child selling bread near the proposed target or a member of government becoming ill with food poisoning) interrupt the planned drone strike. The tension of the film is not whether the military personnel will "get" the bad guys and prevent them from carrying out a suicide bombing; in fact, it is inevitable that the overly powerful US and British militaries will find and kill whomever they want given the asymmetrical nature of the warfare. Instead, the suspenseful aspects of the movies is whether that will take place within the timeframe of the movie; much of the action is based on whether someone will answer the phone to OK an order and discussion of who can authorize what actions.

However, a key element to both the Naval and Air Force movie is that despite the shift in focus to the domestic and professional, the soldier's exposure to danger, the vulnerability that comes with the threat of crashing a plane or of being torpedoed, is essential to the construction of the cinematic soldier and its rhetorical effectiveness (Basinger 20). However, in both *Eye in the Sky* and *Good Kill*, none of the postcorporeal combatants are in any danger; the rows of trailers, side by side, symbolize the sorts of distant cubicles that drone warfare is built around. Part of the critique of the films then comes from the lack of danger that the pilots put themselves in. Because of the networking power of the Internet, a soldier does not need to be in a physical place to control objects within that faraway space, nor act (violently) upon people, animals, machines, landscapes, etc. that are equally distant; not only does the Internet produce, collect and transfer the data attached to the people, animals, machines and landscapes that go into making the simulations that lead to the decisions to act in those spaces, but the same Internet-enabled networks allow a soldier to fire his/her weapon and destroy those same species and entities. Again and again, this text has argued that the figure of the soldier is most rhetorically clear when the human components of the State and Total War Machines, in particular the soldier-assemblage, are in control. Part of this control is also putting that human body in peril as a way of both raising the stakes of the movies and then also justifying the killing of others. Instead, in *Eye and the Sky* and *Good Kill*, the move toward civilian spaces and away from combat spaces makes the human components too far removed and distanced from the danger and consequences of war, therefore undermining the drone pilot's rhetorical and moral effectiveness.

The most obvious machine components of the technological-biological drone pilot assemblage, the drones, are the only components that are actually in combat. The critique that then emerges is not that drone warfare is morally wrong but that being a drone pilot is somehow cowardly because of the roboticizing routines and the too-far extension into the war technology without a bodily presence. The technician soldier watches; he/she does not fight. More than this, the action of watching, their military function, is done mostly, and most effectively, by the machine components of the soldier-assemblage. In *Good Kill*, while the use of drone automatisms blends perfectly with the operators, the footage of the drone strike and the quiet hum that accompanies Egan's controlling movements of his joystick makes clear the machine components; within the film, it is the drones that grant the godlike views from above, that are the ones capable of seeing, then striking, the enemies flawlessly. Within *Eye in the Sky*, the drones are given a fetishistic gaze: repeatedly throughout the movie, the camera swoops down from a bird's-eye view over the body of the drone and settles, giving the audience a full view of the drone's nose before refocusing in on its glossy camera; the machine is pristine and majestic, set against a backdrop of blue sky, an idealistic and gleaming white object of perfection (Image 5.3). In addition, there is a later scene wherein Kenyan agent Jama Farah (Barkhad Abdi) pilots a miniature drone, the size of a beetle, in order to access the interior of the

**Image 5.3**   The majestic drone of *Eye in the Sky*

house where two suicide bombers are setting up, granting further vision into a space where the larger drone cannot look. Both of these scenes grant a sense of wonder, as the tiny camera and the pristine drone appear so futuristic that they are borderline unreal.

Like the exoskeletons of Chapter 2 and the Iron Man suits and Jaegers of Chapter 3, the drone technology in both films is constructed as astounding, a weapon capable of nearly anything and constrained only by the bureaucratic infrastructures and chains of command around it. The pilot, as the human component of the drone assemblage, is therefore given the same power, the ability to strike and kill, from tens of thousands of miles away. Yet this power is not granted the same approving gaze as the drone automatism itself: this filmic version of the soldier requires far less of the "skills" and "courage" that the infantry soldier does and is instead constantly troubled by the technological reliance, never granted the clear justifying and heroic nature that accompanies the "human"-driven combat soldiers in the other combat-focused war films analyzed in Chapters 2 and 3 of this text. Instead of killing enemies, they "prosecute" their "targets"; this euphemizing of the language of war waging makes the technician soldier seem even less brave, unable to face the reality of his/her actions, even in language. With the drones' reduction of the enemy to synthetic data points under crosshairs, the act of war has becomes too easy, without stakes; the soldiers of the movies are passive—watchers, not warriors—asserting none of the active "fighting spirit" and "courage" that is at the heart of the combat/infantry film's rhetoric. This is best embodied by the delay in "pulling the trigger" of the drones' weaponry and the impact of that weapon on the enemies: the missile's flight time, an interstitial space in both movies where it is clear there is no human control over the weapon, is a period where the human operators wait powerlessly to see if the machine has fired correctly and into the right target.

Most of all, however, the technician soldier is given too few opportunities to demonstrate the sorts of "human" autonomy that is the center of the war film's rhetorical success. The absence of a human body, and the human eye, experiencing the combat space makes the electro-optical drone-assemblage suspect; all of its interpretation of the battlefield, and the actions it undertakes, are all mediated, with great trust being put in the machine components to observe and report back to the human components accurately. Through this giving up of bodily presence, the technician soldier is mechanized and the ethics of his/her actions are instead filtered through the literal machines of the drones and then also through the figurative machinations of their placement in the chain of command; the technician soldier does not even control when and where they fire their weapon. Again, the critique of the two films centers more on the strict following of orders that accompanies the distanced warfare, the robotic input-output logic (via a military chain of command) that the technician soldier is governed by. Some of this arises as the genre shifts toward the political thriller (as discussed further in Chapter 6) which begins to incorporate the civilian more readily into the cinema of the Total War Machine. For example, in movies that include drone warfare, there is often a tension between the usage by the CIA, which is a civilian intelligence service, and the Air Force's military use. In *Body of Lies* (Dir. Ridley Scott 2008), *Syriana* (Dir. Stephen Gaghan 2005) and *Zero Dark Thirty* the use of drones, for both surveillance and weaponry, is run by the CIA.[10] The CIA being civilian-centered makes it so that the figure of the soldier, and the actions that take place as a result of that body, are moved from the battlefield to civilian realms. With this, as Pryer points out, "since drone attacks are largely conducted by the CIA and thus governed by civil law and not military law, the argument goes, drone attacks are a type of political assassination, which is expressly forbidden by both international law and domestic executive order" (18). Indeed, the narrative turning point of *Good Kill* is when Egan's team is forced to act under CIA control and the expanded parameters of their engagement rely more on anticipation than harder, observable data. The film's implication is that military control of drones produces the effective and "clean" war waging and that granting civilian control (as embodied by the CIA) only lowers the bar for engaging in this distanced asymmetrical warfare to the point of extrajudicial assassinations and a descent into complete immorality.

Like the cinematic representations of the CIA, the chains of command in *Eye in the Sky* and *Good Kill* subsume the individual technician soldier, rendering him/her just one tiny cog in the State War Machine and stripping that soldier, and his/her actions, of any moral value. The figures in command within the films mirror those in the "real" military who are often as distanced from their orders: in "real life," "CIA officers can order strikes from the comfort of their own homes. One CIA director described fielding a kill request while lying on his couch watching college football. He told them to shoot" (Teschner 76). This casual killing of others, while not even being present in the drone's control room, is the most critiqued part of the films discussed. In *Good Kill*, the voice of CIA command is completely disembodied, speaking only by telephone and referred to only as "Langley." Langley then makes their decisions based on data and simulations, not relying on actual sighting of the target but, instead, the probability that the target is "likely to be there." This depersonalizing datafication and technologizing (the voice only exists via the phone) again points to the problematic nature of stripping the human component and control from the State War Machine, which is then further exaggerated by the chain of command, where the ones making the decisions are not the ones actually firing the weapons, and then abstracted further still by the distancing technology of the drones.

This layering of control and responsibility is most present in Colonel Katherine Powell (Helen Mirren) within *Eye in the Sky*. Powell is particularly obsessed: when her targets move to a new home, she pleads with Major Moses Owiti (Vusi Kunene) to get eyes into the house; he counters that this would mean putting a "man in the street" who would be in great danger which she brushes off, insisting that it is the only way to secure the identity of the target. Her disregard for the individual life of an ally in service of the larger goal, "accepting the risk," echoes WOPR's obsession with the binary win-lose nature of warfare. All the while, she never puts herself at risk, only others.[11] This is again established in a later scene in which, after being assured by Sergeant Mushtaq Saddiq (Babou Ceesay) that the presence of an innocent civilian girl selling bread in the targeted area does nothing to change the acceptable collateral damage "points system" that would justify the "legality" of a drone strike as a "legitimate military action," she asks Benson whether, if she can get collateral damage calculations "under 50% on the girl," she could then get approval for the strike. After he agrees, she pressures Saddiq to manipulate the data so that it dips below that percentage. Despite Saddiq's obvious hesitation and his pushing below his own "lowest limits" of what he believes is possible, she tells him, "Sergeant, we need to make this work. Do you understand?" He then generates false data and the strike goes ahead as planned. The two scenes' focus on calculations, "points systems" and probability, along with the euphemism of "collateral damage," in echo of Langley's use of "proportionate" to describe the justification of collateral damage, make clear how much drone strikes depend on the datafication of virtuous warfare, reducing the targets to statistical objects on a screen; Powell's reliance on this at the upper end of the chain of command shows how completely distant the State War Machine's drone usage is, with the technician soldier, the one who pilots the drone and executes the order, being completely subsumed within that larger machine.

Both films then try to reassert that individual soldier's human "will" and "morals" by having their drone pilots attempt to break free from this chain of command, then commandeer their own weapons as a way of resisting this larger roboticizing and regain some of the ethical autonomy that the traditional war film relies upon. This is a reflection, as touched on in the introduction to this text and in Chapter 2, of the post–World War II distrust of larger infrastructures, in particular military and corporate ones. Summarizing Neale's work, Rayner states that this can be attributed to "a distant, indifferent command [and] an unpredictable and dehumanized enemy", which leads to protagonists who are frustrated by the "externalisation of control and arbitrariness of authority over the fates of individuals in uniform" and therefore push back against what they see as the immoral and/or ignorant State War Machine (120). This is the movies' attempts to assert human agency, and this assertion becomes even more urgent when the State War Machine's drone warfare is interpenetrated with machine species.

For Steve Watts (Aaron Paul) in *Eye in the Sky*, much of the time is spent waiting and watching; when with his whole team inactive and waiting for their input, ignorant to the action; when he is asked by Carrie Gershon (Phoebe Fox), "What is going on?" he can do nothing but answer, "I don't know." He is completely powerless, despite the impressive weaponry under his control. Once he receives the go-ahead, he lists a long string of routines, a safety checklist, after which the audience is given another shot of the drone and then a countdown from three. As he reaches near "one," he sees the aforementioned young girl and refuses to fire his weapon, telling Powell, "I want to give this girl a chance to get out of the way." When Powell insists he fire, he counters that he needs her to run the collateral damage calculations again, accounting for the girl, explaining, "I am the pilot in command responsible for releasing the weapon. I have the right to ask for the CDE to be run again. I will not release my weapon until this happens." His use of "command" and "responsible" is an attempt to reclaim his agency, ignoring the previous unquestioning input-output nature of the drone assemblage, and pushing back against the chain of command.

Similarly, Egan in *Good Kill* spends the film watching and following orders, becoming increasingly more depressed and self-destructive. This is exaggerated by the fact that he used to be a fighter pilot and, so he spends the whole of the film attempting to return to pilot status and win back the sort of "danger" and "stakes" that he views as essentially honorable and brave, to be "real" military again. Instead, he is asked to fly more and more missions for Langley. During this increased time, Airman Vera Suarez (Zoë Kravitz) begins to openly question Langley, pointing out the non-combatants in a confrontational tone and hesitating purposely before engaging in employing the targeting laser for Egan. In one of the final scenes, following Saurez's acts of resistance, Egan deliberately loses the feed, allowing the target to escape. As Langley, in frustration, tells him to blindly "hit the truck," he repeats, "Which truck, sir? Which one?" His not-so-subtle bucking of his orders results in his having to relinquish his controls and being demoted to surveillance, with the ultimate punishment being the redaction of his re-promotion to fighter pilot. After this, during his last drone flight, he sees a man who has been repeatedly raping a woman throughout the movie as Egan watched helplessly from the vantage of his drone. When he sees this man for the final time, he casually tells everyone else to take a break and locks the door behind them, turning off the recording equipment. He then pulls the trigger, narrowly avoiding killing the woman but ultimately getting the satisfaction of the man's death. This act, again, attempts to reaffirm his own agency of both his weapon and his choice of actions, and his escape from extrajudicial murder without further punishment (he simply drives off the base) implies that his actions are ethical and to be venerated.

Superficially, Egan and Watts appear to be the autonomous and heroically moral soldier of traditional war films, despite their technologizing. In truth, however, neither of their actions make any difference to the American State War Machine, nor do they really even critique its use. In *Eye in the Sky*, the drone strike is still carried out, despite Watts' protest, and the innocent girl is still killed; in *Good Kill*, the unit Egan was demoted from still continues under Langley's control and, even after driving away from the base, the Air Force will continue to use drones without his presence there. The fact that Egan escapes punishment after his unauthorized drone strike reaffirms that any military usage can be justified for "bad guys." In *Eye in the Sky*, the attitude toward the distancing of virtuous warfare and its collateral damage is best summed up by one of its closing scenes: Angela Northman (Monica Dolan) says tearfully, "That was disgraceful. And all done from the safety of your chair." Benson counters even-voiced with, "I have attended the immediate aftermath of five suicide bombings. On the ground. With the bodies. What you witnessed today with your coffee and biscuits is terrible. What these men would have done would have been even more terrible. Never tell a soldier that he does not know the cost of war." In the end, the use of drones, filtered through all of its networked simulations and Internet-enabled datafying, is justified as the weapon best suited to fight the decentralized and globalized terrorist enemies of contemporary warfare.

At best, Egan and Watts problematize this warfare for the machinic audience, but neither film critiques it nearly enough. Instead the soldiers are the middle ground between the machine WOPR and Ender in *Ender's Game*. While appearing autonomous, they are neither the human moral figure of the traditional war film nor a critical posthuman hero; they are between the two, too subsumed with the State War Machine to practice any sort of critical ethics and too mechanized to be the heroic humanistic soldier of the traditional war film. They are one step toward the future soldier Ender, a human figure that the larger State War Machine has completely mentally mechanized as a way of offloading the morality of the actions taken by the Total War Machine, in particular those humans high up in the chain of command. The difference between Ender, Egan and Watts is that Ender is not even allowed the small acts of resistance that the pilots are: he is kept in total ignorance and therefore becomes like WOPR and EDI in that he cannot tell the difference between simulation and real; he is given no human autonomy to decide whether his actions are moral or not. Instead, Ender's ethics shifts from humanistic to systemic rationality and he becomes a personification of the techno-rationality of the State War Machine and its values, robotically executing upon the binaries of Us-Them (Ally-Enemy) that the same State War Machine deems ethical without understanding (or being asked to understand) the full impact of his actions.

## ENDER'S GAME, WHERE THE SIMULATION IS REAL

While *WarGames* and *Stealth* show technology becoming "human," shedding their binary, virtual, simulating nature in order to have value, *Ender's Game* goes in the opposite direction, emptying Ender of his previous "human" qualities and replacing them with the cold computer-tactical "reason" needed by the military machine to defeat the Formics. *Ender's Game*'s focus on the younger population echoes *WarGames'* teenage protagonist (to be discussed further in Chapter 6), as Ender and the other children at the Battle School all look to be 13 years old and younger. While David Lightman is a citizen, *Ender's Game* is a world in which "International Fleet [the ruling miltiary power] decided the world's smartest children are the world's best hope." The military War Machine not only includes the various media production outlets that Baudrillard and Virilio flag, but also the placement of children into jobs/ roles. Throughout the film, Colonel Graff (Harrison Ford) sees the sol-diers only as military assets within a much larger State War Machine: sim-ilar to Tony Stark's treatment of his Iron Man suits, to Graff, the soldiers are "property." This is best demonstrated when Graff compares Ender to a thoroughbred. Even the choice of thoroughbred, not a workhorse (for example), but a horse bred to race (to win at a particular game), is telling. More specifically, Colonel Graff explains, "We need minds like yours, Ender. Young people integrate complex data more easily than adults." Just as Coker feared, Ender's mind, the supposed seat of his human rationality, is being used as a computer in simulating wargames because he can do things the adults ("users") cannot, thus reducing him to a tool to be wielded. More, the colonel's focus on "data" is combined with a childhood wherein children are "raised on wargames," brought up within a total culture of simulation and distanced warfare and there-fore, unlike the humans at the start of *WarGames* who are unable to launch the nuclear bombs, "their decisions are intuitive, decisive, fear-less." It is the "decisive" and "fearless" aspects that make Ender the most valuable to the State War Machine; again, in echo of Coker, his intui-tion is less eureka and constructed more through tactical planning and data processing. Immediately, when the audience is introduced to him, he beats an older child at a flying-combat simulator, explaining that he did so, in an affectless tone, because the other child didn't use what was around him and "miscalculated [his] trajectory relative to the incoming asteroid."

Dehumanized from the beginning, then, Ender is the stereotypi-cally stoic solder that is constructed around his data-processing mental machinery via a series of simulating wargames. His education at Battle School only serves to further remove Ender from the "real" conse-quences of war by putting him and his fellow trainees through a series of zero-gravity battles against each other. While in the abstract these are intended to teach (and assess) strategy building and tactical execution, the physical arena and the combat itself are incredibly unlike the actual human-Formic combat situations. There is no physical violence beyond the ability to shoot a "freeze-ray" and incapacitate the opponents. This low-stakes, consequence-free arena teaches its inhabitants that war is, first and foremost, a game built on binary opponents (Ally-Enemy) and clear objectives (a teammate through the opposing gate). Any real violence in the movie takes place outside this space, and even after Ender fights one boy and kills another, he never faces the consequences of those actions beyond his own moral self-flagellation. This oversimplification of warfare, combined with the reduction of all stakes, gives each combatant a dangerously false view of the war they are being trained for: the ability to be "brought back to life" from their "death" in the battle arena, the absence of any blood or physical contact, even the win-lose structure of the simulations (with no middle ground as possible solution), trains the combatants to view warfare as logically simplistic and entirely disembodied and virtual.

The specific scene in which Ender, having been given control of Team Dragon in Battle School, is called to the simulator to take on two other teams that were already prepared showcases how the infrastructure around Ender and the other soldiers-in-training repeatedly aims to strip the "human" out of all the participants through the distanced combat simulations. Ender's solution to winning this seemingly impossible scenario is to surround one soldier with layers of additional soldiers; when the outer soldiers in the formation are sacrificed, they remain in place, frozen but "dead" by the game's rules. Ender effectively sacrifices everyone on his team in order to get one teammate through the opponents' gate and win. Van Creveld's fear of the "binary on-off logic" that rules a computer-structured warfare is at work here: since there are only two outcomes to the game (win or lose), Ender does whatever is necessary to win, even when it means letting his other fellow soldiers "die." If the Battle School exercises are intended to teach the combatants (and the machinic audience by extension) "leadership" and "cerebral control," this particular lesson seems to be about the need for a near-total sacrifice in order to achieve a given goal. Ender, acting within that binary framework, mechanically uses his fellow soldiers as "assets," or cannon fodder, treating them in the same way that the colonel and the rest of the adults treat Ender. In this way, he is demonstrating the essential skills Graff flags in him at the beginning of the movie, justifying Ender's hospitalization of another boy by explaining to Ender's mother, "It's not what he did. It's why." For Graff and the whole military machine, any means are justified so long as they achieve the desired end.

This is only further exemplified by the climax of the film and the specific giant simulator that Ender and his army are put within. Ender moves from the Battle School to what he thinks is the next step in his training at a forward base near the Formics' home world. As Ender leaves, he writes to his sister Valentine that "war seems inevitable." The conflict, from the beginning of the film, is presented in the same binary logic (enemy-ally; win-lose) as the Battle School war game and echoes this text's earlier discussion of *Edge of Tomorrow*'s global enemies, the Mimics (Chapter 2)[12]: the Formics are the clear enemy and must be eradicated, as emphasized by the human president's calls for a "total commitment to the destruction of the enemy" in a televised broadcast at the start of the film. The "total" there is complete, a "win" without any grey middle ground. This is then fought within the postcorporeal, "clean" combat of the simulator that Ender helms. Different from the AR technologies of the Iron Man suits or Jaegers,[13] the simulator in *Ender's Game* itself is really just a collection of chairs and screens. The ships are shown in high definition 3D models but are miniaturized; when the forces are shown on the screens themselves, they are reduced to the bits of data so feared by Coker. In fact, at that stage, it's hard to even tell the enemy ships from ally ships, as each combatant is flattened out into a near-unrecognizable abstraction (Image 5.4). Similar to *Eye in the Sky* and *Good Kill*, the actual "combat" is mostly Ender

**Image 5.4**　Ender commands his simulated army

yelling and people typing in response: there is no blood and very little in terms of explosions or manifestations of the violence being enacted.[14] This virtual distancing by the interfaces is doubled (tripled?) by the chain of command that holds it all together: Ender, as Mazer Rackham (Ben Kingsley) explains, gives commands to his soldiers (his friends from Dragon Team), who then relay those orders to their squadrons. Immediately, then, there are multiple layers of distance from any actual action as each decision passes through at least two people before it is carried out. The soldiers here are cubicle warriors, with the chasm of virtual space and interfaces abstracting the war and their own choices and responsibilities. The climax reveals that the simulator was in fact real, that Ender had been unknowingly commanding a fleet that led to the genocide of the Formics, and brings all the concerns to a head by paralleling Baudrillard's insistence that use of simulating technology conflates the simulation into war so that neither is recognizable (or "real"). Tying back to the discussion of nuclear weapons at the beginning of this chapter, the genocide of the Formics is undertaken with a WMD and his eradication of an entire species and decimation of a planet's landscapes and species recalls a number of other films from this text[15]: even if it is unwitting, he reaffirms human superiority over all other forms of life, undertaking the State War Machine's thinking that obliterating any and all other forms of life is justified when it arrives at the ends of the human species' survival. More than this, the strike is preemptive in that the Formics did not attack the humans, but rather, the human force is convinced they are about to be attacked; Graff justifies these human-centric expansionist actions as a war that is the battle to end all battles, clouding the genocide with the notion that a complete devastation of another species will bring humanity complete peace. In order for Ender to complete the literal "total destruction" of the Formics he has to employ the same lessons from Battle School about sacrifice, ultimately destroying a number of his own men in order to fire the Little Doctor at the Formics' home planet. For Ender, there is no barrier between real and fake war; it is the exact same, as each is simply ordering others to carry out tactics based off data until, as Ender says after destroying the Formics, it is "game over."

Yet, why Ender wasn't told it was a simulation speaks to the larger critique of the movie and Graff and the military machine as a whole. As repeatedly observed, Ender is systematically mechanized and dehumanized and as such becomes a machine capable, both tactically and morally (in echo of Coker), of actually carrying out the total destruction. Like WOPR and other machine-guided systems, Ender is able to actually think of and execute tactics, through the younger person's ability to take in and process extreme reams of data, which adults do not have; in this, he is a super-tool, an exaggerated extension of the military's human brain. After the battle, Graff compliments him by thanking him and then adding, "Brilliant. Absolutely brilliant. Thank God for you, son." Here, Ender is valued most for his intellectual capacities, his tactical abilities made possible by his increased mechanization.

But there is a moral element to it as well. Graff acknowledges that keeping Ender in what he thought was a simulator was the key to this, as he may have "refused to play" had he known it was no game. For Graff and the military, the binary nature of the combat was enough to justify the use of the Little Doctor; as Mazer Rackham explains, "It was them or us. There was no other way"; Graff also repeats, with increasing intensity, "We won," as a way of justifying the decision to keep Ender and his army shielded from the reality of his actions. Yet, as quoted in the introduction to this chapter, when De Landa states that machines are more "reliable" and "willing" to "unleash a third world war," he is, like Coker, questioning whether humans might offload the moral decisions of mass destruction into computerized systems. The entire film, Graff and the Total War Machine have groomed Ender to be the most important part of that State War Machine and therefore to be the one who actually pulls the trigger on the genocide; as Graff explains, "You destroyed them. For all of us." The "for all of us" carries with it an acknowledgement that they themselves were unable to bear the burden of the decision and actual act of genocide and therefore they externalized it further and further down the command chain into the military War Machine, into the mechanized Ender, who becomes even more virtualized by the immersion into the simulator software. The problematic humanism at the center of such an act rejects a critical posthumanism and reduces every component within the State and Total War Machines, including the "enemies" and the species and landscapes within those enemies' territories. While the film does attempt to critique the actions that took place a result of this whole-scale destruction, ultimately, no one within the film is punished and humans continue to live, vindicated by their actions; the transhuman "simulator"/WMD that Ender fires extends his (and his species') power as a tool of total annihilation and thereby underlines a human exceptionalism that places any technology (or other biological or technological entity) as a secondary slave to that human master.

## CONCLUSION: SIMULATIONS AND CIVILIAN-LED CYBERWARFARE

Virilio reframes McLuhan's "global village" in military terms when he explains that

> geographical space has been shrinking with every advance in speed, and strategic location has lost importance as ballistic systems have become more widespread and sophisticated. This technological development has carried us into a realm of factitious topology in which all the surfaces of the globe are directly present to one another. (*War and Cinema* 59)

In terms of drone warfare, *Eye in the Sky* and *Good Kill* critique the militarization of these "factitious" topologies, in that the various State War Machines present in the films use their Internet-enabled networks to extend their military might too far in too cowardly and asymmetrical a fashion and, from this, are engaged in a warfare that is too virtual and distant from the "human" ethics and consequences found in more "traditional" warfare. While this is perhaps true, the more troubling issue may be that in reality, instead of killing all enemy combatants (ISIS and al-Qaeda, for example), the American military's use of drones, according to Lieutenant Colonel Douglas A. Pryer, "[continues] to fuel the anger that provides a seemingly endless supply of recruits and money to anti-American terrorist groups. As the *New York Times* reported, connecting an earlier symbol of moral failure in America's 'war on terror' with the one that persists today: 'Drones have replaced Guantanamo as the recruiting tool of choice for militants'" (17). Drone warfare, powered by Internet-enabled simulations and wargames, provides little opportunity for enemies to surrender and, as such, often appear similar to a "summary execution" (Pryer 19); moreover, the gaping technological divide between those that have extremely high-end technologies (the American State War Machine) in combat with those who have very little makes the one-sided battles seem unfair. For the machinic audience of the films discussed in this chapter (in particular *Eye in the Sky* and *Good Kill*), this sentiment is upheld with an almost nostalgic yearning for the ethics of a "human" and corporeal combat.

In explaining the various State War Machines' shifts toward distanced and virtual warfare, Coker links the drone pilots to government-led hackers engaged in cybermilitary roles, seeing both types of "soldiers" as similarly virtual long distance attackers (120). In reaction to observations like Pryer's, scholars such as Klaus-Gerd Giesen have noted that in the face of such asymmetric warfare, smaller countries' and forces' best weapons might be taking advantage of the very Internet-enabled networks that superpower nations use to run their Total War Machines and launch cyberattacks against those virtual spaces and infrastructures (66). This, of course, doesn't just mean "rogue" hackers or cyber-armies attacking infrastructure and purposely causing one of the aforementioned cyber-Chernobyls that Virilio fears; cyberwarfare also includes the production and distribution of propaganda, espionage, the theft of intellectual property, etc. In Chapter 6 unpacks the cinematic virtual battlefields that emerge within simulacra of cyberwarfare and how the lines between military and civilian spaces and personnel blur further than those of the technician solder: in short, the construction of the hacker-soldier has made drastic shifts in the types of war films that are made and celebrated. In the introduction to this text, Neale flagged a move from the combat nature of the war film to one that looks closer to the espionage and advanced weaponry that marks a political thriller. This sort of paranoiac warfare co-opts the civilian and civilian cyber-spaces and is indicative of the Total War Machine's penetration into all aspects of a contemporary society.

It is interesting to end this chapter thinking about a more "faithful" version of *Ender's Game* in which the movie version recreated some of the subplots of the book version. In Card's novel, Ender's sociopathic brother, Peter, and sister Valentine use a global Internet-like technology ("the nets") to post stylized political speeches. While Ender is away at Battle School, they craft influential political messages online, to the point where they both begin to build up followings of their own, with Peter publishing under "Locke" and Valentine posting opposing points of view under the avatar "Demosthenes." Eventually, the two become incredibly powerful, with each of Ender's siblings' propaganda sparring back and forth until Peter wins out and becomes Earth's ruler, its Hegemon. All the while, Graff and the military know the "true" identities of Locke and Demosthenes but manipulate them, and by extension Earth's citizens, toward a human exceptionalism that results in the Ender-led genocide and the expansion of the human race and subsequent colonization of the galaxy. While the movie strips the entirety of this subplot out, the book acknowledges how powerful the manipulation of civilian information and networks can be toward a military agenda. The films of Chapter 6 recognize the power of the civilian Internet, while also upholding the sorts of networked information-based combat that takes place within a cyberwarfare as a function of the unavoidable and omniscient State War Machine. The data, wargames and military-simulating technologies of this chapter give way to the political thriller's boardrooms and spy equipment, effectively swallowing the civilian into the Total War Machine, entangling them with every cable that constructs the machinic audience's Internet.

## NOTES

1. This need to fight a war without actually fighting a war was long based in "manoeuvres" of actual physical troops; the practice began much earlier but van Creveld states that "eighteenth-century commanders with their standing armies did hold large scale exercises, often on an annual basis" that would "last as long as a couple of weeks" and in which "thousands and even tens of thousands of troops, carrying full pack and equipped for war, took to the field and were put through their paces" (190).
2. Game theory's rise is often attributed to John von Neumann and Oskar Morgenstern's *Theory of Games and Economic Behavior* (1944) and later papers of John Nash. For proof of the intertwining between the military and game theory, Lambertini quotes Isaacs (1965): "Then under the auspices of the U.S. Air Force, RAND was concerned largely with military problems and, to us there, this syllogism seemed incontrovertible:
   a. Game theory is the analysis of conflict.
   b. Conflict is the means of warfare planning.
   c. Therefore game theory is the means of warfare planning."
   From *Game Theory in the Social Sciences: A Reader-Friendly Guide.* Routledge, 2011, 7.
3. In critique, Suid argues that "*WarGames* took the image of the Air Force in Hollywood movies to its actual nadir. Aside from the total implausibility of the story itself, the film's representations of Air Force men and procedures bore virtually no resemblance to the manner in which the service carried out its mission of protecting the nation from nuclear attack" (446). In particular, Suid criticizes the fact that it is Lightman, with the help of Faulken, that is eventually able to convince the military to stand down and not launch and/or counterstrike, and let the simulation run its course; in reality, he contends, a teenager would obviously have absolutely zero say in such an apocalyptic military scenario (450). In actuality,

"NORAD had, in fact, experienced false alarms over the years. But the men operating the system had caught and solved the problems in minutes, not hours" (450).

4. Like *WarGames*, the malfunction in *Stealth* finds echoes in reality: in 2010 "US Navy operators on the ground control lost contact with [an unmanned] Fire Scout helicopter … [and the helicopter], instead of following its programmed flight patterns, steered a course for the capital" (Coker, Christopher. *Warrior Geeks: How 21st-Century Technology Is Changing the Way We Fight and Think about War*. Oxford University Press, 2013, 139).

5. While Lt. Kara Wade (Jessica Biel) shows herself more than capable throughout the film, the choice to specifically gender EDI, and to then gender it male, fits in line with the arguments being made about the hard body's masculinist ethics that run throughout this text. The protagonists of nearly all the war movies discussed throughout the book are male, and most often white male (including *Stealth*'s Lt. Ben Gannon); while there are discussions of female soldiers in Chapter 2 and in this chapter, most often women are restricted to supporting the male soldiers of the film (as wives, girlfriends, sometimes colleagues). Therefore, gendering EDI male fits this pattern. In terms of gendering AI, recent discussions around digital assistants tend to argue that AI assistants (Siri, Cortana, Amy) are problematically gendered female because that meshes with the stereotype of women being subservient (Lafrance, Andrienne. "Why Do So Many Digital Assistants Have Feminine Names?" *The Atlantic*. March 30, 2016. Accessed March 28, 2017. https://www.theatlantic.com/technology/archive/2016/03/why-do-so-many-digital-assistants-have-feminine-names/475884/); therefore, because EDI is an active soldier, he must be gendered male. While further discussion is most definitely warranted, it is beyond the scope of this text. Such work could, however, be further supplemented by Alison Adam's work in "Constructions of Gender in the History of Artificial Intelligence" (*IEEE Annals of the History of Computing* (1996), 18 (3), 47–53, doi:10.1109/MAHC.1996.511944) and her book *Artificial Knowing: Gender and the Thinking Machine* (Florence, US: Routledge, 1998), Donna Haraway's and Rosi Bradotti's theorizing on critical posthumanism, as well as the survey work done in Francesca Ferrando's "Is the Post-Human a Post-Woman? Cyborgs, Robots, Artificial Intelligence and the Futures of Gender: A Case Study." (*European Journal of Futures Research* (2014), 2 (1), 1–17).

6. The threat of terrorism as a way of justifying an evolved version of the hard technological body is a continuing theme through this text. In particular, throughout Chapter 3, the Iron Man suits, more specifically

Iron Patriot/War Machine, are a reaction to the Internet's "globalizing" of the world that reduces the borders of countries, which, in turn, makes unclear who is an enemy and who is an ally. Additionally, at the end of this chapter and into Chapter 6, this text discusses the nature of a contemporary asymmetrical warfare in which the United States is exponentially more technologically powerful. This extreme advantage makes the American State War Machine seem like they are not "fighting fair" and, with that sentiment, the justification for using drone strikes and other technologically advanced tactics and weapons does not carry the "noble" and "human" characteristics that a "justified" war might. Chapter 2 of this text discussed how the binary enemy-ally setup in *Elysium* and *Edge of Tomorrow* was a reaction to this "murkiness" around terrorism and the modern State War Machine, with both films nostalgically clarifying the enemy into an obvious opposite. Further, consistently throughout the films of this text, in order to rationalize the State War Machine's extreme force, the enemy of "terrorism" is created; because terrorism lurks in every space and can mean potential violence at any time, and because terrorists don't "fight fair" when they use human shields and behead civilians in barbaric attacks, the asymmetrical tactics of the modern technologically advanced State War Machine are needed, otherwise the terrorist would win. Following this logic, the terrorist enemy is, as Gabriel Shear states in *Swordfish* (Chapter 6), "Anyone who impinges on America's freedom." Within the American State War Machine, Shear argues, America is therefore always at war, potentially with anyone and everyone.

7. Mead flags the 1988 FOG-M as one of the earliest forms of military drones: "It had a TV camera in the front and a thirty kilometer fibre-optic cable spilling out the back. A soldier watching a video screen would guide the missile with a joystick and crash it into the intended target" (*War Play: Video Games and the Future of Armed Conflict*. Eamon Dolan/Houghton Mifflin Harcourt, 2013, 27).

8. John Kim ("The Origin of the See-through Graphical Interface: World War II Aircraft Gunsights and the Status of the Material in Early Computer Interface Design." *Convergence* (2015), 21 (2)) sees the origins of the military see-through Augmented Reality interface in WWII aircraft gunsights (214). While there is a compelling argument to be made that cinematic drone footage is deliberately set up to visually resemble such an interface so that the drone pilot can be attached to some of the heroics of that more "traditional" pilot, the telepresence of the drone pilot makes the rhetorical effect of footage entirely different. In order to use those WWII gunsights, the pilot, and his liberal human mind, needed to be present in his plane in order to fire the weapon and, as such, his

exposure to danger and bodily harm makes him rhetorically effective and his actions justified. Similarly, the information interfaces in *Gamer*, the *Iron Man* films and *Pacific Rim* all require a human liberal mind in the middle that is also in danger and bodily harm. The telepresent drone pilot, in contrast, sits continents away, and, in many of the films discussed in this text, his/her rationality and liberal mind is reduced to one small link taking orders from a military chain of command.

9. *Eye in the Sky*'s opening similarly argues when it shows Colonel Katherine Powell rising from her bed in her spacious house and walking down the hall to her workspace in her home office, which is a room set up just as one would set up a situation room in a military complex. This scene showcases the complete blending of civilian life and space with military space that comes with drone warfare, effectively arguing that there is no separation between the two.

10. *Body of Lies, Syriana* and *Zero Dark Thirty* all include CIA usage of drone strikes and a large amount of the analysis of this chapter could be applied effectively to those films. However, in the interest of space and scope, this chapter focuses on *Eye in the Sky* and *Good Kill* because of the films' more direct involvement the U.S. Air Force drone pilots and the proximity of the films to the combat aspects, as opposed to the intelligence components, of the State War Machine.

11. The upper levels of the chain of command, government officials, and diplomats are critiqued as too distant and out of touch throughout the film: as an example, throughout the film, between the tense military action, Benson is seen buying children's gifts and ordering other soldiers to organize his civilian life; at the end of the film, after all the violence, he is given back the gift and goes on with his day.

12. In this way, Ender is similar to the hard technological bodies of *Pacific Rim* and *Edge of Tomorrow* in that his enemies are enemies of all humans and that all of humanity must unify into a Total War Machine in order to fight this alien force. As discussed in Chapter 2, this bonding together could be viewed a potential celebration of the globalization that comes with a world-wide Internet network and the machinic audience's expectations that their heroes be globalized heroes. However, as argued in note 6 of this chapter, we might also see this as a nostalgic harkening back to the "clarity" of "traditional" warfare, pre–War on Terror, wherein there were immediately evident markers of ally-enemy.

13. The AR in *Ender's Game* is different from the AR technologies of the Iron Man suits or Jaegers, as Ender uses his interface not to immediately control the materiel and personnel that are on his screen, as the users of the Iron Man suits or Jaegers do, but rather to "give commands" to fleets and individuals who then carry out, in their own individual human ways,

those orders to the best of their abilities. His virtuous distancing via this technology operates similarly to the drone pilot discussed earlier in the chapter in that Ender is telepresent and does not receive the rhetorical weight of a liberal human mind in peril.

14. This cinematic portrayal of "combat-less combat" in cyberwarfare is analyzed further via the "actions" of the hackers discussed in Chapter 6.

15. In complete rejection of a critical posthumanism, as in *Pacific Rim* (Chapter 3) and *The Core* (Chapter 6), the military force in *Ender's Game* uses a WMD in service of humanity's survival with little thought to the environments or species that the weapons were deployed against. The Little Doctor echoes the use of nuclear weapons in the other films, as it too is distanced, non-intimate and indiscriminate in its killing. We might then see Ender (as well as the heroes of *Pacific Rim* and *The Core*) as an argument for Pryer's initial "ethical advantages" for outsourcing the morality of actions to machines: "For one, armed drones and other robots are incapable of running concentration camps and committing rape and other crimes that still require human troops on the ground. Indeed, removing combat operators from the stress of life-threatening danger reduces their potential to commit those crimes that they could still conceivably commit via drones...This means that soldiers under extreme physical duress can commit crimes that they would normally be unable to commit" ("The Rise of the Machines: Why Increasingly 'Perfect' Weapons Help Perpetuate our Wars and Endanger our Nation." *Military Review* (2013), 93 (2), 15).

# CHAPTER 6

# The Civilian Soldiers of Cyberwarfare

## INTRODUCTION: MILITARY AND CIVILIAN CYBERWARFARE AND HACKING

Contemporary definitions of "cyberwarfare" are in great flux among scholars and the American military, partly because the term is so new.[1] Clarke and Knake define it as "actions by a nation-state to penetrate another nation's computers or networks for the purpose of damage or disruption" (6). Their examples include Israeli hacking of Syrian radar systems (7) and the American hack of Iraqi radar bases during the first Gulf War (9), as well as the (likely Russian) DDOS (Distributed Denial of Service) attacks of Estonian servers in 2007 and Georgia in 2008, which effectively crippled the Internet infrastructure of the nations (13; 15). Arno R. Lodder and Lianne J.M. Boer expand on Clarke and Knake's definition by stating cyberwarfare is

> *an attack, originating from abroad, employing virtual means, purporting to damage or disrupt a state's physical or digital infrastructure.* This defini-tion contains the following elements: (1) hostile intent; (2) to damage or disrupt; (3) an opponent's infrastructure; (4) through non-physical means, and (5) involving at least one state. (author's italics 3)

While the Network-Centric Warfare defined in the introduction to this text focused on the principles of a networked information system (an Internet) as a means of communicating and organizing a State War

© The Author(s) 2017
A. Tucker, *Virtual Weaponry*,
DOI 10.1007/978-3-319-60198-4_6

Machine, cyberwarfare is best seen as acts of aggression against enemies by means of a networked information system (an Internet). In contrast to the more "traditional" modes of warfare that have been discussed in this text that use immediately visible hardware (like an exo-suit) and recognizable weapons (a gun), cyberwarfare's shift to "virtual means" targeting "physical or digital infrastructure" complicates the ideas of warfare and, as discussed later in this chapter, the figure of the soldier and the genre of the war film as a whole. Mead argues that "[cyberwar-fare] may have a more pervasive and debilitating effect on countries at conflict than real-world combat" because, quoting Singer, its goal "is not to blow up the enemy tank, but jam it, co-opt it, persuade it" (Mead 166). Similarly, the notion of "attack" from the prior definitions is troubling, as the nature of this type of war waging makes it extremely amorphous and ubiquitous. Klaus-Gerd Giesen states that the notion of "armed aggression" as it applies to cyberspace makes it difficult to pin down what exactly is a "weapon," and when a cyberweapon was used (or installed), and that "the meaning of what can legitimately be considered as a weapon must evolve" (66). From this, Tsirigotis points out that "'cyber' is not just a prefix indicating a new technological war paradigm. It expresses the mate-rialization of physical world through an immaterial way of life and, as far as war is concerned, through an immaterial way for succumbing the adversar-ies" (391). A more "familiar" warfare is in fact present in the "paradigm" of cyberwarfare, in particular in the notion of an "endless" inevitable state of war and the integration of civilians and their resources and infrastruc-tures, "material" and "immaterial," into the Total War Machine.

The most obvious contemporary site of this ongoing and borderless state of war is the contemporary overlap between the War on Terror and the civilian Internet. As touched on in earlier chapters, the technol-ogy of the Internet has created a globalized community while it has also strengthened a globalized enemy of America, often housed under the shifting amorphous umbrella of "terrorism." Writing post-9/11, Žižek argues that the War on Terror is endless in nature: "the first codename for the US operation against terrorists, 'Infinite Justice'" is important because it argues that

> the Americans have the right ruthlessly to destroy not only all terrorists but also all who gave them material, moral, ideological, etc., support—and this process will be, by definition, endless … there will always be another terrorist threat. (71)

to underline this, he refers to former Vice President Dick Cheney's assertion that "the 'war on terrorism' will probably never end, at least not in our lifetimes" (71). The rising use and normalization of cyberwarfare, post-9/11, parallels this: Klaus-Gerd Giesen adds that "cyberwars tend not to stop, i.e. to continue almost endlessly, interspersed with more or less long intermissions" (67). Like the War on Terror, the decentralized nature and constant expansion of the Internet as a technology makes it so that cyberwarfare is composed of mysterious and omnipresent weapons that are then a component of a set of tactics that are impossible to contain or halt. Part of this endless state of war, a mindset that is a crucial driving force of the Total War Machine, is that the Internet is deeply woven into both civilian and military infrastructures, and, because of this, cyberattacks are not limited to military assets.

Cyberwarfare brings to the forefront the notion that digital information and the production, consumption, storage, etc. thereof are as crucial a resource for military and civilian infrastructure as ever. While the digital computer has long been an important component of the modern State War Machine,[2] the ability to connect computers into a network has greatly expanded the might of American military. However, it is useful to remember that while the US Department of Defense funded and created the first Internet (van Creveld *War and Technology* 239), it is its contemporary massive civilian user base that sustains and expands the Internet. However, since civilian targets are often much less fortified, cyberwarfare often moves military actions sharply into civilian realms. The Internet, as a potential cyberwarfare battlefield, "is denominated by computer algorithms and codes. The weapons [are] built from binary '1's and '0's, bits and bytes that allow a variety of actors—state and nonstate—to attack computer systems on which we increasingly rely" (Coker 113). With this, the hijacked civilian computer becomes the main weapon in Botnet DDOS attacks and any example of "cyberspace," shopping for airline tickets or using Facebook or civilian corporate sites and databases, for example (Coker 113), are potential places of militarized conflict and control, especially in 2017.[3] This blurring of civilian and military in digitally networked spaces is further demonstrated by, again, the slippery definition of cyberwarfare. Lodder and Boer make the point that the term "cyberwarfare" along with "'cyberwar,' 'information operations,' and 'computer network attacks' are used interchangeably" (2). Clarke and Knake point out that some in the military "did not fully understand what cyber war meant and thought of it as 'info ops,' part of psychological warfare, or 'psyops' (using propaganda to influence the outcome of wars)" (35); Der Derian in *Virtuous War* also adds that the terms "infowar" (118) and "netwar" (163) were often used interchangeably with cyberwar. However, it is true that since its inclusion in the American State War Machine cyberwarfare has been of particular interest to its intelligence communities, like the CIA and NSA, "as a bonanza for electronic espionage" (35).

This "bonanza" begins to manifest in post-Vietnam war films that show computer and Internet usage (like *WarGames* and *Sneakers*, discussed later in this chapter), but it explodes once the Internet moves into being a popular technology in the mid-1990s. Within the genre of the war film, as mentioned in the introduction to this text, Neale points out that during the turn of the millennium in particular, he noticed the trend of post–Gulf War war films, such as *Enemy of the State* (Dir. Tony Scott 1998) and *Swordfish* (Dir. Dominic Sena 2001), being largely based around espionage and surveillance and drawing upon conventions traditionally seen in the thriller (126). Post-9/11, the move to include cyberwarfare has blended the war film with that of the political thriller, moving a portion of the war film genre away from the traditional depictions of combat and direct military actions to movies based upon the control and circulation of information, paranoia and conspiracy. Žižek argues that the "paranoiac perspective" that emerged post-9/11 expands the use of digitalizing technologies that, in turn, generate an extreme familiarity with virtualworlds that then creates "the awareness that we live in an insulated artificial universe which generates the notion that some ominous agent is threatening us all the time with total destruction" (41). With this "we are entering into a new era of paranoiac warfare in which the greatest task will be to identify the enemy and his weapons ... all this forming an ideal breeding-ground for conspiracy theorists and generalized social paranoia" (46). This leads to "war deprived of its substance—a virtual war fought behind computer screens, a war experienced by its participants as a video game, a war with no casualties (on our side at least)" (46). While Chapter 4 takes apart the "video-game" notion of war waging and Chapter 5 began to complicate the "war fought behind computer screens" in its analysis of cinematic forms of war simulations and drone strikes, the films of this chapter, and their edging toward the political thriller genre, are driven by the fact that, as Žižek argues, "[ordinary citizens] are totally dependent on the authorities for information about what is going on: we see and hear nothing; all we know comes from the official media" (46–47). In some senses, the movies of this chapter resemble the "naval film" elements of *Eye in the Sky* and *Good Kill* in their shared focus on civilian life and bureaucratic procedures (Chapter 5). Yet movies like *Blackhat*, *The Fifth Estate* and *Snowden* are much more interested in the notion of surveillance than military actions; from this, the movies center on the tensions that arise from digital information that straddles the lines of private and public existence, with secrets then becoming key to the plots and arguments that the movies are making.

The shift of war films toward the political thriller is important to note. As Castrillo and Echart argue, "The political thriller in Hollywood appears as an important cultural artifact, displaying a close connection between its narratives and the current events at any given point in the history of the United States" (109); the authors continue, arguing that "very much like war films, political thrillers tend to avoid the construction of dystopian or fantasy story worlds and instead take as a starting point for their narratives certain historical events that have left a significant imprint in the history of the U.S." (119). The intersection between the two genres in the aforementioned movies is important within the paranoiac warfare that constructs their plots: the leaning toward the political thriller highlights recognizable environments containing "a world gone awry, taken over by the modern, senseless chaos of a life without meaning and a social community without reliable moral standards. Such an off-balance, ambiguous state forcefully engenders, in both characters and audiences alike, an inescapable feeling of vulnerability" (112). What makes war films that incorporate elements of the political thriller so resonant in 2017 is that the cinematic worlds that are "threatening to collapse into chaos [remain], however, within the boundaries of the daily, ordinary, urban reality. The thriller is a genre grounded in our shared perception of a realistic setting" (112). For *Snowden* and *The Fifth Estate*, films that blend in elements of the biopic, their relationship to "actual events" double this effect: the events of the film take place in the exact same narrative world as the movie-watching audience. By moving from the "naval film" into dramatic "realism," such war films tunnel further into civilian life and reinforce the Total War Machine: "ordinary citizens" and their "daily, ordinary, urban reality" are constantly on the battlefield, potentially under attack by an amorphous and invisible enemy, an "ominous agent," with their Internet-enabled technologies the vulnerable points of surveillance.

As opposed to "traditional" warfare and soldier-to-soldier combat, paranoiac cyberwarfare often involves civilian "soldiers" and the targets are also often civilian rather than military. This makes sense when we consider that, as Lodder and Boer state, in reaction to the previous definitions of cyberwarfare, "[those definitions contain] one major flaw in that [they require] a cyberattack to be attributable to a state—which is seldom the case. Cyberattacks are difficult to trace, and even if governments or three computer scientists succeed in doing so, it often proves hard to attribute the actions of those responsible for the attack to a specific state" (2). Der Derian calls these non-state enemies "faces without states" (*Virtuous War* 102), and they are often civilians, and because they are often civilians, they are not bound by the larger infrastructures of a military, and are therefore able to be more nimble and immediately aggressive. In reaction, because of this shifting between military and civilian realms and personnel, Coker argues that "[in] cyberspace the [American] military may come to rely more and more on civilian skills" (116). In particular, Mead contends that "[the] Pentagon could more sensibly follow the example of Russian and China and harness the power of independent hackers, whose expertise often far outshines that of government employees" (167). Therefore, "independent hackers," at the center of both the history of cyberwarfare and civilian computer use, are uniquely able to move between both military and civilian worlds effectively.

Within the world of American cinema, there are already models for the hacker-soldier[4]: In films like *Iron Man 3, The Core* and *Swordfish* (to name only a few), the figure of the hacker is repurposed from his/ her civilian life into the Total War Machine, often as too-simple assemblages, like a literal phylum of Iron Man suits or unthinking human-military weapons, which resist a critical posthumanism. While the romantic notion of the hacker has roots in a 1980s ethos of technological exploration and techno-utopia, the repurposed military hacker, with no military training, seamlessly folds into the State and Total War Machines. This shift reflects one of the key aspects of an Internet-enabled State War Machine that is shifted toward an increasingly globalized enemy, wherein information and data of citizens and military, and the protection/privatization thereof, are of prime importance to warfare infrastructure and effectiveness. In contrast, within *Blackhat, Snowden* and *The Fifth Estate*, the figures of the hacker and the whistleblower clearly resist their military masters and, with this resistance, a "new" form of heroic techno-soldier emerges. As these war films move closer to the political thriller genre, the hacker and whistleblower are celebrated as figures capable of slicing through misinformation, exposing harmful secrets, and providing the "ordinary citizen" with "truthful" information outside of "official media."

With the figure of the hacker broadly outlined, the movies can be seen as documents that are part of the recent trend of war films wherein, Gooch argues, "surveillance combines the explicit threat of violence with an implicit reorganization of power and knowledge through the gaze," adding that "this cycle's expansive and explicit representation of surveillance and its concomitant fantasies of disciplinary power also point to anxieties about the effectiveness of this power and its need for ever-more-fine-grained mechanisms of social control" (156). From this vantage, the aforementioned cinematic hacker-soldiers are in direct reaction to Deleuze's notion of a "society of control," which he outlines in "Postscript on the Societies of Control" (1992). Beginning by summarizing Foucault's understanding of "*disciplinary societies*," in which "the individual never ceases passing from one closed environment to another, each having its own laws" (author's italics 3), he states that this prior construction of society has been replaced by one marked most clearly by the idea of control. A society of control is built around a language which is "*numerical*" and where "controls are a *modulation*, like a self-deforming cast that will continually change from one moment to the other, or like a sieve whose mesh will transmute from point to point" (author's italics 4). The use of the word "mesh" echoes the digital networks of the Internet and its numerical structure, pointing toward the digitizing of humans into informational forms, what he calls codes or passwords (5). Like the State War Machine and cyberwarfare, "in societies of control, one is never finished with anything," and he speaks specifically to "the armed services" as being "metastable states coexisting in one and same modulation, like a universal system of deformation" (5). Further, "the numerical language of control is made up of codes that mark access to information and reject it" and this society creates "*dividuals*," which are "masses, samples, data, markets, or '*banks*'" (author's italics 5). In particular, "the societies of control operate with ... computers, whose passive danger is jamming and whose active one is piracy and the introduction of viruses," which are always tethered together in a "continuous network" (6). Linking back to the political thriller's focus on surveillance and paranoia, Kristy Best explains then that within control societies "information is ritually and relentlessly extracted from those who wish to participate in almost any form of citizenship or consumption" (8); this extraction is "dispersed, slippery and leak into everyday practice" (5), which leads to the fact that "facilities for information collation and tracking provided by digital technology amplify state and corporate capabilities for surveillance and control, which are particularly problematic for the maintenance of democracy, civil liberties and citizenship capabilities" (6). This happens for Deleuze, as Best explains, in the third stage of the control society, where "the institutional sites that held this disciplinary gaze have been dissolved, leading to an even more dispersed form of surveillance. ... The sites dissolve further, according to Deleuze, to include whole populations, who become even more enthusiastically involved in their own self-discipline" (9).

Gooch, also referencing Deleuze, argues that "surveillance does not simply coincide with sight's increasing centrality in postmodern warfare; it is also part of this larger skein of social controls" (156). It is from within this paranoiac environment of constant surveillance that the techno-soldier, the hacker and/or whistleblower, emerges as a heroic liberal figure; s/he is no longer the "dividual" of a military or corporate system, but instead asserts his/her "nonstate" power and humanity by harnessing the digital technologies, and the numerical language inherent within, redirecting it back, most often, at the military system itself. Unlike the drone pilot, who is maligned for the remote, distant nature of his objectified weaponry,[5] the hacker-soldier revels in the hidden and remote ways of accessing and redistributing information; because the information is virtual, and not human (biological), the weaponized tactics that the hacker/whistleblower uses in combination with a computer do not come across as cowardly but rather as masterfully genius and borderline magical.

However, like the previous depictions of cinematic hackers,[6] their moral systems look a lot like the previously discussed hard body's: there is a consistent rejection of ineffectual military infrastructures and an upholding of individual and liberal ethics. This echoes the genre conventions of the political thriller, as the hacker of the war film is constructed similarly:

> At the heart ... lies a conflict that confronts an individual with the system, the ordinary citizen against the institutions, the human being against the inhumanity of political and/or corporate power. Governments and companies are presented as forces bent on protecting their interests at any cost, to the extent of eliminating any opposition, even when such policy involves murder. (Castrillo and Echart 120)

When considering paranoiac cyberwarfare, non-state hacker whistleblowers are heroic actors protecting and empowering the civilian population; the "ordinary citizen" hacker's positive use of, and often exposure of the military use of, digital information makes them, like the hard technological body, a sole combatant against larger, seemingly unbeatable systems.

Like the problematic hard technological body, however, the hacker is much like the "hero of the political thriller" in that he "nearly always fits the prototype of the male, white American" (115) and the reinforcing of traditional white masculinity and patriarchy do little to move the figure toward a critical posthumanism that recognizes more of a globalized society. Rosewarne expands further by arguing that "while the idea of hacking as something *men* do is a common portrayal, a more interesting aspect to this is hacking as *masculine*: that it isn't only conducted by men but that the practice actually shares attributes most commonly associated with *maleness*"; she ties this more precisely to a "frontier masculinity" wherein the hacker, specifically Julian Assange (Benedict Cumberbatch) in *The Fifth Estate*, is portrayed as the cowboy of the virtual Wild West that is "defined by individualism" and "the male interest in power" (author's italics 132–134). While physically "softer" than the traditional hard body soldier, the hacker-soldier still reinforces problematic ideals of violent masculinity. This is further compounded when this masculinity is combined with Internet-enabled technologies: much like Deleuze outlines, because the Internet-enabled computer technologies of the films are treated as passive at best, predatory at worst, the networked nature of a civilian user is treated like a weakness and point of vulnerability; it is their deep symbiotic relationship that makes them lesser as the computer technologies are viewed as inherently corrosive and vulnerable, as viral carriers of infection. However, when the technologies are portrayed positively in the hands of the hacker-soldier, they are problematically treated as enslaved property, weapons or tools, the code the bullets and the punch of the keyboard the pulling of the trigger. In opposition to a critical posthumanism, the technological co-species in the films, when not maligned as the vulnerable and diseased portions of the biological-technological user assemblage, are weaponized in total service of a human master. While the interfaces that the hacker-soldiers of the films utilize are realistic, and the films bear little of the "special effects" that have traditionally marked Internet use,[7] their masterful use by the biological portion of the soldier-assemblage reinforces human superiority and, unlike the exoskeletons or Iron Man suits discussed in earlier chapters, the biological soldier's rational mind and skills are the spectacular part of the State War Machine.

Using the weapons and tactics of cyberwarfare, Nick Hathaway (Chris Hemsworth) in *Blackhat*, Edward Snowden (Joseph Gordon-Levitt) in *Snowden* and Julian Assange in *The Fifth Estate* all show themselves to be the "ordinary citizen" outside of the corrupt corporate and military infrastructures. Much like the hard technological bodies of Cage and Max discussed in Chapter 2, they all provide humanistically ethical resistance to the surveillance intrinsic to the control society and the conspiracies of power that emerge from control of digital information. The soldier-hacker's resistance upholds the values of "democracy, civil liberties and citizenship capabilities" and is anchored in the civilian liberal individual at the center of the technological-biological assemblage of the computer user.

## EARLY CINEMATIC CIVILIAN-MILITARY HACKERS

The initial attitudes toward hackers, especially in their relation to cyberwarfare, can be explained further by van Creveld:

> Since 1945, the term 'war' itself has acquired an unsavory connotation. Following the rules that govern the usage of all dirty words, it has tended to be taken out of the vocabulary and to give way to euphemisms. ... Thus, changing the name of the thing represented one way by which military affairs could be made palatable to contemporary tastes. (*Technology and War* 292)

In particular, he argues there is an attempt to "turn weapons into toys" and that "the word 'weapons' itself, incidentally, is increasingly being replaced by the term 'systems' which are 'optimized' for this mission or that" (292). Weapons are then promoted in publications (and movies) "for boys of all ages" and "are presented much like stereo sets and lawn mowers and motorcycles. Like any other gadget, weapons are considered to derive their fascination from the sheer engineering skill that went into them, and of course from the power ('capabilities') which result from this skill" (292). Residual effects of this are certainly present in the spectacular depictions of the gadget-hardware of the previously discussed EDI in *Stealth*, the exosuits in *Edge of Tomorrow* and *Elysium*, and the Iron Man suits: the machinic audience's joy in watching those films is, at the very least, tethered to the appreciation of those high-tech weapons and the craftsmanship ("engineering") that went into their construction. The early figure of the hacker was often constructed using the same language to describe their computer use as van Creveld uses to explain the popular "marketing" of technological weapons. Multiple histories of hackers, like *Hackers: Heroes of the Revolution* (Levy 1984), *The Hacker Crackdown* (Sterling 1992) and the more recent *Exploding the Phone* (Lapsley 2013), stress the narrative of the hacker as explorer and prankster, as an ethical exploiter of machines and machine systems, not of human beings. The main weapon of the phone phreaks, hackers of the telephone system, was a children's toy, a Captain Crunch whistle that could be acquired from a cereal box; when blown into a phone receiver, its specific frequency signaled to the computer routing the phone call that the call was to be forwarded without any charges. Likewise, the computers that early hackers used were "gadgets" and their use of computers was often dismissed as immature hijinks. There are multiple examples of this in Hollywood cinema pre-Y2K,[8] but in focusing on war films, the hacker-soldier is most clearly defined by the rascals of *Sneakers* (Dir. Phil Alden Robinson 1992), the juvenile David Lightman in *WarGames* and Rat in *The Core* (Dir. Jon Amiel 2003).

As discussed at the end of Chapter 4, past depictions of "hackers" using the Internet have relied on cartoonish graphics and filmic effects because "programmers tapping on keyboards or staring at screens of code are invariably boring displays" (Rosewarne 119). Yet in all three movies discussed in this section, there is little of the visual effects surrounding computer use and the Internet that populate other films; additionally, the interfaces that the hackers use look relatively similar to what an Internet user of that time period would have used. As such, with very few exceptions, the viewer doesn't "enter" the computer as they do in *The Lawnmower Man*, or zoom along the cables as if they are a piece of data, both of which are common visual tropes in movies involving the Internet in the 1990s.[9] Instead, the user, like Rat, is shown typing at a screen and the viewer sees the screen over that character's shoulder, "uses" the Internet as the character of the movie uses it (Image 6.1). Paralleling the rise in home computers in the decades leading up to Y2K, the networked computer and the Internet are integrated into the Total War Machine of these films as an everyday device. Despite being weaponized, it is treated much like a stereo or a TV might be in other "real-world" genres like dramas, comedies, etc. Within the paranoiac

**Image 6.1**   Rat hacks the Internet in *The Core*

political thriller/war film, there is very little (if any) of the double frame that takes place in the movies discussed in the first four chapters of this text.[10] In addition, unlike the slow motion surrounding the exosuits of *Elysium* (Chapter 2) or the extreme haptic interfaces of *Ender's Game* (Chapter 5), the lack of visual effects and the naturalistic portrayal of Internet usage splits the focus and heroic gaze between the computer and its user: the computer is the gadget-weapon that makes it possible for its hacker-soldier to do almost anything; also, the expert user and their mastery and control of the computer is the weapon. With this, everyday users, including the machinic audience, are encouraged to treat their computers as slavish gadget-weapons that serve the users' ends.

Keeping this in mind, David Lightman is the best, and perhaps most influential, example of this figure. But it is his treatment of his computer as a toy, which he uses to access the military "systems" of NORAD, that nearly sets off WWIII. This is further underlined by the shots of his home computer: the machine sits in the middle of a messy room, where other gadgets, stereo equipment, books and dirty clothes are cast about; in contrast to the sterile military environment of NORAD, the hacker's home computer is casually integrated into civilian space as one of many personal belongings. When Lightman is hacking his school records to change his and Jennifer's (Ally Sheedy) grades, or reserving plane tickets for the two of them, the audience is given a mischievous scamp; as

Thomas illustrates, "The harmlessness of Lightman's actions early on …
is made clear by his good nature and his curiosity" (25) and, as such, his
"weapon," his computer and his connection to the Internet, is treated
similarly, even in a military environment. Building on Chapter 4's discussion of the film and video games, Lightman immaturely thinks that his
Internet-enabled computer is a toy and that his actions with it are without consequences: when Jennifer confronts him by telling him he could
"go to jail" for his hacking, Lightman grins and says, "Only if you're
over 18." Again, it is because he is a teenager "goofing around" that
he thinks he is absolved of any responsibility as it relates to his cyberweapon. This attitude continues despite the very dire consequences that
his "play" brings about, as the climax of the film still has the computer
being tricked into playing a game as a way of defusing the impending
nuclear war.

This is, of course, not a critique the film makes; as the protagonist,
it is because he is outside the military system and command structure
that he is able to both expose the weakness and ineptitude of the military infrastructure, as well as control/master WOPR. Despite his immaturity, what makes him heroic is at the core of much of the ethos that is
to be folded into further cinematic versions of the hacker: like the hard
technological body, he is able to make individual and liberal choices that
lead to rational and honorable human actions that are not constrained by
the control societies represented by the military or the binary-only computer, WOPR. From this, Thomas argues that "in the film, the hacker
is positioned as dangerous because he is exploring things about which
he has little or no understanding" (25), not because he is a deliberately
malicious threat; in reaction to this, Suid worries that such a treatment
makes it so that "[the audience] might even have applauded David for
averting a nuclear holocaust, irrespective of his having initiated the threat
through his illegal actions" (448). This is especially true as "technology is infantilized in the film (underscored by the use of the name of
Faulken's deceased son, Joshua)" and David is then recast as "the most
appropriate educator for the technology of the future" (Thomas 26). In
this, WOPR is an infantile toy and Lightman is the figure best attuned to
its gadget-nature. Deliberately, while he uses some of the techniques that
would be appropriated into later cyberwarfare tactics, Lightman is not a
soldier. However, as is consistent with the cinematic hacker and hacker-
soldier, he is given the same amazed gaze as one might imagine a civilian
giving the engineer of one of the high-tech gadgets van Creveld flags,

and is subsequently admired not only for his skills but for "the power ('capabilities') which result from this skill." While, again, not a soldier, his version of the hacker is in echo of the hard body's ethical system based around liberal, human action, and, as such, the film then treats WOPR as an unthinking, war-obsessed marvel of engineering while it treats Lightman as the impish civilian whose weapon-toy use exposes the weaknesses of an Internet-enabled military system.

David Lightman was very influential in hacker culture: despite the "the story's dramatic implausibilities, inaccurate depictions of the military, and criminal actions" that led many within the military community to dismiss it as a "complete fantasy" (Suid 448), Thomas goes to great lengths to explain how "the film had a greater impact on hacker culture than any other single media representation" (26), leading to a moment in the zeitgeist in which, dismissively, "hacking [became] just another manifestation of the post-industrial phenomenon of 'youth' as a distinct period in life" (Rosewarne 142). Lightman was more or less the only cinematic representative of an Internet user in the 1980s, as in the decade that followed the film's release, there was scant representation of the Internet in Hollywood cinema, with a renewed presentation of it following the lead-up to and the explosion of the Internet's population after the release of the popular GUI Netscape.[11] Most portrayals of the Internet in the 10 years leading up to the turn of the millennium tended to be within the science fiction or horror genres, though there were some initial forays into other more "realistic" civilian spaces like the thrillers *Disclosure* and *The Net* (Dir. Irwin Winkler 1995) and the romantic comedy *You've Got Mail* (Dir. Nora Ephron 1998).[12] Unlike *WarGames*, the computer use in those films is relatively accurate to its era and the interfaces the characters use, and the sorts of information they are able to access, are in line with an Internet of the era; in this, the machinic audience sees a slight move away from the Internet-connected computer as fantastic "gadget" and towards it being portrayed as a commonplace object with access to a normalized network of virtual worlds. In terms of hacking, *Sneakers* (1992) stands alone in its era as a "naturalistic" movie that addresses hacking in a positive light. The fact that the film is described on both Wikipedia and imdb.com as a "comedy" makes it more unique but also situates the film, and the relationship between hacker and the military, on a lighter note, similar to *WarGames*.[13]

The basis of the dynamics between computers and users is established in the opening scene: taking place in 1969, it has the college-aged

Martin Bishop (Robert Redford; the character also goes by Martin Brice) and Cosmo (Ben Kingsley) hacking and rerouting money from various bank accounts as a sort of prank. Immediately, the computer is an impish device used to carry out "jokes," like having the Republican National Committee "donate" a large sum to the Black Panthers. While the computers begin in the realm of Lightman's immature gadget, the film turns more serious when Cosmo is arrested for this computer use and Bishop escapes and assumes a new identity. When the film picks up again, it is 20 years into the future, and Bishop is an adult running a business that tests banks' security flaws. Bishop/Redford, 56 at the time of the film's release, is hardly the clueless teenager that Lightman is: his "adult" problems include running a small business, dating, and, for the majority of the film, using all means of technological and espionage surveillance to clear his name from his and Cosmo's original crime.[14]

Like *Brainstorm* and *The Lawnmower Man* (Chapter 4), *Sneakers* is a war film insomuch as the military lurks around the edges of the Internet-enabled technologies of the film, trying to claim them for their own. The representations of the Internet in the film are encapsulated by the mysterious "black box" that mathematician Dr. Gunter Janek (Donal Logue) designs. After the team acquires the black box, they find out that it is a code cracker that allows them access to a number of Internet-enabled infrastructures like power grids, flight control towers and the Federal Reserve. The black box is presented like a super-powerful magical gadget, capable of hacking into any database and retrieving any secret information; the housing of all these important pieces of infrastructure on the Internet, the film argues, makes them especially vulnerable to such miraculous devices and any potential nefarious users. As opposed to Deleuze's "dividual," it is up to the individual Bishop, who is framed by the criminal Mafia on one side and the NSA on the other, to regain control of the black box technology for ethical uses. This is especially true at the end of the movie when it is revealed that the box is only good for decoding American codes, not foreign ones, and, as such, is only good for "spying on Americans." The black box then becomes a (civil) cyberwarfare weapon, with the film attempting to undermine the machinic audience's trust in the Internet and the American government and corporate agencies that dominate those virtual spaces. Control of the Internet, as a gathering place for secret digital information, is essential and it is Bishop and his team's resistance to freely giving over this device that makes them heroic at the end; their assertion of their free will over the criminals and the control societies that buttress them on either side affirm the need for a civilian and human liberal mind at the center of any technological assemblage as a trustworthy check and balance. That the movie takes place with "adult" characters in a world more recognizable to the audience of the time shifts *Sneakers* from the sci-fi roots of *WarGames* into the more "realistic" and serious genre of the political thriller, and, with this change, it becomes a harbinger of later cyberwarfare cinema.

In fact, it is Cosmo's speech to Bishop at the end of the movie that sets up the future of cyberwarfare films. He tells Bishop that

> the world isn't run by weapons anymore, or energy, or money. It's run by little ones and zeroes, little bits of data. ... There's a war out there, old friend. A world war. And it's not about who's got the most bullets. It's about who controls the information. What we see and hear, how we work, what we think ... it's all about the information!

In this quote, though the machinic audience is given no combat and only intelligence officers as representations of the military (not soldiers, pilots, etc.), Cosmo argues that the background of war is ever present in all the "little bits of data," wherever the audience sees and hears and works, and that sense of constant electronic warfare leaks into every system via Internet connections. The goal of this ever-present "world war" is control of information/data, not traditional weapons, and whoever is able to manipulate, produce and distribute that information/data is the most powerful.

This sense of information control is central to the hacking that takes place in *The Core*, a movie that returns to the archetype of Lightman to construct its hacker figure, Theodore Donald "Rat" Finch. In the movie, the Earth's core has stopped rotating and the Earth's population has only a year to tunnel into its center and lay a series of nuclear explosions that will hopefully restart the planet. The military, headed by General Purcell (Richard Jenkins), must put together a team that includes engineers, astronauts, geophysicists and a hacker. With the military in the peak power positions, the movies echoes the building of the atomic bomb (and the construction of the Jaegers in *Pacific Rim* [Chapter 3]) in the ways in which it shows the Total War Machine utilizing all of the civilian resources, human, natural, technological, etc., in order to save humanity. While the mission at the hub of the plot is not a combat one, it overlaps with *Pacific Rim*'s human exceptionalism and the movie's detonation of a series of under-ocean nuclear bombs in that the humans in *The Core* care little for any other species or for ecological concerns; similarly, the heroic act that ensures humanity's survival in *The Core* is literally the bombing of the center of the earth.

Within the Total War Machine of the movie, unlike the civilian non-soldier versions of the hacker in *Sneakers* and *WarGames*, Rat is a techno-soldier and he engages in cyberwarfare. He does begin as a civilian: his introductory scene is the FBI bursting into his apartment; his home is in a similar state to Lightman's chaotic and immature room, and it is clear that Rat is meant to be thought of as juvenile. Later, in exchange for his skills, he talks about losing his virginity and then demands "xeno-tapes and Hot Pockets." After being taken in for an interview, he tells Zimsky (Stanley Tucci), "One Zero One Zero Zero. With that I could steal your money, your secrets, your sexual fantasies, your whole life. Any country, any place, anytime I want. We multitask like you breathe. I couldn't think as slow as you if I tried." With this, the audience is given the beginnings of the techno-soldier, a civilian appropriated into the State and Total War Machines, whose extreme skills and obsessive nature make him an asset, and a person whose virtuosity is admired like a sharp-shooter's would be. More than that, as evidenced by the American flags that populate his apartment, his skills are meant to be wielded by the United States.

Unlike the "cyberattacks" that target another computer system, Rat's skills are in access to and distribution of information. As he brags, access-ing a person's money, sexual fantasies and whole life is easy and in line with previous versions of the attacking or intruding hacker. Because of these skills, he is in charge of "information control, the flow of informa-tion on the Internet." As such, Rat's hacking, though benevolent, is simi-lar to the cyberwarfare "info ops" or "psyops" that aim to control the creation, the spread and the type of information on the Internet. Rat then stops the spread of "panic and chaos" in the civilian realm by creating a "virus bot" that "seeks out any files contained on the Web with key words [the military] designates, and wipes them out." Rat's earlier mentioning of secrets becomes ironic as he is now tasked with covering up the real dangers and "what's really going on" as an active and powerfully restrict-ing agent of the control society. Later in the film, however, he reverts back to the civilian liberal roots that the hackers of earlier films demon-strated. After San Francisco is destroyed and the Californian power grid is knocked offline, Rat becomes involved in a much larger government-military conspiracy: in the case of the team's failure, Zimsky and Purcell made a back-up plan to employ a weapons system called DESTINI, originally meant to fight an enemy by creating targeted seismic events; however, the testing of the weapon is what caused the earth's core to stop rotating in the first place. Rat hacks the electrical grid to delay the application of DESTINI, effectively giving the drilling team time to restart the earth's core themselves and escape. Not only does Rat disobey his military orders, he releases all of the information about the DESTINI system to the public at the very end of the movie.

By the end of the movie Rat returns back to the hacker-hero of Deleuze's society of control. However, at the beginning of the film, he is incorporated into the Total War Machine and manipulates the numerical language of the Internet and its populations of "dividuals"; he is a figure "who [has] become even more enthusiastically involved in [his] own self-discipline" (Best 9). His initial choice to align himself with Žižek's "authorities" allows for the Total War Machine to manipulate who is allowed to accesses "truthful" information, and, therefore, his walling off of the general public from that apocalyptic information puts him at odds with the hacker (and hard body ideals) of "democracy, civil liberties and citizenship capabilities" (Best 6). Yet he ends up acting out of a sense of humanistic duty: Josh (Aaron Eckhart) laments to Beck (Hilary Swank), thinking he is going to die, that it is a shame that no one will know the sacrifices that they all made for humanity's survival nor that the American government and military were to blame, "unless it got out somehow." The last heroic action of the film, in reaction to the governmental and military societies of control that cannot be trusted, is Rat's exposure of DESTINI and the whole drilling operation: importantly, the final shots of the movie are the visualization of Rat sending out the top secret documents on a computer screen, with excited newscasts underneath explaining the documents' contents. This is the crowning moment of the film's humanist ethics: not only do the humans dominate nature (wreck, then fix the Earth's core), but the species also masters the computer and machine species to promote and distribute secret documents as a liberal and democratic act of resistance.

With this act, Rat moves from the immature Lightman to the "adult" Bishop and provides a cinematic template for the hackers and whistle-blowers of the movies discussed later in this chapter. The fact that the documents go to multiple civilian (news outlets) and military (the

Pentagon) sites of control is important, as it establishes how top secret the information was and the depths of conspiracy that was undertaken to protect that information, even as, literally, the world was ending. Considering its genre, *The Core* would likely be labeled first as a disaster movie, then perhaps a thriller, with the elements of a war film lingering around its fringes. However, the American military is at the heart of the plot machinations, and, while little "traditional" military action (combat) takes place, the types of tactics that the Total War Machine of the movie employs signals the shifts in the war film genre that come with a State War Machine increasingly reliant on digital information: the cyberwarfare of *The Core* is first an act of surveillance (monitoring public Internet traffic) then conspiratorial restriction (creating and maintain secret information). This is the manipulation of "dividuals" that takes place in a paranoiac warfare, where those that regain the most authority are the ones best able to master, often through digital means, the information gathered from the "leaky" and "dispersed [forms] of surveillance" that is "ritually and relentlessly extracted," primarily from civilians.

In films that showcase cyberwarfare, clandestine information is central. Secrecy in *WarGames* is tied to the juvenile gadget-weapon computer user: Lightman hacks in order to get at a number of videogames that have yet to be released. However, in his discussion of Lightman, Thomas then hits on one of the key components of a society of control in later war films: with information being housed in numerical systems that are "nearly identical" and in a "continuous network," the Total War Machine depends on the complete intermingling of civilian, corporate and military, and, in particular, the fact that "corporate and military secrets are, at some level, indistinguishable" (30). However, the hacker that emerges in the late 1980s, "without military funding and without corporate secrets to protect," provides the template for the cinematic hacker's ethics (Thomas 14): this is first clear in *Sneakers* when the "corporate tool" of SETEC Astronomy, funded by the NSA, can only snoop on other American governmental institutions. The civilian figures of *Sneakers* are able to trick and resist both the corporate (Ben Kingsley) and military uses of the machine, and are early precursors for Rat in their resistance of societies of control and reassertion of individual, civilian free will. Thomas explains that the cinematic hacker operates with the ethical framework that "secrecy creates a space for the worst kind of criminality, which, because of the culture of secrecy, can only be exposed by another type of criminality—hacking" (31), which, when represented cinematically, Rosewarne flags as creating the archetypical "hacker as criminal outsider" (122). The cinematic hacker is transformed by her/his dual nature of righteous criminality, an idea that is at the heart of *Blackhat, The Fifth Estate* and *Snowden*, where the protagonists must consistently undertake criminal acts to expose the (civilian) surveillance and secrets, larger criminal acts and figures, that arise in digital worlds of a society of control.

## THE CYBERWAR FILM AS POLITICAL THRILLER

While the introduction to this book quoted Neale's observation that the war film was blending with the techno-thriller, a number of the more recent films that feature cyberwarfare (which includes military surveillance) fall closer to the political thriller genre. While little scholarly research has been done defining the genre,[15] the techno-thriller is marked by a fusion of "military action/adventure, science fiction and espionage fiction with a dose of social realism" (Moore para. 2). The films discussed in this chapter do begin with some of the markings of science fiction (*WarGames, The Core*) and action-adventure (*The Core, Swordfish*) in their representations of Internet and computer technology; *Blackhat, Snowden* and *The Fifth Estate*, as products of a continuous civil and international cyberwarfare environment, represent the tensions between civilian and military Internet users and the struggle for information in an age of near-total surveillance, and, as such, are more in line with the political thriller.

Like the war film, the political thriller is especially astute at capturing "the fears, paranoia and fantasies of their era" (Kellner 165). The post-9/11 political thriller[16] is defined most clearly by its concerns with the expanded domestic and international surveillance that becomes possible through the ubiquity of digital information environments, and with who gathers, accesses and controls that information. In particular, Ian Scott sees a move toward a focus on the "'heroic quest' model of conspiracy thriller … the moral fortitude of the chasing protagonist seeking to discover the secret plots and deception" (103); Castrillo and Echart add that "these films generally focus on the dilemma between trust and distrust, and the protagonist's quest for a liberating truth, which can only be attained by confiding in other characters and exposing oneself to the risk of betrayal" (114). The political thriller's

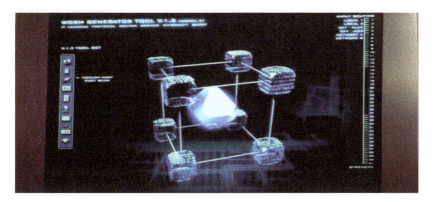

**Fig. 6.2** *Swordfish*'s Jobson's virus-building interface

> main dramatic question or main tension of the story revolves around the hero's search for the truth, that is, for information, for knowledge. … Therefore, political thrillers are at their core investigative narratives in which the protagonist must face physical and moral threats so as to retrieve a hidden truth and hand it over to the people. (114)

Scott points out, however, that for many of the films of the contemporary era, "intuitional power [is] a source of danger in American society" (107). Because military agencies, specifically American, are institutional powers engaged in cyberwarfare tactics, they are the main authorities of control in the discussed films of this chapter; as the "action" of the war film moves from combat to politics and civilian realms, there is a strong mix between the political thriller and the war film, in particular at the focus points of cyberwarfare: secret information and surveillance.

In terms of filmic effects, as mentioned previously, there is a relative lack of visual effects that are meant to illustrate Internet use. There are two brief scenes in *Blackhat* that are meant to show the interior of an Internet network and how a virus spreads: in each, the viewer sees the wires and devices and then watches them get overwhelmed with the bytes of light that are meant to represent the malicious code; in *The Core*, there is a brief shot of Rat "underneath" a layering of multiple computer screens that is meant to portray his anxiety as he tries to stop DESTINI from being used. Of all the movies analyzed in this chapter, *Swordfish* has arguably the least realistic interfaces, blending lines of code with odd visualizations of program executions (Fig. 6.2). More commonly, though, the computers of the political thriller/war film are treated much like those devices found in spy films, "such as photo cameras and disguised microphones, interrogation rooms, etc." (Castrillo and Echart 119). The authors continue: "These [devices] are essential elements of the investigative plot, since they are ultimately tools for obtaining information or evidence" (119) or unpacking and revealing the conspiracy and secret information at the heart of the discussed films. With the computer-as-espionage tool, the movies of this chapter attempt to represent naturalistic computer use, and their presence as common objects in homes, military spaces and workplaces normalizes them so that their ubiquity becomes part of the terror of constant surveillance. The move away from the doubling of Butler's frame (outlined in Chapter 3) implies a reversal in attitudes when it comes to Internet and computer usage in the Total War Machine: instead of framing and looking "into" the Internet (as a screen for example), the frame dissolves and the Internet permeates all of the environment without restrictive portals. In the war films of this chapter, this implies then that the battlefield is everywhere and that every person populating that environment is a military subject.

Within this environment of complete and ongoing war, as argued in the previous section, the secret and unraveling and preservation of it is at the center of the political thriller as a genre, and the war film's move from a subset of the cinematic genre, is indicative of the paranoiac cyberwarfare that arises from societies of control. Adding to this, it is surveillance, and the paranoia and conspiracy theorizing that comes from feeling forever watched in a continuous environment of potential terrorist attacks and/or war, that drives the political thriller/war film hybrid. Using the NSA spying revelations and the establishment of WikiLeaks as primary motivations, the cinematic hacker-soldier, as an expert in accessing and disabling the systems of large-scale information control around her/him, is the ideal cinematic hero to unravel and expose the secrecy and criminality arising from cyberwarfare. As such, the worlds of the films are "governed by forces larger than the individual, the community, and sometimes even the state" (Castrillo and Echart 116). Growing from the "conspiracy thrillers" in the 1970s (Scott 120), it is often government and military forces working together, under the guise of national security, that hide and conspire to trick the general public about their own obtaining and manipulating of digital information. The character of

Mother (Dan Aykroyd) in *Sneakers* is played for laughs: when he states that the CIA caused earthquakes in Nicaragua (which *The Core* affirms) or that the US government faked the moon landing, the other characters roll their eyes or slide uneasily away from him. However, many movies post-9/11 embrace the conspiratorial elements of constant military and civilian digital information production and distribution. Within this paranoiac setting, the hacker/whistleblower protagonist is, like the hero of the political thriller, in echo of the hard body's ethics: the figures stress that "individualism [is] the driving force for liberty and equality" (Scott 20), and that is the singular figure's humanistic responsibility, in the face of "forces larger than the individual," to "liberate" the information, exposing secret conspiracies and "the worst kind of criminality," and make it public to all.

*Swordfish*, released just before 9/11, takes Cosmo's argument from *Sneakers* into the realm of secret government operations and the beginning of the Web 2.0 world. The film centers on former Mosad agent Gabriel Shear's (John Travolta) plans to rob secret American government funds, long leftover from covert money-laundering operations in the 1980s. To do this, he must hire Stanley Jobson (Hugh Jackman) to provide a virus that will "tunnel" into the funds via a bank on the "backbone" of the banking network, and funnel the 9.5 billion dollars to Shear. Kellner calls it an "elaborate political conspiracy drama" in which the film then becomes a navigation in trust and double crossing, akin to the political thriller (16): Shear reveals himself to be working for a secret government agency, set up by J. Edgar Hoover, called Black Cell and under the direction of United States Senator Reisman (Sam Shepard); his colleague and pseudo–love interest Ginger (Halle Berry) confesses that she is DEA, but working undercover; Jobson is then chased and briefed by J.T. Roberts (Don Cheadle), who works for the FBI cyberdefense task force. Like in the political thriller, Jobson must cycle between characters to decide who to side with and what tasks he must undertake, while the larger mechanisms of infrastructure (secret government military operations, the FBI, the US government) whirl around him. Jobson is heroic in part because he has just finished a multi-year jail sentence because he hacked the FBI's databases in retaliation for the government secretly reading civilian emails, undertaking criminal action in order to expose a larger criminality. The machinic audience is meant to side with him as he has his daughter kidnapped and held in order to force his continued hacking of the bank; additionally, his computer skills, with which he hacks the Department of Defense mainframe along with the banking network, are presented as heroic and virtuous. As a civilian, one whose moral fortitude has already been proven by his jail sentence, he is the one outside of the control societies that is able to recontrol that information and redirect it for his own purposes.

Yet the original theatrical release makes Shear's development the film's "heroic quest" and justifies his murderous actions as part of a larger "patriotic" campaign against the amorphous globalized force of terrorism within which Jobson, despite his resistance, is just one part of the American State War Machine. When Jobson exposes the control society for what it is, adjusting his hack so that the money jumps infinitely from one bank to the next and therefore effectively making the money impossible to find, he shows that the money is purely virtual, pure information, and by writing a script that harnesses that nature, he shows how powerless both the Black Cell and the US government are. However, he eventually has to give into these control societies in order to save his daughter and then Ginger, ultimately being folded back into the larger machinic phylum of the State War Machine by returning the money to Shear; his individual compassion and morality make him vulnerable to the societies of control, and his computer, once his own weapon, is given back to the State War Machine it came from. Shear then emerges victorious, faking his death and making off with all the money. Like Cosmo in *Sneakers*, who argues that the world is engaged in an unknowing digital war, Shear argues that his actions are justified because he has a strict code of ethics guided by an extreme patriotism. Because America is still in a constant state of war, he is willing to sacrifice anything and anyone (including Senator Reisman) in the preservation of American values. As referenced earlier in Chapter 5, when Stanley asks, "War? Who are we at war with?" Gabriel answers, "Anyone who impinges on America's freedom. Terrorist states, Stanley. Someone must bring their war to them." Shear's use of violence and the appropriation of Stanley's cyberwarfare skills are justified in order to protect the millions of Americans who take their "freedoms" for granted. As such, the original cut of the movie ends with Ginger withdrawing all the money from a bank in Monte Carlo and sailing off on a yacht with Shear; just before the end credits the audience hears from a news report offscreen that a terrorist mastermind has been killed in an "unexplained explosion," implying that with the money taken from the bank robbery, Shear is able to continue on with his black ops. Jobson is far from the immature Lightman version of the hacker and closer to the "adult" hackers of *Sneakers*. However, he provides little of the resistance that Rat or Bishop do and instead takes his 10 million dollars at the end and happily tours the United States with his daughter.

In many ways, his moral system is closer to Tony Stark's in the *Iron Man* films. As argued in Chapter 3 and my other work,[17] despite Stark's best intentions as a civilian hacker, he is unable to completely free himself from the military roots of his weaponized suits and, in fact, develops deeper bonds with the American military as the films progress. Robson is similar to Iron Man and the drone pilots discussed in Chapter 5 in that he recognizes the failings of the control societies and their mass surveillance, resists it and enacts vigilante justice against it in order to halt the American government from spying on its own citizens. However, like Stark and those drone pilots, he is subsumed within the military system, ultimately overpowered, as the American State War Machine takes his cyberwarfare labor/hacking and uses it for its own purposes. *Swordfish*'s focus on conspiracy and double crossing moves it from the (cyber)war film toward the political thriller, but its spectacular combat and car chase scenes situate parts of it within the action-adventure genre. This broad mix is reflective of the messiness of a contemporary State War Machine that utilizes combat from Shear's mercenary army alongside Jobson's cyberwarfare tactics in order to fight an amorphous and ever-present "terrorist" force or, even more broadly, against "anyone who impinges on America's freedom." Such warfare, the movie argues, is ubiquitous, inescapable and patriotic, and so any resistance is not only fruitless, but un-American.

With this understanding of civilian resistance to omniscient cyberwarfare, *Blackhat* is a middle ground between the war film as technothriller and political thriller. The film opens with the hacking of a nuclear plant in Chai Wan, Hong Kong; as a result, one of the plant's reactors explodes. Initially painted as a terrorist attack, the film gradually unfolds to reveal a web of criminal elements that are manipulating various infrastructure sites like the stock market, nuclear facilities and mining operations, like the list that the hackers of *Sneakers* find, in order to make themselves hundreds of millions of dollars. As a Hollywood war film, *Blackhat* is somewhat unique in that there is little of an American military element; instead, one of the main characters, Captain Chen Dawai (Leehom Wang), is a member of the Chinese cyberwarfare unit. The film's casting of Wang and Tang Wei (playing Chen Lien), and its use of English subtitles, which allows characters to speak in multiple languages, along with the international filming locations (Hong Kong and Malaysia), extend the film beyond the scope of the American State War Machine and, in this, is similar to *Eye in the Sky* in its portrayal of a global Total War Machine that interchangeably swaps different weaponry, information and personnel among countries; while there is tension about sharing information with other nations, such a depiction also attempts to give a sense of the borderless nature of terrorism, hacking and cyberwarfare and how the enemies are often not nationally affiliated but rather individuals attacking state and/or corporate targets via the global Internet. Like *Eye in the Sky*, a number of scenes feature the inner workings and political maneuverings that take place at the bureaucratic level of the State War Machines: such scenes are meant to illustrate the politicized nature of the virtual worlds, information and warfare that surround those government infrastructures, and the film's inclusion of this non-combat reminds that the political thriller's "central conflict is political in nature. Politics, therefore, cannot be just the backdrop or setting, but have to be inherently associated to the criminal source of conflict that creates the dramatic premise of the film" (Castrillo and Echart 113). While the "political" nature of the film wanes in the second half, as the film focuses more on the action-adventure elements of gunfights with semi-automatic weapons, the boardroom scenes and various phone calls seek to give some sense of how the many layers of various State War Machines work beyond the immediate theater of war.

The cyberwarfare of the film again places at the center the expert civilian who must uncover a series of secret information, puzzle through clues and unravel the larger conspiracy. The protagonist, Nicholas Hathaway, begins the movie in prison and, like *Swordfish*'s Jobson, Hathaway is the aforementioned "criminal" in search of exposing larger criminality. It is revealed that he is one of the world's foremost hackers and is one of the cowriters, along with Captain Dawai, of the core of the script that provided the backdoor into the Chai Wan nuclear power plant's system. The viral script, now decades old, has been sloppily modified and Dawai and Hathaway must work together to figure out who the new author is. The distinction between "script kiddies" and writer of actual code is illustrative: the "script kiddy" simply takes prewritten code and executes it; Duwai and Hathaway, by writing the actual code, demonstrate a superior expert knowledge of their virtual environment that is essential to heroically re-hacking their enemies. Still, the ability of anyone with an Internet connection to "pick up" and wield these weaponized

scripts is part of the horror of a networked digital information environment: within the film, the user does not have to understand even a line
of the program in order to use it, and the ease of use and the preva-
lence of such scripts is meant to underline how terrifyingly "easy" it is to
engage in cyberwarfare. In the opening scene, after the Remote Access
Tool (RAT) has opened a backdoor, the malicious hacker on the other
end types for only a few seconds and hits "enter," and the power plant
explodes. In contrast, the reason why Hathaway is heroic is because he
understands and can manipulate the computer as a weapon and so he
is repurposed into a global Total War Machine in order to fight the terrorists with their own weapons. As such, he is the liberal human actor,
outside of the military societies of control, who cuts through the ineffective military system's barriers in order to catch the murderers and
thieves. This is best exemplified by the scene where FBI Agent Carol
Barrett (Viola Davis) asks the NSA if they can use their "Black Widow"
tool to de-corrupt a set of recovered data so that they can track the terrorists' IP addresses. Such a super-tool is not only kept secret, but kept
in close possession by the government agency: the administrator at the
NSA refuses, not because it is in use, but because of fears of sharing the
classified technology with the Chinese, and because, as he says, he simply doesn't "want" to. Barrett then leaves the room and willfully turns a
blind eye as Hathaway hacks into the NSA with a phishing scheme, and
utilizes the tool himself. Hathaway, much like in *Sneakers* and *The Core*,
is an individual figure best suited to a "justified" criminality, and one that
is in pursuit of the truth, knowledge and information being kept hidden
by the societies of control that surround the digital world. Like Bishop,
he is the self-interested adult hacker: Hathaway wants his own freedom from jail, but continues on his pursuit of the terrorist after Duwai
is killed, more out of revenge, justice and his love for Duwai's sister;
this shift towards the hard body's values, and away from the blind and
violent patriotism of Shear, makes him heroic and his quest less about
American superiority and preservation, dangerous "intuitional powers,"
and more about an individual (civilian) moral system dedicated to right-
eousness and duty. While the elements of the action-adventure make it
much different than *Snowden* and *The Fifth Estate*, the political elements
surrounding the use of the technology, the crossing of secret information
across national borders, and the unraveling of the terrorist conspiracy
make Hathaway the civilian hacker-soldier best suited to fight for liberty
and equality against the larger (global) societies of control.

*The Core, Swordfish* and *Blackhat*, and their portrayals of cyberwarfare, provide elemental templates for the later *Snowden* and *The Fifth Estate* in their increased inclusion of political elements and the move toward "naturalistic" representations of military and civilian Internet usage.[18] *Blackhat* then also contributes to the acknowledgment of a global Total War Machine that is also reflected in the two whistleblower films. However, *Snowden* and *The Fifth Estate* move solidly into the political thriller, while still grounding themselves in the electronic and cyber aspect of a contemporary Total War Machine and war film. The most striking distinction, however, is the move toward the biopic and the reflection of the "real world." Broadly, Castrillo and Echart argue, political thrillers are "(1) films based on actual events; (2) fashioned narratives that reference actual events and institutions in a more veiled manner; and (3) fictional storylines that reference not actual events but rather an atmosphere of concern or anxiety over a political or social issue" (118). While many war films have long purported to be about "real" events and people, and in fact draw rhetorical strength from the portrayals of heroic actions from "real people," *Snowden* and *The Fifth Estate* are unique in that they involve aspects of cyberwarfare that, as previously mentioned, were usually relegated to science fiction (*The Core, WarGames*), comedy (*Sneakers*) or action-adventure (*Blackhat*); instead, the two films are non-fictional in their reconstruction of "real" events and people. More, those "real" people and events are centrally "political in nature" and the films' concerns and anxieties are, like the political thriller, the criminality that arises from the digital information system's control by institutional (political) powers. The two films then aim to didactically reflect "real-world" topics and ramifications in the ways that both the political thriller and the war film excel at and aim to "educate" their reader about the "true" workings of the societies of control, and "hand over" those truths to the machinic audience through their protagonists' heroic quest of investigation and exposure. In particular, more so than the aforementioned films, the two films are political thrillers before they are war films, in that their focus is on actual figures and events.[19]

The two films in particular begin with Best's understanding of societies of control: "Contemporary control is postmodern, and thus automatic and bodily, impacting on everyday life rather than institutional sites such as workplaces" (14); such an environment is without the "earlier forms of controls … limits, barriers, insides and outsides" and highlights the notion that in 2017, digital information systems are completely

ubiquitous and integrated into every aspect of life and that all information gathered in that space is equally public. The techno-soldier also
recognizes the tools of a continuous and all-surrounding cyberwar battlefield, and utilizes those same systems to also watch, gather and then
expose corruption. *The Fifth Estate* focuses on Julian Assange and the
creation and rise of the website WikiLeaks. The film resembles, in some
ways, *The Social Network* (Dir. David Fincher 2010) in that it is also a
film about the "true story" of creation of a digital information organization with a controversial figurehead; its use of actual historical people
and events move it toward the non-fiction drama with its elements of
suspense and paranoia also establishing it as a political thriller. Its inclusion as a war film has to do with the involvement of various global military forces, but predominantly the American military, and the release of
various databases of information, including the Afghan War Logs that
WikiLeaks titled "Collateral Murder." Like *Blackhat*, its near-constant
shift between locales (Iceland, Norway, Kenya, the US, Egypt, etc.), give
the viewer the sense that the events, and the Total War Machines that
they are exposing, are global in nature; when the film shows the flow of
information from the site in glowing arcs from continent to continent,
it does so to show the worldwide nature of both the information distribution and also the scale and scope of the warfare that it is exposing.
Multiple characters within the film characterize these arcs, reminiscent of
a missile's parabola, as part of an "information war," one that is fought
by controlling, hiding and revealing various parts of the societies of control, including the military.

In particular, it is the hacker figure of Assange, operating as a "civilian
journalist," that is the driving force of the "political decision making"
taking place. He is introduced as a hacker grounded in 1980s mythol-
ogy: he manually splices his computer into a printer in one of the opening scenes, hijacking it to make flyers for his upcoming talk; he talks
about his previous hacking of NASA's website as well as his creation of
the software that keeps the whistleblower submissions to the website
completely anonymous. He begins the film as the master computer user,
and, more than this, a mature adult engaged in protest against the injus-
tices he sees around him; as he walks through the Chaos Communication
Congress, which is littered with bright colors and exactly the sorts of
gadgets and toys van Creveld flags as central to the immature hacker, he
looks on in disgust, describing the intelligence dedicated to their creation and production as "a waste." Instead, Assange is dedicated to the

early hacker ethical system that contends that all information should be free and that computers are tools to release and maintain that information; most clearly, he states and repeats his thesis: "Free people must have knowledge." The movie is not a political thriller in the sense that there is a secret to unveil; rather, the film is a delicate, balanced understanding of secrecy as the heart of resistance to a society of control and cyberwarfare: there is a need to keep the whistleblower's identity secret in order to expose the larger secret information and conspiracies attached to the larger infrastructures of control present in an information war, in particular government agencies.

He explains his mission at the start of the film:

> When new information comes to light, it can bring about great change. Two people and a secret. The beginning of any conspiracy and all corruption. And as it grows, more lies, deceits, more people and more secrets. But, if we can find one moral man, someone willing to expose all these secrets, that man could topple the most repressive of regimes.

Assange's ethics are based around the notion of the "one moral man," the individual within the society of control using the digital systems to cloak themselves in order to release evidence of larger secrets and corruption. As such, he explains that he is "fighting for freedom, for privacy, for the right to remain concealed in clouds of codes." For him, freedom is privacy, and within an extremely public information-saturated digital environment, he has an obligation, as a liberal human, to act outside those control infrastructures, to infiltrate, expose and "topple" corruption within, in turn giving rise to what he calls "a whole new form of social justice." The hacker, as the supra-knowledgeable manipulator of such an environment, is just the figure to lead that new form of justice. The movie then paints the release of the War Logs and various other leaks as heroic, cutting in real news footage that explains that the organization has publically uncovered senseless civilian deaths and American soldiers committing war crimes. The argument is, then, that making this information public, by utilizing the tactics of cyberwarfare as a lone private (hacker) civilian, the "one moral man," is the best way to fight back against the societies of control.

This massive amount of information collected in a society of control actually contributes to the downfall and climax of the film. Assange's argument from the start of the film is that older "traditional" forms of media, namely newspapers, are too centralized and slow to deal effectively with the fast and widespread contemporary digital environment. WikiLeaks then is a "revolution," a word the film repeats multiple times, in digital information distribution. As such, he advocates taking all of the sensitive American government cables and emails he receives, including the 91,000-plus documents he gets from Bradley Manning (now Chelsea Manning), and simply dumping them onto the Internet for all to see and sort through. The other central character of the film is Daniel Berg (Daniel Brühl), who, throughout the film, tries to convince Assange to be "more responsible" and release only the information they can verify after they have redacted sensitive information (such as American spies' identities) to save their and the whistleblowers' lives. However, because the trove is so incredibly large, three gigabytes of text files, he does not want to spend the time doing it. Eventually, because Berg sees it as his duty to protect the human lives of those included in the to-be-leaked documents, he destroys the privacy creation system that allows whistleblowers to upload their secret information, effectively disabling the site.

With this, the disassembling of the site casts Assange as a figure similar to the military personnel he critiques in that, for him, the people within the documents are not humans but rather information ("dividuals"). This flattening of these human lives is constructed as horrific and critiques the hacker as one that is so deeply integrated into the digital computer systems around him that his brain is transformed into a similarly efficiently and robotic calculating machine. Ultimately, however, despite perhaps the personal character and ego of Assange, the film does uphold the actions of the site and the act of leaking and civilian cyberwarfare as ethical and moral. In one of the final scenes of the film, Nick Davies (David Thewlis), an editor at *The Guardian* and one of the consistent mainstream media publishers of WikiLeaks' information, tells Berg that there is

a new information revolution, this one more powerful and terrifying than the last. A fifth estate ... which is why we need more responsible men, men of purpose, to harness its power, to lead us into the future. Daniel, you and Julian gave us a glimpse of what the future could be ... to demand the waves of information that one day soon will wash all their evils away.

In the end, the movie confirms that it is Assange's ethical system, in parallel to the hard technological body (Chapter 2), based around the

**Image 6.3**   The many Julian Assanges of WikiLeaks

singular and liberal individual "responsible man," that can harness the revolutionary digital information systems in order to combat larger evils for the good of humanity. Earlier in the film, Assange reveals to Berg that WikiLeaks doesn't have "hundreds of volunteers" as he claims, but it is only Assange by himself that is creating and controlling multiple email and chat accounts; when he does this, the movie visualizes this by having multiple rows of Assanges all seated at desks, gleefully typing away, an army of virtual versions of him engaged in the urgent combat brought about by an information war (Image 6.3). In this moment, the film most clearly illustrates its central theme: that Assange's greatest and most noble strength is the ability to harness his digital selves (avatars), the virtual parts of his biological-technological assemblage; he is still the center and controlling force of this fleet of selves and as such they are rhizomatic versions fanning out in information combat, heroically exposing the larger criminality through this multipronged attack. While Rosewarne would rightly explain Assange as an egotist and power-monger as, by doing so, he becomes "more interesting than a mere net-geek and is framed as a worthy protagonist" (138), most clearly he is representative of the hacker as the individual civilian outsider with the essential liberal human at the center of his virtual parts, breaking apart the larger societies of control for the good of humanity.

*Snowden* carries many of the same themes as *The Fifth Estate* but differs in its recounting of Edward Snowden's history as a military-trained soldier that exits the American State War Machine in an act of resistance and public defiance against its domestic use of mass surveillance tools on its own citizens. He is the reverse of the civilian-hacker-made-military-weapon and his military history puts him closer to the hard body's ethics, a whistleblowing Rambo, in that he similarly sees the ineffective and unjust military infrastructure and reacts against it as a liberal individual. The film takes the time then to show Snowden training for American Special Forces with a series of boot-camp scenes that fall in line with the stereotypical war film; the inclusion of these scenes bestows Snowden with the ethos of the "traditional" soldier, granting him the same level of patriotism as the combat soldier, while also bestowing on him the values of courage and grittiness that the postcorporeal drone pilots of *Good Kill* and *Eye in the Sky* do not receive for their remote virtuous killing (Chapter 5). He turns from the infantry soldier to the techno-soldier when a series of stress fractures are discovered in his legs and he is told he cannot put the necessary weight on them to continue down that branch of a military career. Instead, he joins the CIA as a system analyst, later working for the NSA, and then the CIA again, before he carries out his hack and leak of the Heartbeat program, a set of software designed to store and index all Internet communications.

The movie establishes itself as a war/political thriller blend with its repeated shots of cameras and the constant revelation of government authorities lurking voyeuristically within every virtual space. The other military characters of the film justify this invisible intrusion and gathering by gesturing to the paranoiac cyberwarfare that covers and structures every civilian and military space. His instructor at the CIA school, Corbin O'Brian (Rhys Ifans), explains that "the front lines on the War on Terror are not in Afghanistan or Iraq. They're here. London. Berlin. Istanbul. Any server. Any connection. The modern battlefield is everywhere." He later repeats his assertion that the "battlefield is everywhere" and the film argues that this sentiment is used as justification for a series of surveillance tactics, such as remotely turning on the microphone and cameras of any Internet-connected devices; the reading and indexing of any Internet communication; and the geo-tracking of any Internet-connected device. The fact that the vast majority of spying is done by America on its own citizens is justified under the broad umbrella of National Security and the notion that the enemy, like Shear states, is "anyone who impinges on America's freedom," regardless of citizenship. Snowden begins the film as a conservative, arguing for governmental rights to such surveillance tactics. However, as he is exposed to the true tactics of the American military, he softens, with the turning point being when O'Brian informs him that he and his girlfriend Lindsay Mills (Shailene Woodley) have been surveilled as well. His shift in ideologies is meant to be a model for the machinic audience, but also illustrate the dire nature of the governmental and military exploitation of the digital control apparatus that blends into everyday life. The movie argues that the paranoia that comes with cyberwarfare and the societies of control in general is proven to be horrifyingly real.

This shared revelation between *The Fifth Estate* and *Snowden* manifests in similar depictions of the Internet within their cinematic worlds. As mentioned previously, there is no "entering" into the computer and the shots of Internet use are mostly over the shoulders of characters; the interfaces, software and websites that the characters use are the same as the machinic audience's. These naturalistic shots show the computer as an ever-present common object and the Internet as a near-invisible and ubiquitous technology. *The Fifth Estate* emphasizes this in the brief scenes where the text of digital conversations, as Assange is walking through an airport for example, is laid over the screen: here, the digital nature of his communication weaves entirely into the world, so that it actually manifests physically for the viewing machinic audience as if it is an object in the world.[20] Additionally, within both films, there is inclusion of drone footage that is similar to that discussed in Chapter 5, although the two films do treat it quite differently. In *The Fifth Estate*, the audience is given the prerecorded drone footage from "The Afghan War Logs"; the inclusion of it as a historical document, rather than a "live feed," makes the footage akin to the troubling double frame of the war photo that is discussed in Chapter 3, making the document  that much more horrific because of the attempts to keep it secret. In contrast, *Snowden*'s usage almost mirrors *Good Kill*'s or *Eye in the Sky*'s usage and is done to show how the technicians that feed intelligence, such as the location of an Internet-connected phone of a suspect to drone pilots, combine with the State War Machine. The intelligence officers, and then the movie's audience, are given the view that the pilots get in order to critique the dehumanizing effect that their information is having on the lives of others around the world; the camera of the drone is then no different, in the world of the movie, than the repurposed civilian cameras, weaponized by Snowden's and the military's civil spying software, as each are both enacting violence on civilians, every day on the ever-present cyber-battlefield, through their distanced watching. With this, these films, more than any others in this chapter, treat the computer as the spy devices of the political thriller, as tools of disguise and deceit and as "tools for obtaining information or evidence" (Castrillo and Echart 119).

The lack of cinematic effects and digital techniques around the representation of the Internet in the film is meant to underline how omnipresent computers and digital networks are, but also that they are viral devices that make the human element vulnerable; the technological aspect of the technology-biology assemblage of the hackers, and all the characters in general, infects the rational and private biological element, putting them in constant risk. When Snowden explains how the web of surveillance spreads out in digital spaces, how one user/node in the network very quickly and easily links to 2.5 million other users/nodes, he highlights how the dense connections enabled by the Internet are actually dangerous and overwhelming because they are effective weapons for those empowered by a society of control. Computers and the Internet are tools of domestic cyberwarfare and similarly, the hacker is a figure that can subvert those tools to expose those control systems. However, for both the hacker and the military, the Internet is a tool/weapon that is to be wielded; it bears none of the markings of a cooperative co-species that is found in a critical posthumanism and, instead, is subservient to the human users.

*Snowden*'s ethical system, as portrayed by its protagonist, is like *The Fifth Estate*'s in its problematic human-centric aims. Snowden's protagonist has none of the ego of the character of Assange and instead is far more like the hero of the political thriller in his purity and urgency to "retrieve a hidden truth and hand it over to the people." His exposure of mass surveillance is painted as an untainted and self-aware sacrifice as he is forced to give up his American citizenship, resigning himself to a life of exile in Russia. More than this, when he does release the information, in an attempt to ensure that his friends at the NSA do not get caught up in a "manhunt," he leaves a deliberate "digital footprint" so that the investigators know that it is only him that is responsible and so that he can then take the full blame and punishment. As he explains to *The Guardian* reporter Glenn Greenwald (Zachary Quinto), "This is not about money or anything for me. There is no hidden agenda. I just want to get this data to established journalists like yourself so you can present it to the world and the people can decide." This apparently selfless act is meant to speak as much to a larger liberal heroism as it is to the massive corruption taking place within the American State War Machine. In a later scene, he sits in the backyard drinking beer with one of his colleagues, trading war stories with the other technicians, which, like the earlier training scenes, is a familiar trope in the traditional war film. His NSA boss Trevor James (Scott Eastwood) comments, "You make it sound criminal. It's war. It's a job," and Snowden counters by detailing the Nuremberg Trials, explaining that after the "the Nazi big shots" were tried and hung, "the next trial was for the judges, lawyers, policemen and guards. Ordinary people just doing their jobs and following orders. That's where we got the Nuremberg principles, which then the UN made international law just in case ordinary jobs become criminal again." The film criticizes the normalization of this state surveillance and society of control and shows that Snowden is the voice of reason and compassion against the massively criminal enemy of his own government. Again, the film establishes the liberal human, the hard body ethics: his instructor near the beginning of the film quotes Ayn Rand's *Atlas Shrugged* (1957) by saying, "One man can stop the motor of the world"; later in an argument with Mills, Snowden tells her that he alone is moral and responsible enough: "I feel like I'm made to do this. And if I don't do it, I don't know anyone else who can." In both of these quotes, the hacker figure is the only person, the single man, capable enough to act outside the other infrastructures of control and liberate the human element inside and reaffirm the humanistic qualities of freedom and individuality. With this cinematic celebration of Snowden, the cinematic hacker's transformation from David Lightman in *WarGames*, an immature kid mucking around with mischievous danger, to an ethical adult is complete. The film's use of a Rubik's cube as a central symbolic object makes this clear: at the beginning of the film, Snowden is seen carrying it to meet Greenwald and Laura Poitras (Melissa Leo) as they plan to release the data; it turns out that he received the cube from Hank Forrester (Nicolas Cage), who was his ethical role model during his initial CIA training and the person who pushed him to challenge what exactly he was being asked to do as part of the American State War Machine; that same Rubik's cube is then used to smuggle the data out, as Snowden copies it onto an SD card and slides it under one of the squares. If the military computer begins as a gadget, as van Creveld argues, and the hacker the immature child, then the film's reoccurring use of a toy, the Rubik's cube, as the central metaphoric object shows how far the hacker figure has come, reappropriating his toys and gadgets for greater ethical purposes.

The film is a didactic document and intends to make an argument for the exposure of such societies of control and promote the heroism of Snowden in the face of those larger machines and infrastructures. The film goes to great lengths to attempt to teach its audience about the FISA and to detail the Espionage Act as a way of showing what exactly Snowden sacrificed; the film is meant to educate its readers in this way, arguing for a greater awareness of the constant digital surveillance done under the guise of the American State War Machine and the fight against terrorism. To further stress its relationship to the world of the machinic audience, the film collages in real news footage and TV interviews with various governmental and military figures; this tethers the film to the real world to further strengthen its rhetoric. This culminates in the ultimate endorsement of its protagonist when, at the very end of the film, the real Edward Snowden seamlessly replaces the actor Joseph Gordon Levitt in between scenes, and he speaks to close the film (Fig. 6.4). This unites the actor, and the fictional world of the movie, with the "real" world so that there is no difference, attempting then to establish that the movie's

**Image 6.4** The real Edward Snowden gets the last word

narrative is the truth; the dramatization of the events were not fictional at all and Snowden is the ultimate hero, the single liberal human hacker-soldier who revealed the military's information weapons to the world. The computers of the "real world," the technological aspects of the machinic audience assemblage, are either corrosive and intrusive weapons used against the user or subservient tools to be mastered and brandished against any enemy.

## CONCLUSION: THE CIVILIAN AT WAR FOREVER?

That hacker-soldiers are portrayed as the main heroes of most of the films of this chapter ultimately speaks to what might be the American military's ultimate weakness: "Growing connectivity over an insecure internet multiplies the avenues for e-attack; and growing dependence on computers increases the harm they can cause. ... Cyber-weapons are most effective in the hands of big states. But because they are cheap, they may be most useful to the comparatively weak" (*The Economist staff* para. 25). Mead (170), van Creveld (*Wargames* 299–305) and Giesen (66) express the similar fear that cyberweapons are actually quite useful for terrorists and smaller nations engaged in a guerilla-style asymmetrical warfare. As such, films that feature cyberwarfare that then focus on the individual's ability to cripple and resist the larger American War Machine are accurate in the sense of exposing the ultimate vulnerability ingrained in such warfare.

However, Best explains that when asking contemporary citizen Internet users about stopping using the technology, or perhaps using it with more awareness, "respondents voice a fatalism in their responses, suggesting that not only is stopping participating in digital life unpalatable, as it is for respondents in the second category, but that it is in fact impossible" (19). It seems too that the films, by promoting a humanistic ethical system, insist that only those with an extreme amount of skill, the hacker techno-soldier, are able to resist, and any resistance is met with the full force of the Total War Machine in the form of exile and criminal prosecution. While the films do critique the military infrastructures and argue for more critical awareness of the societies of control, the heroes of *Snowden* and *The Fifth Estate* are left stateless martyrs who have, at best, momentarily fractured the American State War Machine without being the singular person who actually stops "the motor of the world." Future films may adopt a more critical posthuman perspective in encouraging the collective might of a citizenship in cooperation with their machine co-species. Such positive portrayals of technology, separated from the supra-user hacker, may give the machinic audience models for new forms of digital space and protest against a variety of forms. The fatalism of the movies throughout this book, toward the ongoing state of global war, toward the surveillance of all moments of everyday civilian life, toward American and human exceptionalism, can be broken, and perhaps the machinic audience will see some of the films in this text, and this chapter specifically, by being willing to at least superficially and messily critique the societies of control, as causing some of the small initial cracks.

## NOTES

1. To get a sense of the history, Martin van Creveld argues that cyberwarfare begins with the WWI use of a transmitter on the Eiffel Tower to jam German wireless communications and then later with WWII uses of ELINT (ELectronic INTelligence) which encompassed devices like the codecracking bomb, as well as electronics aimed at interfering with enemy radio transmissions and radar (*War and Technology* 270–271). In the past 25 years, in reaction to this "new" form of warfare, Clarke and Knake outline the nationalized creation of cyberarmies that led NATO to open a cyber defense center in 2008 (17); the United States officially entered with a "multiservice, joint U.S. Cyber Command" in 2009, but as the authors point out, this attention to cyberwarfare started much earlier, as "[in 1995] National Defense University graduated its first class of officers trained to lead cyber war campaigns" (34); Further history can be found in Mead's *War Play* (168), as well as *Cyber Warfare and Cyber Terrorism* (Colarik, Andrew M., and Lech Janczewski. Idea Group Reference 2007) and *Cybersecurity and Cyberwar* (Singer, P.W., and Allan Friedman. Oxford University Press, 2014).

2. Van Creveld flags the information that comes with rising complexity and the need to manage the increasing biological and technological populations of the State War Machine as one of the main factors for using computers as organizing military tools; he also flags the information that arises with an enlarged reliance on computers to calculate and carry out much of the automated tasks of a modern State War Machine (*War and Technology* 236–237).

3. This has become even more obvious in the wake of the 2016 American presidential election as potential Russian acts of cyberwarfare included the creation and distribution of "fake news" about Democratic nominee Hillary Clinton and the release, via WikiLeaks, of John Podesta's and the Democratic National party's emails.

4. I analyze *Iron Man 3*, *The Core*, and *Swordfish* in the chapter "Hacking Against the Apocalypse" in *Interfacing with the Internet in Popular Cinema* with an eye toward how the civilian hacker is repurposed in the State War Machine.

5. Further discussion of drone warfare and cinematic representations of drone pilots can be found in Chapter 5 of this text.

6. See note 4 of this chapter.

7. I discuss the "trucage" of special effects surrounding cinematic portrayals of Internet usage in the chapter "The Reel/Real Internet" in *Interfacing with the Internet in Popular Cinema*.

8. While I discuss the hacker at various points in my own *Interfacing with the Internet in Popular Cinema*, the chapter "The Cables In, Under and Around Our Homes" would likely be of particular interest as it takes up the movie *Hackers* (Dir. Iain Softley, United Artists 1995) in detail.

9. Despite attempts at "realism," Hollywood has long taken the view that they must make computer use "interesting" by creating dramatic interfaces like the tie-dyed screens of *Hackers*. Relating to this chapter, at the end of *The Core*, Rat sends out all the secret information he has hacked from the military in a .doc file: while Rat is essentially sending an email to a number of recipients, the movie shows an interface in which the messages arc all over the planet and "land" in their destinations in a way that no email service has ever done. See note 7 of this chapter for discussion of the special effects that usually accompany "entering" the Internet.

10. Chapter 3 of this text further explains Judith Butler's frame as it relates to war photography and how that effacing frame doubles when it is included in the war film.

11. A brief history of the Internet and the introduction of the popular GUI interface can be found in my introduction to *Interfacing with the Internet in Popular Cinema* (6–22).

12. As the chapter "The Reel/Real Internet" in *Interfacing with the Internet in Popular Cinema* argues, just the inclusion of the Internet in pre-Y2K films was often enough to mark the movie as science fiction.

13. I have done prior analysis of *Sneakers* in the chapter "Hacking Against the Apocalypse" in *Interfacing with the Internet in Popular Cinema* (117–118 and 127–128).

14. In a nod to *WarGames*, the teenaged Carl Arbogast (River Phoenix) is portrayed very similarly to Lightman: like Lightman, the audience is told Arbogast was caught for "adjusting" his grades via computer.

15. Some work defining the techno-thriller genre has been done by Nader Elhefnawy in the articles "Science Fiction and the Post-Cold War" (*The Internet Review of Science Fiction*, January 2009, Accessed March 29, 2017, http://www.irosf.com/q/zine/article/10498#f13) and "The

Rise and Fall of the Military Techno-Thriller" (*The Internet Review of Science Fiction*, November 2009, Accessed March 29, 2017, http://www.irosf.com/q/zine/article/10603).

16. After 9/11, the American Congress passed the Patriot Act, which expanded the power of various government agencies, the NSA in particular, to collect information from its citizens, especially on the Internet; in addition to this, the 2002 Department of Homeland Security Act established the department as a domestic agency designed to fight and prevent terrorism, ultimately relies heavily on the information gathered as part of the expanded powers granted by the Patriot Act. For more: https://www.justice.gov/archive/ll/highlights.htm (Accessed March 29, 2017).

17. See note 4 of this chapter.

18. An expanded version of this chapter might consider analyzing the political thriller elements of *Zero Dark Thirty* and *Eye in the Sky* as well.

19. Though it is beyond the scope of this book, there is more work to be done on the different biopics of figures that were key to the construction and rhetoric surrounding Internet usage, including *The Social Network*, *Jobs* (Dir. Joshua Michael Stern, Open Road Films 2013) and *Steve Jobs* (Dir. Danny Boyle, Universal Pictures 2015). Within the war film, there is a long history of mixing biography into the genre, and although it did not fit into this chapter, there are arguments to be made about the ways in which the biopic/war film is changed by the Internet, using *The Fifth Estate* and *Snowden* as evidence.

20. A similar technique is used in the movie *Trust* (Dir. David Schwimmer, Millennium Films 2010) and is now a semi-common visualization across movies and TV. I write more about *Trust* and the notion of text conversations overlaying the cinematic world in "The Reel/Real Internet" in *Interfacing with the Internet in Popular Cinema* (204–208).

# Conclusion: What Might a War Film Look Like Going Forward?

This text began from a broad perspective that was very much in line with Kellner's understanding of the power of cinema:

> Films can also provide allegorical representations that interpret, comment on, and indirectly portray aspects of an era. Further there is an aesthetic, philosophical, and anticipatory dimension to film, in which they provide artistic visions of the world that might transcend the social context of the moment and articulate future possibilities, positive and negative, and provide insight into the nature of human beings, social relationships, institutions, and conflicts of a given era. (14)

From this point of view, this book considered the movies that it analyzed within the technological and military "eras" they were made and first viewed within, and considered the ways in which the war film most often undermined the potential cooperative power of Internet-enabled machine species with a continued focus on the humanistic ethics laid out by Jeffords' Reagan-era hard body. The "insight" the movies provided reified the fears and concerns found in the moviemaking machinic phylum of Hollywood and its overlap with the American State War Machine, all the while deconstructing the documents as windows into "the nature of human beings, social relationships, institutions, and conflicts" as it related to the civilian machinic audience of war films.

© The Editor(s) (if applicable) and The Author(s) 2017                    229
A. Tucker, *Virtual Weaponry*,
DOI 10.1007/978-3-319-60198-4

This book is being published with the knowledge that, like *Interfacing with the Internet in Popular Cinema*, it is far from comprehensive and with the hope that other scholars might pick up some of the initial or underdeveloped thoughts that were begun with this text. For example, there likely should have been an entire chapter dedicated just to drone warfare, as there is more to be written about *Furious 7* (Dir. James Wan 2015), *Body of Lies*, *Syriana* and *Zero Dark Thirty*, with more critical attention paid to the influential visual template of *Enemy of the State*. Likewise, there could easily have been another chapter built out of the spy thriller's quasi-military use of Internet-enabled technology that is on display in the *Mission Impossible, James Bond* and *Bourne* films. Alongside this, there are a number of films, like the more contemporary *13 Hours* (Dir. Michael Bay 2016) and *Whiskey Tango Foxtrot* (Dir. Glenn Ficarra and John Requa 2016), as well as the older *Wag the Dog* (Dir. Barry Levinson 1997), *Live Free or Die Hard*, and *Redacted*, that deserve further analysis. Additionally, the *Terminator* franchise, in particular how *Terminator 3: Rise of the Machines* (Dir. Jonathan Mostow 2003) explains how Skynet was constructed from the civilian Internet, could be expanded upon. Most glaringly, though the text does address some of the concerns around the white male masculinity of the 1980s hard body, there is a great deal more to be written about the role of gender, race and class as they relate to the cinematic representations of Internet-enabled technologies in war films.

So, with this regretful acknowledgment, this book ends by considering the future of the war film and how it might best construct relationships between all the varying species, biological and technological, and how the machinic audience might view and think critically through those war films. These concerns are especially important considering the protracted, ubiquitous and likely never-ending War on Terror that the machinic audience lives with every day. Urgently then, as LaRocca maintains,

> If war is now perpetual, something we assume to be an ongoing, even permanent part of the domestic life of the nation (perhaps especially since 9/11) and taken for granted in the course of wider geopolitics, then it is analytic that we are in or at war at all times, subject to its traumas, and called upon—almost incessantly—to think through our positions as citizen-combatants. (23)

When Basinger explains that "World War II films were all about living and dying" (73), this conclusion counters by asking, "What are War on Terror films about?" Žižek calls this contemporary virtuous war waging "a virtual war fought behind computer screens, war experienced by its participants as a video game, a war without casualties" (37). Using 9/11 as an example of "a spectral apparition on the (TV) screen," Žižek illustrates that what makes this war different is that "it is not that reality entered our image; the image entered and shattered our reality" (19). This porous relationship between mediated-reality and reality leads to physical and virtual spaces in which the synthetic images of cultural interfaces, like Internet-enabled browsers and applications and movies, are aggressively disrupting the machinic audience's understandings of their reality. From within these battering environments, when looking specifically at War on Terror films, such movies are likely repeating some of the questions of the WWII film: "What makes a good life and what makes a good person? What should we be willing to die for—and how do you die right? ... What about killing? If you had to do it, did that make you a killer? Would it change you forever?" (Basinger 73). This conclusion would add: what does it mean to live without traditional modes of territory as the State War Machine becomes increasingly networked and digitized? How can "citizen-combatants" resist the "participation" in war waging that is thrust upon them by the various societies of control that surround them? What role will our Internet-enabled technologies play in this resistance? Is there a space, virtual or physical, to escape the omnipresent battlefield of the War on Terror?

We should begin to end this chapter by acknowledging that

> representation, no matter its quality of image or insight, is an insufficient means for conveying the reality of first-person experience. In this respect, it is worth emphasizing how the representation of war on film is not a representation of war; a war film is very much its own kind of thing and is not, regardless of manifold creative or constitutive achievements, war. (LaRocca 39)

A critical posthumanism, first and foremost, is focused on the realities of its ethics on actual species and landscapes. However, while "the telling and teaching of war's realities, it would seem, is never finished and never complete ... [and] film, notwithstanding our neglected admission of its limited gifts, will not be the means for finishing the job" (LaRocca 42), war films can be cultural interfaces where initial attitudes and arguments about past, current and future warfare and conflicts can be made and then manifested in the "real" world. Recalling the introduction to this text, Kellner's "future possibilities," and the potential paths that Haraway lays out for the cyborg, the answers to these questions will likely decide whether the machinic audience will find themselves embroiled in "a Star Wars apocalypse waged in the name of defence" or a "joint kinship with animals and machines, [where they are] not afraid of permanently partial identities and contradictory standpoints" (295). The path to "joint kinship" depends upon the future understanding of the ethics of warfare. Lieutenant Colonel Douglas A. Pryer explains, "Ethics begins with the judgment that all human beings have something in common. … The commonality of this … means that principles of conduct can be formulated that guide anyone to live their life in the best possible way" (19). He then hones in on what "the ethic of reciprocity" (19) is as an understanding of warfare that acknowledges the other opposing forces as equally deserving of sovereignty and respect as one's own forces. While Suid argues that "war films will remain popular so long as men love war itself" (12), this text ends by considering how then the machinic audience might complicate their watching of the war films and enact an ethics of reciprocity based in a critical posthumanism. In a basic way, this means a return to Eisenhower's assertion that "only an alert and knowledgeable citizenry can compel the proper meshing of the huge industrial and military machinery of defense with our peaceful methods and goals, so that security and liberty may prosper together" (para. 14). In 2017, "an alert and knowledgeable citizenry" must know that for both the military and for citizens "the virtual has shared an isomorphic relationship to the dream. And like the dream, it requires critical interpretations if we are not to sleepwalk through the manifold travesties of war, whether between states or tribes, classes or castes, genders or generations" (Der Derian 774). The reciprocal and critical interpretations of the "dreams" of war, in whatever cultural interface they may take the form of, likely mean, as Žižek champions, resisting the "impossible universality" of American- and human-centric ethics that the war films of this book often impose on their audiences. Overlapping with Pryer's call for an ethics of reciprocity, Žižek then says that instead of "imposing our notion of universality … universality—the shared space of understanding between different cultures—should be conceived as an infinite task of translation, a constant reworking of one's own particular position" (*Welcome* 83). This idea of translation could encompass watching war movies from other countries in other languages; it could mean augmenting one's viewing experience with multiple histories and texts; it could also mean reclaiming certain literal and visual vocabulary and stripping out their euphemisms. Revisiting Chapter 6's quote from van Creveld when he contends that "changing the name of a things represented one way in which military affairs could be made palatable to contemporary tastes" and that "our age seems to be the first which systematically attempts to disguise the true nature of weapons even as it remains obsessed with their performance" (292), the machinic audience should counter with their own translations that name military violence with actual vocabulary that describes them. This does not just mean problematizing drone warfare's use of the word "prosecuted" instead of "kill" or "assassinate," but also looking through the various visual effects, tropes and manipulations that create the spectacular war film. These reciprocal translations puncture the universal dream of the virtual (of the humanistic ethics of the war film, the human-centric applications of cybernetics, the distant othering of virtuous war) and push the machinic audience to approach all their cultural interfaces with critical skepticism and, ultimately, care and compassion for all the species and landscapes with which they cooperatively interact, both physically and virtually.

# FILMS CITED

*13 hours*. 2016. Dir. Michael Bay. Paramount Pictures.
*Alien*. 1986. Dir. James Cameron. 20th Century Fox.
*American Sniper*. 2014. Dir. Clint Eastwood. Warner Bros. Pictures.
*Apocalypse Now*. 1979. Dir. Francis Coppola. United Artists.
*Avatar*. 2009. Dir. James Cameron. 20th Century Fox.
*Batman*. 1989. Dir. Tim Burton. Warner Bros. Pictures.
*Blackhat*. 2015. Dir. Michael Mann. Universal Pictures.
*Body of Lies*. 2008. Dir. Ridley Scott. Warner Bros. Pictures.
*Brainstorm*. 1983. Dir. Douglass Trumbull. MGM Grand Entertainment.
*Die Hard*. 1988. Dir. John McTiernan. 20th Century Fox.
*Die Hard 2: Die Harder*. 1990. Dir. Renny Harlin. 20th Century Fox.
*Die Hard with a Vengeance*. 1995. Dir. John McTiernan. 20th Century Fox.
*Disclosure*. 1994. Dir. Barry Levinson. Warner Bros. Pictures.
*Edge of Tomorrow*. 2014. Dir. Doug Liman. Warner Bros. Pictures.
*Elysium*. 2013. Dir. Neill Blomkamp. Sony Pictures Home Entertainment.
*Ender's Game*. 2013. Dir. Gavin Hood. Lionsgate Films.
*Enemy of the State*. 1998. Dir. Tony Scott. Touchstone Pictures.
*Eye in the Sky*. 2015. Dir. Gavin Hood. Entertainment One.
*First Blood*. 1982. Dir. Ted Kotcheff. Orion Pictures.
*Furious 7*. 2015. Dir. James Wan. Universal Pictures.
*Fury*. 2014. Dir. David Ayers. Columbia Pictures.
*Gamer*. 2009. Dir. Neveldine & Taylor. Lionsgate.
*Ghost in the Machine*. 1993. Dir.Rachel Talalay. 20th Century Fox.
*Good Kill*. 2014. Dir. Andrew Niccol. IFC Films.
*Hackers*. 1995. Dir. Iain Softley. United Artists.
*Her*. 2013. Dir. Spike Jonze. Warner Bros. Pictures.

© The Editor(s) (if applicable) and The Author(s) 2017
A. Tucker, *Virtual Weaponry*,
DOI 10.1007/978-3-319-60198-4

*Iron Man.* 2008. Dir. Jon Favreau. Paramount Pictures.

*Iron Man 2.* 2010. Dir. Jon Favreau. Paramount Pictures.

*Iron Man 3.* 2013. Dir. Shane Black. Paramount Home Entertainment.

*Jarhead.* 2005. Dir. Same Mendes. Universal Pictures.

*Lawnmower Man.* 1992. Dir. Brett Leonard. New Line Cinema.

*Lawnmower Man 2: Beyond Cyberspace.* 1996. Dir. Farhad Mann. New Line Cinema.

*Live Free or Die Hard.* 2007. Dir. Len Wiseman. 20th Century Fox.

*Lone Survivor.* 2013. Dir. Peter Berg. Universal Pictures.

*Pacific Rim.* 2013. Dir. Guillermo Del Toro. Warner Bros. Pictures.

*Rambo: First Blood Part II.* 1985. Dir. George P. Cosmatos. TriStar Pictures.

*Rambo III.* 1988. Dir. Peter MacDonald. TriStar Pictures.

*Redacted.* 2007. Dir. Brian De Palma. Magnolia Pictures.

*Rendition.* 2007. Dir. Gavin Hood. New Line Cinema.

*RoboCop.* 1987. Dir. Paul Verhoeven. Orion Pictures.

*RoboCop.* 2014. Dir. José Padilha. MGM Pictures.

*RoboCop 2.* 1990. Dir. Irvin Kershner. Orion Pictures.

*RoboCop 3.* 1993. Dir. Fred Dekker. Orion Pictures.

*Saving Private Ryan.* 1998. Dir Steven Spielberg. Dreamworks.

*Shaun of the Dead.* 2004. Dir. Edgar Wright. Universal Pictures.

*Sneakers.* 1992. Dir. Phil Alden Robinson. Universal Studios.

*Starship Troopers.* 1997. Dir. Paul Verhoeven. Columbia-TriStar Pictures.

*Stealth.* 2005. Dir. Rob Cohen. Columbia Pictures.

*Stop-Loss.* 2008. Dir. Kimberly Pierce. Paramount Pictures.

*Strange Days.* 1995. Dir. Kathryn Bigelow. 20th Century Fox.

*Superbad.* 2007. Dir. Judd Apatow. Columbia Pictures.

*Surrogates.* 2009. Dir. Jonathan Mostiw. Touchstone.

*Swordfish.* 2001. Dir. Dominca Sena. Warner Brothers Pictures.

*Syriana.* 2005. Dir. Stephen Gaghan. Warner Bros. Pictures.

*Terminator 2: Judgment Day.* 1991. Dir. James Cameron. TriStar Pictures.

*Terminator 3: Rise of the Machines* 2003. Dir. Jonathan Mostow. Warner Bros. Pictures.

*The Birth of a Nation.* 1915. Dir. D.W. Griffith. D.W. Griffith Corp.

*The Cell.* 2000. Dir. Tarsem Singh. New Line Cinema.

*The Core.* 2003. Dir. Jon Amiel. Paramount Pictures.

*The Deer Hunter.* 1979. Dir. Michael Cimino. Universal Pictures.

*The Fifth Estate.* 2013. Dir. Bill Condon. Dreamworks Pictures.

*The Hurt Locker.* 2008. Dir. Kathryn Bigelow. Summit Entertainment.

*The Last Starfighter.* 1984. Dir. Nick Castle. Universal Pictures.

*The Matrix.* 1999. Dir. Andy Wachowski & Lana Wachowski. Warner Brother Pictures.

*The Matrix Revolutions.* 2003. Dir. Lana and Andy Wachowski. Warner Bros. Pictures.

*The Net.* 1995. Dir. Irwin Winkler. Columbia Pictures.
*The Social Network.* 2010. Dir. David Fincher. Columbia Pictures.
*The Thirteenth Floor.* 1999. Dir. Josef Rusnack. Columbia Pictures.
*Top Gun.* 1986. Dir. Tony Scott. Paramount Pictures.
*Total Recall.* 1990. Dir. Paul Verhoeven. TriStar Pictures.
*Unbroken.* 2014. Dir. Angelina Jolie. Universal Pictures.
*Virtuosity.* 1995. Dir. Brett Leonard. Universal Pictures.
*Wag the Dog.* 1997. Dir. Barry Levinson. New Line Cinema.
*WarGames.* 1983. Dir. John Badham. MGM/UA Entertainment Company.
*Whiskey Tango Foxtrot.* 2016. Dir. Glenn Ficarra and John Requa. Paramount Pictures.
*Zero Dark Thirty.* 2012. Dir. Kathryn Bigelow. Columbia Pictures.

## Works Cited

Annadale, David. 2010. Visions of War and Terror. Avatars of Destruction: Cheerleading and Deconstructing the "War on Terror" in Video Games. In *Reframing 9–11: Film, Popular Culture and the 'War on Terror'*. ed. Jeff Birkenstein, Anna Froula and Karen Randell, 97–106. New York: Continuum.
*After Burner.* 1987. Sega.
*America's Army.* 2002. United States Army.
Aukstakalnis, Steve, and David Blattner. 1992. *Silicon Mirage: The Art and Science of Virtual Reality.* San Francisco: Peachpit Press.
Barfield, Woodrow. 2015. *Fundamentals of Wearable Computers and Augmented Reality.* Oakville, CA: CRC Press.
Barker, Martin. 2011. *A Toxic Genre: The Iraq War Films.* London: Pluto Books.
Basinger, Jeanine. 2003. *The World War II Combat Film: Anatomy of a Genre.* Middletown, CT: Wesleyan.
*Battlezone.* 1980. Atari.
Baudrillard, Jean. 1995. *The gulf war did not take place,* trans. Paul Patton. Bloomington: Indiana University Press.
Bell, Mark. Towards a Definition of 'Virtual Worlds'. *Journal of Virtual Worlds Research* 1 (1): 1–4.
Best, Kristy. 2010. Living In The Control Society: Surveillance, Users And Digital Screen Technologies. *International Journal of Cultural Studies.* 13 (1): 5–24. doi:10.1177/1367877909348536.
Blum, Andrew. 2012. *Tubes.* New York: HarperCollins Publishers Ltd.
Brady, Sara. 2012. *Performance, Politics, and the War on Terror: Whatever it Takes,* Palgrave Macmillan.
Braidotti, Rossi. 2013. *The Posthuman.* Cambridge: Polity Press.
Butler, Judith. 2009. *Frames of War.* New York: Verso.
Card, Orson Scott. 1985. *Ender's Game.* New York: Tor Science Fiction.

Carmigniani Julia, and Furht, Borko. 2011. Augmented Reality: An Overview. In *Handbook of Augmented Reality*. ed. B. Furht, 3–46. New York: Springer.

Castrillo, Pablo, and Pablo Echart. 2015. Towards a Narrative Definition of the American Political Thriller Film. *Comunicación y Sociedad* 28 (4): 109–123. doi:10.15581/003.28.4.109–123.

Cavell, Stanley. 1979. *The World Viewed: Reflections on the Ontology of Film*. Boston: Harvard University Press.

Clarke, Richard A., and Robert Knake. 2011. *Cyber War: The Next Threat to National Security and What to Do About It*. New York: Ecco.

Clearwater. David A. 2010. Living in a Militarized Culture: War, Games and the Experience of the U.S. Empire. In *Cultures of Militarization*. ed. Berland, Jody, and Blake Fitzpatrick: 260–285. Cape Breton University Press.

Clynes, Manfred E., and Nathan S. Kline. 1960. Cyborg and Space. *Astronautics*.http://web.mit.edu/digitalapollo/Documents/Chapter1/cyborgs.pdf. *Accessed 4 May 2016*.

Coker, Christopher. 2013. *Warrior Geeks: How 21st Century Technology is Changing the Way We Fight and Think About War*. Oxford: Oxford Press.

Cook, Michael. 2004. Hollywood Joins Abe Underway to Film 'Stealth'. America's Navy. http://www.navy.mil/submit/display.asp?story_id=13848. Accessed 16 April 2017.

Craig, Alan B. 2013. Understanding *Augmented Reality: Concepts and Applications*. Saint Louis: Morgan Kaufmann.

DARPA. 2013. Warrior Web Prototype Takes Its First Steps. *darpa.mil*.http://www.darpa.mil/NewsEvents/Releases/2013/05/22.aspx. *Accessed 23 Feb 2015*.

Daston, L., and Gailson, P. 2010. *Objectivity*. New York: Zone.

Deleuze, Gilles and Felix Guattari. 1987. *A Thousand Plateaus*. trans. Brian Massumi. Minneapolis: University of Minnesota.

Deleuze, Gilles. 1992. Postscript on the Societies of Control. *October* 59: 3–7.

De Landa, Manuel. n.d. Economics, Computers and the War Machine. http://www.t0.or.at/delanda/netwar.htm. Accessed 10 April 2017.

De Landa, Manuel. 1991. *War in the Age of Intelligent Machines*. New York: Zone.

De Landa, Manuel. 1997. The Machinic Phylum. *V2*.http://v2.nl/archive/articles/the-machinic-phylum. *Accessed 11 April 2017*.

De Landa, Manuel. 2002. *Intensive Science and Virtual Philosophy*. New York: Continuum.

Demczynski, S. 1969. The Tools of the Cybernetic Revolution. In *Survey of Cybernetics*. ed. J. Rose. London: ILiffe Book Ltd.

Der Derian, James. 2000. Virtuous War/Virtual Theory. *International Affairs* 76 (4): 771–788.

Der Derian, James. 2009. *Virtuous War: Mapping the Military-Industrial-Media-Entertainment Network,* 2nd Edition. New York: Routledge.

Eberwein, Robert. 2010. *The Hollywood War Film*. Oxford: Backwell.

Eisenhower, Dwight D. 1961. *American Rhetoric*.http://www.americanrhetoric. com/speeches/dwightdeisenhowerfarewell.html. *Accessed 18 April 2017*.

Fear, David. 2013. No 'Tomorrow': Doug Linman on the Blockbuster than Almost Broke Him. *Rolling Stone*. http://www.rollingstone.com/movies/news/no-tomorrow-doug-liman-on-the-blockbuster-that-almost-broke-him-20140606?page=2. Accessed 6 June 2014.

Fahey, Chris. 'Stealth' Films Aboard Vinson. *America's Navy*. http://www.navy.mil/submit/display.asp?story_id=11862. Accessed 18 April 2017.

*Gears of War*. 2006. Epic Games.

General Electric Company 1971. Final Report on Hardiman I For Machine Augmentation of Human Strength and Endurance. www.dtic.mil/cgi-bin/GetTRDoc?AD=AD0739735. Accessed 23 Feb 2015.

Gibson, William. 1984. *Neuromancer*. New York: Ace Books.

Giesen, Klaus-Gerd. 2014. Justice in Cyberwar. *Ethic: International Journal for Moral Philosophy* 13 (1): 27–49. doi:10.5007/1677-2954.2014v13n1p27

Glass, Fred. 1985. Sign of the Times: The Computer as Character in "TRON, War Games", and "Superman III". *Film Quarterly* 38 (2): 16–16.

Gooch, Joshua. 2014. Beyond Panopticism The Biopolitical Labor of Surveillance and War in Contemporary. In *The Philosophy of War Films*. ed. David LaRocca, et al., 155–178. Lexington: The University Press of Kentucky.

Gronke, Paul and Peter D. Feaver. Uncertain Confidence: Civilian And Military Attitudes About Civil-Military Relations. Triangle Institute for Security Studies. http://people.reed.edu/~gronkep/docs/uncertain.pdf. Accessed 23 April 2017.

Hafner, Katie and Matthew Lyon. 1996. *Where the Wizards Stay up Late*. New York: Simon and Schuster Ltd.

Haraway, Donna. 2000. A Cyborg Manifesto. In *The Cybercultures Reader*. ed. D. Bell and B. Kennedy. New York: Routledge.

Hayles, N. Katherine. 1999. *How We Become Posthuman*. Chicago: University of Chicago Press.

Herbrechter, Stefan. 2013. *Posthumanism: A Critical Analysis*. New York: Bloomsbury.

Heims, Steve. 1991. *The Cybernetic Group*. Cambridge: MIT Press.

Heim, Michael. 1993. *The Metaphysics of Virtual Reality*. New York: Oxford.

Hightower Jr., O'Dell. 2000. Virtual Reality in Military Simulations. *Allied Academies International Conference. Academy of Information and Management Sciences. Proceedings* 4 (1): 11.

Hubbard, Ben, and Michael R. Gordon. 2017. U.S. War Footprint Grows in Middle East, With No Endgame in Sight. *The New York Times*.https://www.nytimes.com/2017/03/29/world/middleeast/us-war-footprint-grows-in-middle-east.html. *Accessed 18 April 2017*.

Hullmund, Chris. 1993. Masculinity as Multiple Masquerade. In *Screening the Male: Exploring Masculinities in Hollywood Cinema.* ed. Steven Cohen and Idna Rae Hark, 213–229. London: Routledge.

hooks, bell. 2009. *Reel to Reel.* New York: Routledge Classic.

Isenberg, M. T. 1981. *War on Film: The American Cinema and the First World War, 1914–1941.* London: Associated University Press.

Jeffords, Susan. 1988. *The Remasculinization of America: Gender and the Vietnam War.* Bloomington, IN: Indiana University Press.

Jeffords, Susan. 1994. *Hard Bodies: Hollywood Masculinity in the Reagan Era.* New Brunswick, NJ: Rutgers University Press.

Kellner, Douglas. 2010. *Cinema Wars: Hollywood Film and Politics in the Bush-Cheney Era.* New York: Wiley.

Kim, John. 2015. The Origin of the See-through Graphical Interface: World War II Aircraft Gunsights and the Status of the Material in Early Computer Interface Design. *Convergence* 21 (2): 213–227. doi:10.1177/1354856514543249.

King, Mary Sterpka. Preparing the Instantaneous Battlespace: A Cultural Examination of Network-Centric Warfare. *Cultures of Militarization.* ed. Berland, Jody, and Blake Fitzpatrick: 304–329. Cape Breton University Press.

Krushner, David. 2013. Ender's Game is Already a Reality for the U.S. Military. *IEEE Spectrum.* http://spectrum.ieee.org/computing/software/enders-game-is-already-a-reality-for-the-us-military. Accessed 11 April 2017.

Kurzweil, Ray. 1990. *The Age of Intelligent Machines.* Cambridge, MA: MIT Press.

Kurzweil, Ray. 1999. *The Age of Spiritual Machines: When computers Exceed Human Intelligence.* New York: Viking.

Lambertini, Luca. 2011. Game Theory in the Social Sciences: A Reader-friendly Guide. New York: Routledge.

Langford, Barry. 2005. *Film Genre: Hollywood and Beyond.* Oxford: Edinburgh University Press.

Lapsley, Phil. 2013. *Exploding The Phone: The Untold Story of the Teenagers And Outlaws Who Hacked Ma Bell.* New York: Grove Press.

LaRocca, David. 2014. Introduction: War Films and the Ineffability of War. In *The Philosophy of War Films.* ed. David LaRocca, et al., 1–80. Lexington: The University Press of Kentucky.

LaRocca, David. 2014. The Multifarious Forms of War Films: A Taxonomy of Subgenres. In *The Philosophy of War Films.* ed. David LaRocca et al., 489–501. Lexington: The University Press of Kentucky.

Lele, Ajey. 2013. Virtual Reality and its Military Utility. *Journal of Ambient Intelligence and Humanized Computing* 4: 17–26.

Le Roux, Willem. 2011. The Use of Augmented Reality in Command and Control Situation Awareness. *Scientia Militaria - South African Journal of Military Studies* 38, 115–133. doi: 10.5787/38-1-82.

Levy, Steven. 1984. *Hackers: Heroes of the Computer Revolution*. New York: Dell.

Lodder, A., & Boer, L. 2012. Cyberwar? What War? *Justitiele Verkenningen* 38 (1): 52–67.

*Magazine*. 2017. https://www.wired.com/2008/03/darpa-wants-con/. Accessed 11 April 2017.

Manovich, Lev. 2017.Database as a Genre of New Media. *AI and Society*.http://vv.arts.ucla.edu/AI_Society/manovich.html. *Accessed 11 April 2017.*

Manovich, Lev. 2001. *The Language of New Media*. Boston: MIT Press.

Mbembé, J. 2003. Necropolitics. Trans. Libby Meintjes. *Public Culture* 15 (1): 11–40.

Mead, Corey. 2013. War *Play: Video Games and the Future of Armed Conflict*. New York: Eamon Dolan/Houghton Mifflin Harcourt.

Milgram, et al. 1994. Augmented Reality: A class of displays on the reality-virtuality continuum. *SPIE 2351*. 282–290. http://etclab.mie.utoronto.ca/publication/1994/Milgram_Takemura_SPIE1994.pdf. Accessed 11 April 2017.

Mirrlees, Tanner. 2013. The Economics, Geopolitics and Ideology of an Imperial Film Commodity. *Cineaction*.http://www.cineaction.ca/wp-content/uploads/2013/05/CA92_IronMan.pdf. *Accessed 11 April 2017.*

*Missile Command*. 1980. Atari.

Moravec, Hans. 1988. *Mind Children: The Future of Robot and Human Intelligence*. Cambridge: Harvard University Press.

Moschovitis, Christos J.P., et al. 1999. *History of the Internet: A Chronology, 1843 to the present*. Santa Barbara, CA: ABC-CLIO.

Nayar, Pramod K. 2014. *Posthumanism*. Madlen, MA: Polity Press.

Neale, Steve. 1991. Aspects of Ideology and Narrative form in the American war Film. *Screen* 32 (1): 35–57.

Neale, Steve. 2000.*Genre and Hollywood*. New York: Routledge.

Neale, Steve. 2004. Action Adventure as Hollywood Genre. In *Action and Adventure Cinema*. ed. Y. Tasker. 71–83. New York: Routledge.

Nilges, Mathias. 2010. The Aesthetics of Destruction: Contemporary US Cinema and TV Culture. In *Reframing 9–11: Film, Popular Culture and the 'War on Terror'*, ed. J. Birkenstein, A. Froula, and K. Randell, 23–34. New York: Continuum Books.

O'Day, Marc. 2004. Beauty in Motion: Genre, Spectacle and Action Babe. *Action and Adventure Cinema*. ed. Y. Tasker, 201–218. New York: Routledge.

Parkin, Simon. 2015. How VR is Training the Perfect Soldier. *Wearable*. http://www.wareable.com/vr/how-vr-is-training-the-perfect-soldier-1757. Accessed 17 Oct 2016.

Platoni, Kara. 1999. The Pentagon Goes to the Video Arcade. *The Progressive*.https://www.thefreelibrary.com/The+Pentagon+Goes+to+the+Video+Arcade.-a054618060. *Accessed 16 Oct 2016.*

Poeter, Damon. 2014. Call of Duty Sales Top $10 Billion. *PC Magazine*. http://www.pcmag.com/article2/0,2817,2472593,00.asp. Accessed 17 Jan 2016.

Pryer, Douglas A. 2013. The Rise Of The Machines: Why Increasingly "Perfect" Weapons Help Perpetuate Our Wars And Endanger Our Nation. *Military Review* 93 (2): 14–24.

Rayner, Jonathan. 2007. *The Naval War Film: Genre, History, National Cinema*. London: Manchester University Press.

Rheingold, Howard. 1991. *Virtual Reality*. New York: Touchstone Books.

Robb, David. 2004. *Operation Hollywood*. Amherst, NY: Prometheus Books.

Roderick, Ian. 2008 Putting the Post-Human in the Loop: Future Combat Systems and Post-Disciplinary Training. *Journal for Cultural Research* 12 (4): 301–316.

Roderick, Ian. 2010. Mil-bot Fetishism: The Pata-physics of Military Robots. *Cultures of Militarization*. ed. Berland, Jody and Blake Fitzpatrick, 286–303. Cape Breton University Press.

Rodowick, D.N. 2007. *The Virtual Life of Film*. Boston: Harvard University Press.

Rosewarne, Lauren. 2016. *Cyberbullies, Cyberactivists, Cyberpredators: Film, TV. And Internet Stereotypes*. Santa Barbara, CA: Praeger.

Ryan, Johnny. 2010. *A History of the Internet and the digital future*. London: Reaktion Books.

Scott, Ian. 2000. *American Politics in Hollywood Film*. Edinburgh: Edinburgh University Press.

Shachtman, Noah. 2008. Pentagon: 'Augment' Reality with 'Videogame' Contact Lenses. *Wired*.

Shain, R.E. 1976. *An Analysis of Motion Pictures Released by the American Film Industry, 1930–1970*. New York: Arno Press.

Shields, Rob. 2003. *The Virtual*. New York: Routledge.

Singer, P.W. 2009. *Wired for War: The Robotics Revolution and Conflict in the 21st Century*. New York: Penguin Books.

Sneakers. 2017. imdb.com. http://www.imdb.com/title/tt0105435/. Accessed 18 April 2017.

Sneakers. 2017. Wikipedia. https://en.wikipedia.org/wiki/Sneakers_(1992_film). Accessed April 18 2017.

Sontag, Susan. 1978. *On Photography*. London: Penguin Books.

Stewart, Garrett. 2009. Digital Fatigue: Imaging War in Recent American Film. *Film Quarterly* 62 (4): 45–55.

Stirling, Bruce. 1992. *The Hacker Crackdown*. New York: Bantam

Stirling, Bruce. 1993. War is Virtual Hell. *Wired Magazine*. https://www.wired.com/1993/01/virthell/. Accessed 16 Oct 2016.

Suid, Lawrence. 2002. *Guts and Glory: The Making of the American Military Image in Film*. Lexington, KY: The University Press of Kentucky.

*Survey of Cybernetics.* 1969. ed. J. Rose. London: ILiffe Book Ltd.

Swofford, Anthony. 2003. *Jarhead.* New York: Scribner.

Tasker, Yvonne. 1993. *Spectacular Bodies: gender, genre and the action cinema.* New York: Routledge.

Tasker, Yvonne. 2004. Introduction. In *Action and Adventure Cinema,* ed. Y. Tasker, 1–13. New York: Routledge.

Taylor, Giles. 2013. A Military Use for Widescreen Cinema: Training the Body through Immersive Media. *Velvet Light Trap* 72: 17.

ter Haar, René. 2005. Virtual reality in the military: present and future. *3rd Twente student conference on IT.*

Teschner, John. 2013. On Drones. *The Iowa Review* 43 (1): 74–81.

Thomas, Douglas. 2002. *Hacker Culture.* Minneapolis, MN: University of Minnesota Press.

Tucker, Aaron. 2014. *Interfacing with the Internet in Popular Cinema.* New York: Palgrave Macmillan.

van Creveld, Martin. 1989. *Technology and War: From 2000 B.C. to the Present.* New York: Free Press.

van Creveld, Martin. 2013. *Wargames: From Gladiators to Gigabytes.* Cambridge University Press.

Virilio, Paul. 1989. *War and Cinema.* New York: Verso Books.

Virilio, Paul. 1997. *Pure War.* Trans. Mark Polizotti. New York: Semiotext(e).

Virilio, Paul. 1998. Military Space. In *The Virilio Reader.* ed., James Der Derian. New York: Blackwell.

Virilio, Paul. 2000. *Strategy of Deception.* trans. Chris Turner. New York: Verso Books.

von Neumann, John, and Morgenstern, Oskar. 1953. *Theory of Games and Economic Behavior.* Princeton: Princeton Press.

War in the Fifth Domain. 2017. *The Economist.*http://www.economist.com/node/16478792. *Accessed April 18 2017.*

Weber, Cynthia. 2006. *Imagining America at War.* New York: Routledge.

Wendle, John. 2011. U.S. Men at War: BlackBerrys and iPads on the Afghan Front. *Time.*http://content.time.com/time/world/article/0,8599,2089184,00.html. *Accessed 16 Oct 2016.*

Wiener, Norbert. 1961. *Cybernetics, or Control and Communication in the Animal and Machine Second Edition.* Cambridge, MA: The MIT Press.

Wiener, Nobert. 1967. *The Human Use of Human Beings.* New York: Avon.

Žižek, Slavoj. 1997. *The Plague of Fantasies.* New York: Verso.

Žižek Slavoj. 2013. *Welcome to the Desert of the Real: Five Essays on September 11 and Related Dates.* New York: Verso.

Zocco, Alessandro, and Lucio Tommaso De Paolis. 2015. Augmented Command and Control Table to Support Network-Centric Operations. *Defence Science Journal* 65 (1): 39–45. doi:10.14429/dsj.65.6713.

# INDEX

© The Editor(s) (if applicable) and The Author(s) 2017
A. Tucker, *Virtual Weaponry*,
DOI 10.1007/978-3-319-60198-4

GPSR Compliance
The European Union's (EU) General Product Safety Regulation (GPSR) is a set
of rules that requires consumer products to be safe and our obligations to
ensure this.

If you have any concerns about our products, you can contact us on

ProductSafety@springernature.com

In case Publisher is established outside the EU, the EU authorized
representative is:

Springer Nature Customer Service Center GmbH
Europaplatz 3
69115 Heidelberg, Germany

*9 7 8 3 3 1 9 6 0 1 9 7 7 *